London: the Art of Georgian Building

LONDON: THE ART OF GEORGIAN BUILDING

by Dan Cruickshank and Peter Wyld

The Architectural Press Ltd: London

DEDICATION

To the builders, craftsmen and architects of Georgian London

A Note About Scale: in the new measured drawings in this book a major division on the scale bar represents 1 foot and a minor division represents 3 inches

First published 1975 by The Architectural Press Ltd., London.

Reprinted 1986

ISBN 0 85139 371 8

All rights reserved. No part of this publication may be reproduced, stored in a retrieval system, or transmitted, in any form or by any means, electronic, mechanical, photocopying, recording or otherwise, without the prior permission of the publishers.

© Text and photographs Dan Cruickshank 1975
© New measured drawings Peter Wyld 1975

Printed in Great Britain by BAS Printers Limited, Over Wallop, Hampshire.

CONTENTS

PREFACE 1

PART I FAÇADES
Introduction 18
Illustrated Development 40

PART II ELEMENTS: DETAILS
Doors 82
Windows 154
Roofs 166

PART III ELEMENTS: MATERIALS
Brick 178
Stucco 192
Stone 194
Coade Stone 198
Wood 202
Metalwork 210
Glass 220
Paint 221

PART IV AXONOMETRIC SUMMARY 222

BIBLIOGRAPHY 226

STREET INDEX 231

PREFACE

Surprising as it may seem to late 20th-century pedestrians in pursuit of ever-diminishing elegance in Britain's capital city, Georgian London was formed not by great architects but by master builders, entrepreneurs and all kinds of speculators. Yet the coherence it had, both in construction and design, belies this curiously multiple parentage and reveals that a great binding force was at work: the orderly flexibility of 18th-century architectural classicism. This book, which begins in 1680 when Wren was at the height of his powers and closes about 1830 when the classical discipline of 200 years was suddenly shattered, sets out to investigate in photographs, measured drawings and contemporary quotations how this order worked, how it originated and how eventually it was dissolved, by an analysis of the most typical building type of the age: the speculative terrace house. As 18th-century architecture's lowest common denominator the terrace house reflects more truly the basic level of contemporary understanding, invention and interpretation of classicism than a study of the great pioneering buildings of the age.

Most of the period's visual coherence then, stems from the fact that classically derived proportion and details were universally accepted by craftsmen and builders as a standard discipline and to the present-day eye (though certainly not to the Georgian eye) houses built between 1700 and 1830 have a pleasing homogeneity. Yet, as we examine them in detail and begin to see them as those who built them saw them, we realise that change was constant, reflecting subtle but ever-present shifts in the contemporary understanding of classicism, of fashion and of building technology.

Although the great mass of Georgian London was not built by the great architects of the day, their influence was profound in the development of the terrace house as a living art form, for the average terrace house was to a certain degree a scaled-down version of the fastidiously elegant town houses which eminent architects built for the rich and powerful. London, unlike Paris, was never a city where the wealthy had free-standing *hôtels*. They lived like the artisan and the shopkeeper in terrace houses, a practice which happily facilitated the movement downwards of new fashions to the more modest terraces of poorer citizens, although this filtering process sometimes took years. Indeed in some cases the movement of architectural fashion down the economic scale happened only when a new vogue had become established enough to be almost vernacular. Obviously, it was cheaper to employ a builder to execute details he was used to than getting him to understand and practice the newest fashion; an economic fact which has caused houses in many parts of London to appear archaic in design simply because they were so modestly built.

From the technical point of view a revolution took place during the period covered by this book. In 1700 the building trade was still almost medieval. Structures were conceived in timber-frame and brick and decorations were individually hand wrought. By the end of the period the modern age had arrived with mass-production, standardisation and economy of individual works ruling the design and building processes. But it is important to remember that in no way were the wares of mass production thought to be unpleasant or second-rate. To the optimistic and rational 18th-century mind it was sensible and realistic to improve building techniques and the mass production of architectural motifs occurred only when architectural taste was ready for it. This perfect attuning of architectural taste to mass production had taken place by the 1770s, when a feeling for external simplicity and a repetition of units had triumphed in the mind of the architect. Since architectural classicism by its nature demanded the identical repetition of objects and a symmetrical arrangement of them, what could be better both aesthetically and practically than well designed and relatively cheap mass-produced ornaments? It was against this background that Coade artificial stone shot to success (see pages 198–201).

As well as reflecting technical, economic and social change in Britain, architecture was also a victim of them. The growth of architectural styles in London was closely controlled by the wealth and political stability of the country. When there was a boom and money was invested in house building, many architects and builders had the opportunity to express and develop the current architectural ideas. When there was depression ideas withered for want of opportunity. One of the most obvious ways in which the economy was reflected in architecture was in the number of houses built in particular periods. The firm establishment of the Hanoverians on the throne of England in 1714 heralded a period of economic stability and encouraged investment in tangible real estate. Accordingly, from 1715 to 1730 a vast number of rural estates bordering on London were covered with grids of terraces. In the west the great estates enforced a high standard of town planning, while in the east the estate owners (who usually owned small parcels of land big enough only for a couple of streets) were merely concerned with squeezing as many plots out of their sites as possible and here such land-consuming ornaments as squares and avenues were abandoned. During this same period many existing areas were rebuilt and improved so that, even now, a high proportion of surviving Georgian London was built between 1715–30.

1730–40 saw a slowing down of this development of new land (although parts of the west end were rounded off in this decade) but infilling and rebuilding continued.

The 1740s were the years of greatest uncertainty since the Georges were established on the throne. There was an unsuccessful political war with France in Europe, a continuing colonial war with France in America and in 1745 the old Catholic bogey came marching south once again in the form of Bonnie Prince Charlie. The lack of building in London during the decade 1740–50 reflects this general loss of confidence and it is very difficult practically anywhere in London to find even individual houses of this period. In the few streets where they may be found as, for example, in the vicinity of Berkeley Square and Southampton Place, off Bloomsbury Square, they represent the tail-end of earlier developments rather than new initiatives.

In 1750–60 there was an upsurge and the Roman austerity then in fashion and which had been trying to assert itself in the few buildings of the previous decade, became fully developed. The typical 1760 house with its Roman block cornice, muted grey bricks, assertive *piano nobile* and restrained door case had ample chance of developing from 1770 through to 1790, a period of Neo-Classical revolution and also of a general expansion in the size of London.

The war with France and Napoleon brought this boom to an end and impetus alone kept building enterprise going until *circa* 1800, when fear of invasion, shortage of Scandinavian timber, high taxes on building materials and the gearing of the nation to total war brought practically all new development to a standstill. Many speculative builders went bankrupt and accounts of terraces standing unfinished for years are common in newspapers and pamphlets of the period.

From 1810 onwards despite the continuing war, the economy became more stable and personal fortunes were being made by war profiteering. The increase in building in London reflects the security felt after 1805 when it became obvious that the French could not invade England nor even disturb British trade with the colonies.

From 1810–30 much of London's development took the form of lining the existing country roads radiating out of the capital with neat terraces and cottages. New roads were also constructed to link expanding industrial areas such as the docks or new suburbs with the city centres. These new roads, such as the Commercial Road and Camberwell New Road, opened up previously inaccessible land for building. Squares and terraces were laid off the new highways and gradually the fields between the built-up roads were covered with grids of brick terraces, cottages, villas and semi-detached houses.

The influence of town planning on the façade design of 18th-century London terrace house was very great, both because of the limitations it imposed and the possibilities it offered. At the beginning of the 18th century the greatest area of London was built on land that had been covered with building since medieval times, where houses had been repeatedly rebuilt on the same street pattern. This meant that since houses in a terrace were individually designed and built in a piece-meal fashion when the expiration of individual leases permitted such remodelling, the transition of London streets from one architectural fashion to another was very sporadic. However, the few new large-scale fashionable developments that there had been—such as Inigo Jones' Covent Garden Piazza of the 1630s, Bloomsbury Square in the 1660s and St James's Square of the 1660–80s indicated the direction that town planning would take during the 18th century.

In its ideal form 18th-century town planning was concerned with the submergence of the varied façades of individual units into one grand design or palace front, the creation of vistas via an ordered grid of streets, avenues and lanes. This grid would be interrupted logically by events such as squares, circuses or crescents. Simply, as Palladian designs became the fashionable thing after 1715, a system of symmetrical and related town planning was evolved to complement the order of the Palladian façades. This was the ideal and the Cavendish–Harley Estate, the development of which began in 1719, reflects to a large degree this ideal. But it is worth remembering that despite our veneration of the geometrical repose of Georgian town planning, some of the inhabitants of 18th-century London found the grid-iron approach rather depressing. John Gwynne, whose influential *London and Westminster Improved* was published in 1766 said, "Had the parish church of Mary-le-bone been rebuilt in a magnificent manner and well placed it would have answered the purpose both of a commodious place for public worship to the numerous families in that parish, and at the same time in the view of the town from the adjacent country, would have broken the line of new buildings, which as they at present stand give no better idea to the spectator than that of a plain brick wall of prodigious length."

But in most of the then rapidly growing London the amount of control necessary to create this sort of aesthetic over-view was just not available. Speculative builders who were financing the development of London, were then as now motivated by the urgent desire to run up houses as quickly as possible and were not interested in palace fronts and squares. It was not until the early 19th century when developers such as the Lambeth born John Nash and James Burton, father of the better-known Decimus, were building in London that the uniform terrace as an architectural whole became the standard speculative form. They operated in a bigger way than their earlier counterparts with an eye for larger-scale general effects and leased whole streets to develop rather than a couple of house plots, a mode of economic operation which facilitated the creation of the regular terrace as a distinctive urban unit.

Apart from its adverse effect on the uniformity of development there were other aspects of the pre-Nash and Burton development system that worried builders and architects during the 18th century. The parallel with today's speculative building is again appropriate because due to the stringently economical basis on which terrace houses were run up, the houses themselves were often thought to be technically ill-built. R. Neve wrote in 1703 that, "The greatest objection against London houses (being for the most part brick) is their slightness, occasioned by the fees exacted by the landlord. So that few houses at the common rate of building last longer than the ground lease and that is about 50 or 60 years. In the mean time, if there happens to be a long fit of excessive heat in summer, or cold in winter, the walls being but thin, become at last so penetrated with the air that the tenant must needs be uneasie in it; but those extremes happen but seldom. And this way of Building is wonderful beneficial to Trades relating to it, for they never want work in so great a City, where houses here and there are always repairing or building up again."

And Isaac Ware in his *Complete Body of Architecture* supported Neve's view, "We see a strange difference between the buildings of earlier ages and those of the present time, in respect of the article of strength ... the nature of the tenures in London has introduced the art of building slightly. The ground landlord is to come into possession at the end of a short term and the builder, unless his grace tyes him down to articles, does not choose to employ his money to his advantage ... It is for this reason we see houses built for 60, 70 or the stoutest of the kind for 99 years. They care they shall not stand longer than their time occasions, many to fall before it is expired; nay some have carried the art of slight building so far, that their houses have fallen before they were tenanted."

After this analysis of bad building, Ware made a few predictions which one hopes could also be heeded in present-day London, " ... Perhaps the modesty of our generality of architects contributes to this practice. The Greeks and Romans built for succeeding ages, because their works would be the admiration of all time; our people are not so sanguine in their hopes, and therefore not so solid in their structure ... It is certain the present methods of running up houses in London, not only disgraces us in the eyes of strangers, but threatens continual disasters. Till such a control shall be laid upon bad builders by public authority, those who have more skill and integrity should distinguish themselves from them by their work."

These views were so generally held that the Building Act of 1774 took some measures to rectify them. The Act created Rates or categories into which all types of building could be fitted. The first four Rates related to types of domestic building, the other three to non-domestic forms (see pages 24–29). Each Rate carried with it certain structural conditions and regulations which had to be complied with by the builder of a house falling into its category. Which Rate a given house fell into was decided by its cubic capacity and the expense of its construction.

In the 18th century the unit for measuring the cubic capacity of buildings was called the square: 1 square equalled 100 square feet. Therefore a house of 9 squares or over and valued at £850 was categorised as First Rate; a house consisting of 5 squares was Second rate, $3\frac{1}{2}$ squares a Third Rate and a house under $3\frac{1}{2}$ squares valued at less than £150 was a Fourth Rate building.

Whilst this brief chronological outline shows the bursts and slumps in the building activity of expanded Georgian London, the stylistic characteristics of that activity and the aesthetic principles which informed it, are most accurately conveyed in the numerous books of architectural plates through which contemporary architects and theorists influenced their fellows and after the passage of centuries, still speak most clearly to us.

The key book that moulded the classical architect's mind was Andrea Palladio's *Quattro Libri dell'Architettura* which appeared in 1570, its first English translation being published in 1715 by Palladio's Venetian-born apostle Giacomo Leoni who had settled in England at an unconfirmed date before 1715. At that time the English Palladian movement was taking over from the Baroque school of Wren and the more idiosyncratic Baroque of such men as Nicholas Hawksmoor, Sir John Vanbrugh and Thomas Archer, the only English Baroque architect to have studied the monuments of continental Baroque at first hand. Leoni's Queensberry House, London built in 1721 provided the prototype English Palladian town house and gradually the highly individual approach to classicism practised by English architects and builders in which the vernacular and the new classicism were synthesised naturally, was replaced by the authoritarian dogma of Palladio.

Palladio, in his turn, had interpreted Roman remains— often inaccurately—and he had very little concern with actual Greek remains. However, despite his lack of archaeological consistency, to the early 18th-century Englishman Palladio supplied the required ideals of classicism. His plates and words were totally convincing in communicating order, control, discipline, repose and ancient precedent. It was totally accepted by all layers of fashionable society as well as by architects and builders and Palladio's works became the measure by which to judge all new works, as well as for providing precedents and inspiration.

Plate **1** shows a detail of an elevation and section of a palace front and contains many motifs that were picked up by 18th-century Palladians and adapted to the English climate and interpretation. The giant composite column, encompassing two stories, became the ideal treatment for grand fronts and the rusticated ground floors, with mask keystones, became the standard way of visually strengthening the ground floor. The first floor is the *piano nobile* with a balustered veranda, the attic storey, with square windows, being placed above the cornice. Interestingly, this particular plate shows that the arches above the windows are made of bricks keyed to form arches—a technique that became standard in 18th-century London.

Plates **2** and **3** show the standard of Palladian details. Plate **2** gives a very enriched Ionic specimen: its proportions are Roman, as are its members—such as the pulvinated frieze. Plate **3** shows a Corinthian column and

1, 2, 3 Plates from Andrea Palladio's *Quattro Libri dell' Architettura* published in 1570. **1** shows the courtyard elevation of the Palazzo Iseppo Porto in Vicenza

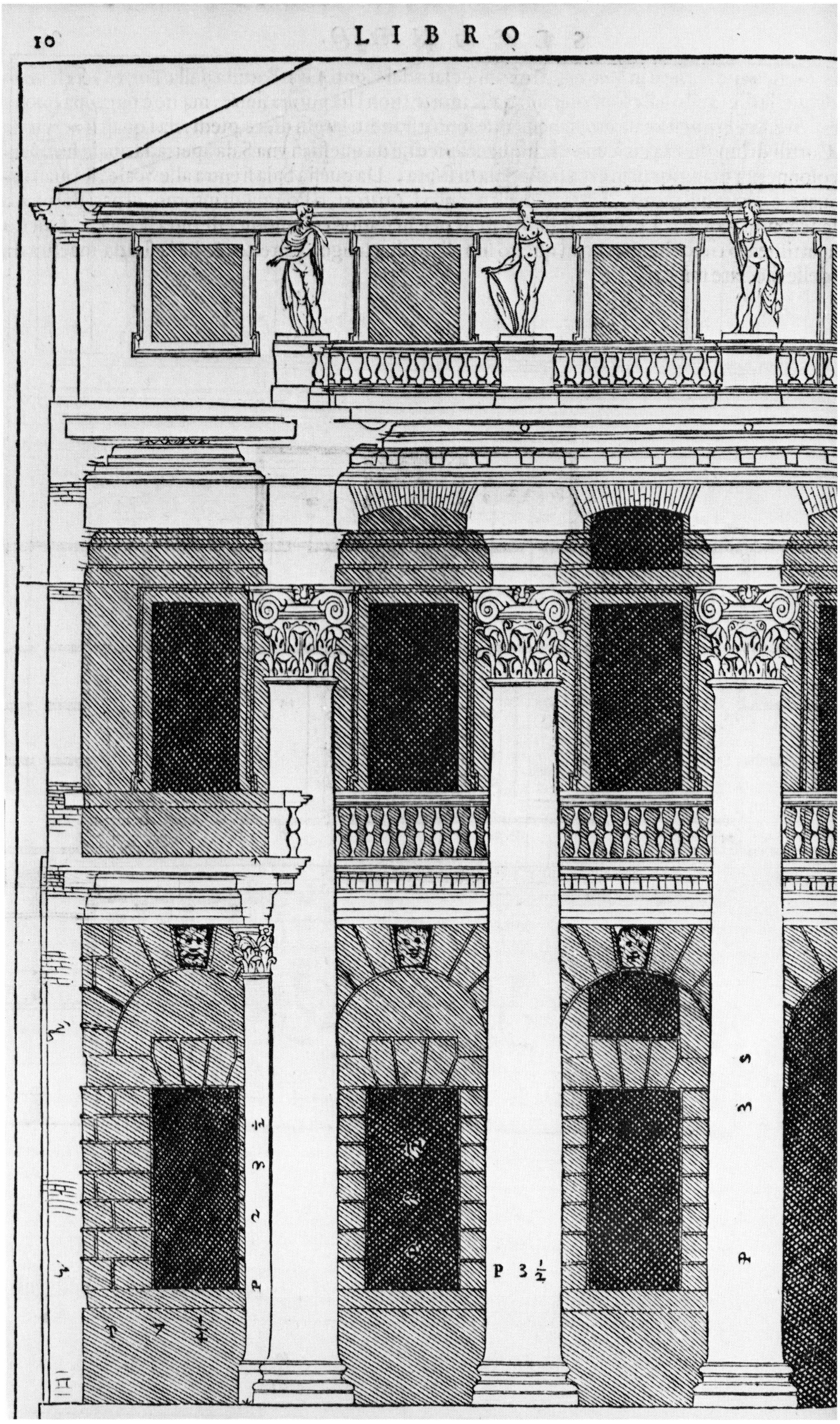
10
LIBRO
P 3 1/2

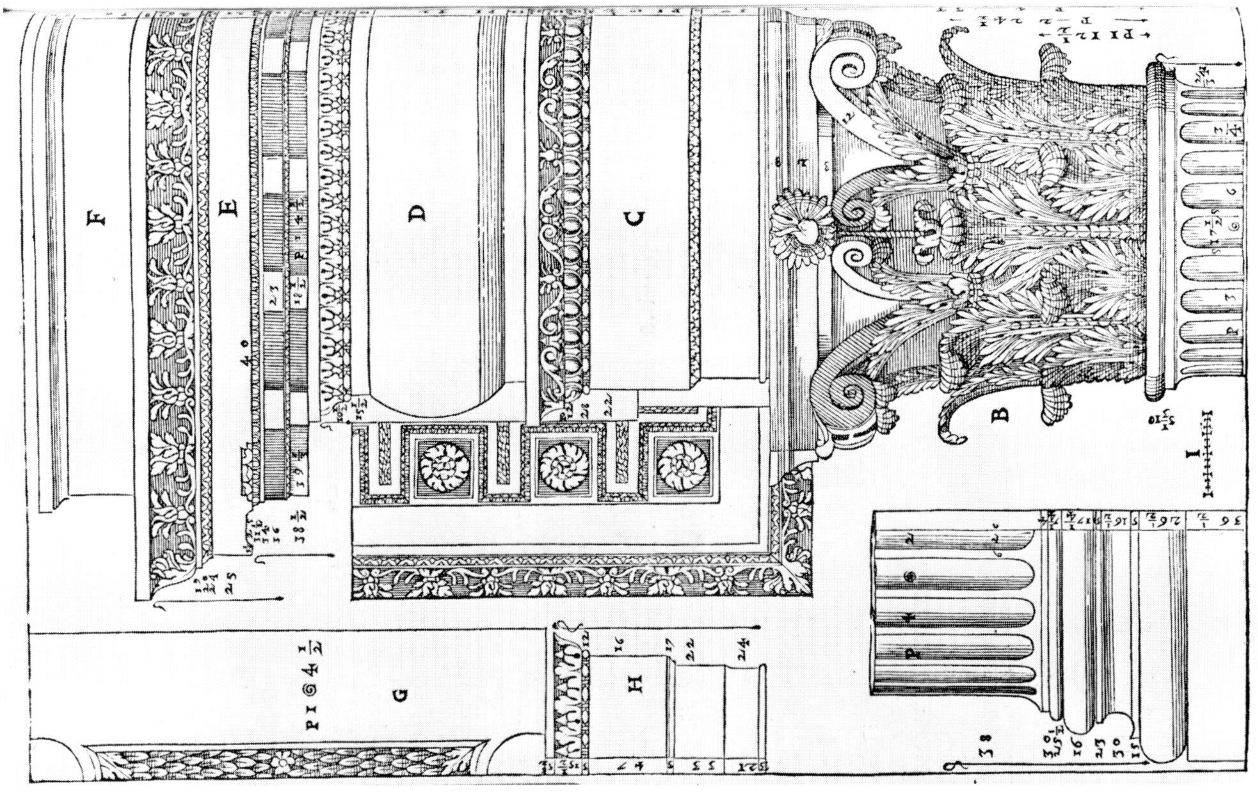

3

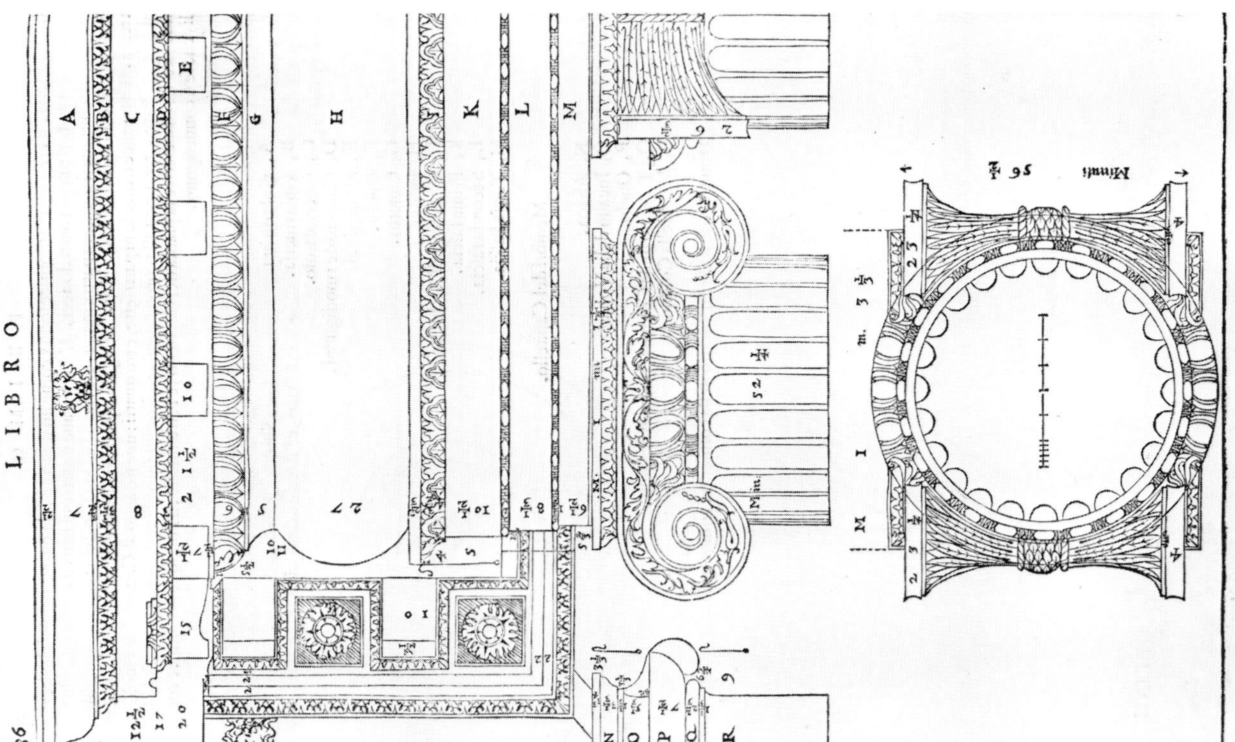

2

entablature drawn by Palladio but based on the Temple of Mars, Rome.

Besides the work of Palladio, other Renaissance architects were used for inspiration during the 18th century. In 1702 Joseph Moxon published *Vignola or the Compleat Architect* and a plate and its description from this book is shown in plate 4. It is redrawn from Jacopo Barozzi da Vignola's original and shows a very perfect and enriched Roman Doric capital and entablature. Despite the fact that he published this plate during the heyday of English Baroque, Moxon was obviously not concerned with promoting the free interpretation of the Orders. To see the result of free expression look at plate 37 on page 105 in which the door was constructed about 20 years after Moxon's plate was published. For further comparison plate 5 shows the enriched Doric as it was conceived in 1757 by Abraham Swan in his *Designs in Architecture*. Here the motifs and proportions are still Roman via the Italian Renaissance.

Plate 6 was published in 1756 by Isaac Ware in his *Complete Body of Architecture*. A comparison of the Five Orders is given and all are still based on Palladio's interpretation of Roman relics. Isaac Ware was a Palladian theorist, architect and builder. A protégé of Richard Boyle, third Earl of Burlington, and the builder of Chesterfield House, London and Wrotham Park he was, like his patron, dogmatic in his theories about architectural design. Yet it was a dogma laced with reality and not suppressive of it for he was, after all, a builder as well as a Palladian scholar and had to put up with the whims of his clients. When Ware's patrons demanded some incorrect but fashionable folly he was obliged to build it for them and his book reflects the professional annoyance he felt as he built:

"In houses which have been some time built and which have not an out of proportion room, the common practice is to build one on to them ... the custom of routs has introduced this absurd practice. Our forefathers were pleased with seeing their friends as they chanced to come and with entertaining them when they were there. The present custom is to see them all at once, and to entertain none of them; this brings in the necessity of a great room,

4 Plate from Joseph Moxon's *Vignola or the Compleat Architect* published in 1702 and based on Jacopo Barozzi Vignola's popular interpretation of the architectural orders, *Regole delli Cinque Ordini* published in 1562

5 Plate from Abraham Swan's *Designs in Architecture* published in 1757

Plate IV

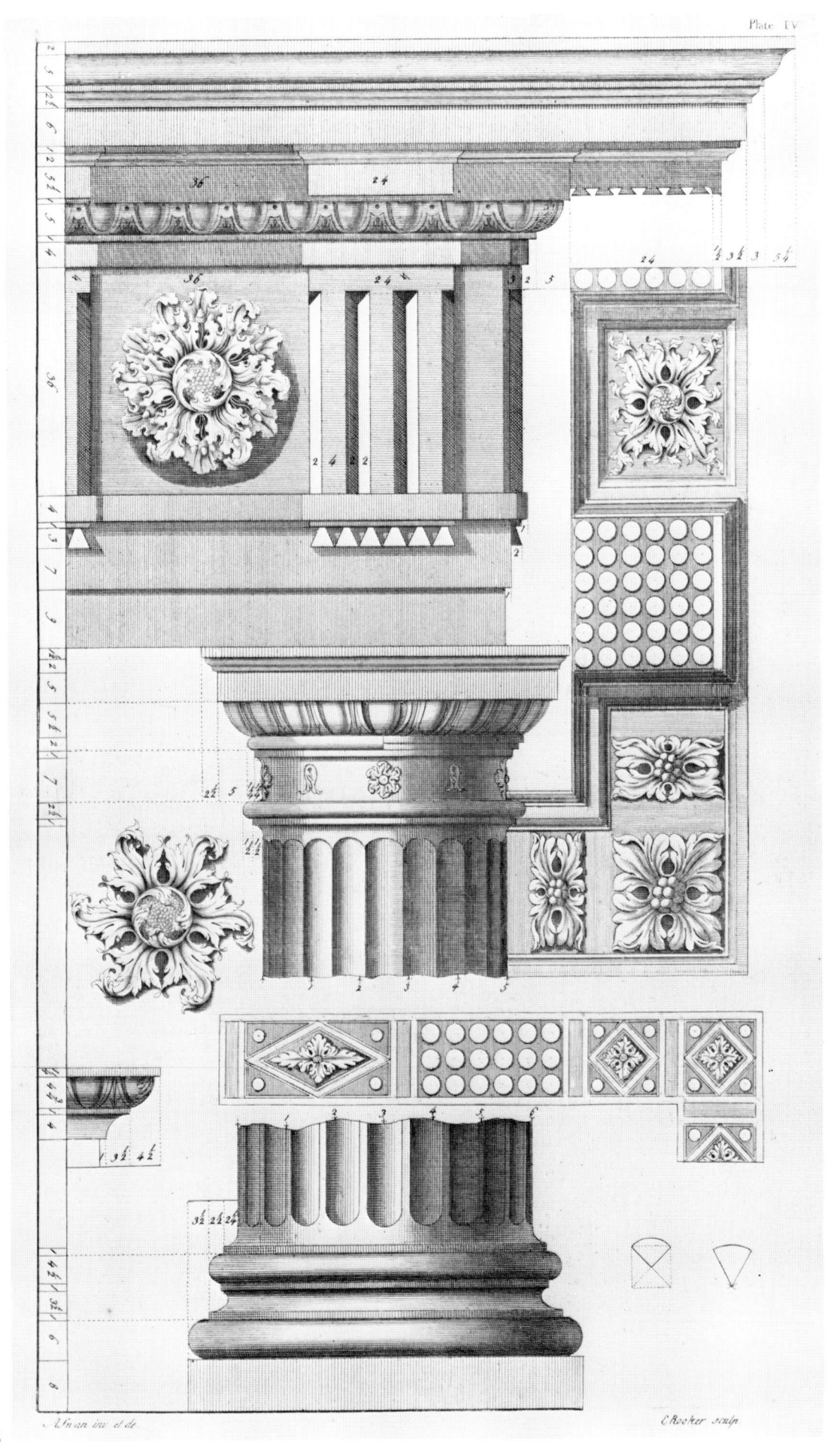

The Five Orders of ARCHITECTURE with their PEDESTALS.

TUSCAN. DORICK. IONICK. CORINTHIAN. COMPOSITE.

Cornice. Frize. Architrave. — ENTABLATURE
Capital. Shaft. Base. —
Cap. Base. Pluth. — PEDESTAL

6

7

8

which is opened only on occasions, and which loads and generally discredits the rest of the edifice....

"This is the reigning taste of the present time in London, a taste which tends to the discouragement of all good and regular architecture, but which the builder will be often under a necessity to comply with, for he must follow the fancy of the proprietor, not his own judgement....

"What ever the false taste of any proprietor time may adopt, the builder, though he complies with it from the orders he receives yet he must never suppose that the caprice or fashion can change the nature of right and wrong. He must remember that there is such a thing as truth, though the present mode will not follow its steps; and establish it as a maxim in his own mind, that proportions and regularity are real sources of beauty and always of convenience."

What the Palladians would not admit was that their architectural aesthetic was really as arbitrary as anything that had preceded it. As far as they were concerned, the ancients had found an architecture in total alignment with the laws of nature and Palladio was their prophet and they his disciples.

Just about the time Isaac Ware was publishing his great book on Palladian building practice, an architectural revolution was brewing. This was the beginning of the Neo-Classical movement and it led to the rethinking and re-assessment of all the old accepted concepts about classicism. New sources of information about classical architecture were found, examined, recorded and spread throughout Europe. The new ideas reached England bound up in large and expensive books which were produced by young architects and dilettante historians and artists who, on their Grand Tour, studied ancient remains in Italy, North Africa and Greece. Instead of taking Palladian interpretations of Roman remains as the basis of their concepts about ancient architecture, they investigated the actual relics for themselves. They also studied Hellenistic and Greek remains—which Palladio had not—and came up with startling results. The effect of the new information was, at first, only to change and enlarge the repertoire of decorative motifs, but ultimately it changed attitudes both to proportion and form.

In 1757 Robert Wood published his *Ruins of Balbec*, a sequel to his *The Ruins of Palmyra*. The books consisted of many huge and finely engraved details, elevations and plans and a wealth of new decorative ideas.

The classical architecture Wood recorded was very un-Palladian. Plate **7** shows a niche with a segmental pediment with its typanum filled by a shell motif. The capitals are composite, but of an unusual design with simple, well-defined acanthus leaves licking up from the astragal. The pilaster shafts have recessed panels filled with vegetable decoration—in this case oak leaves. This was a motif picked up by Robert Adam during the 1760s.

Plate **8** shows a detail of blind arcading between columns. The decoration on the cornice above the arch became typical of Neo-Classical work during the 1770s. The top member is decorated with anthemions and the bottom member is fluted.

In 1762 James 'Athenian' Stuart, whose temple at Hagley built in 1758 was the earliest Doric Revival building in Europe, published in conjunction with N. Revett the influential *Antiquities of Athens*. Like Robert Wood's work, it was the fruit of the researching and recording of ruins, undertaken in this instance during a visit to Greece between 1751–55. This work also included scholarly reconstructions, but however more acceptable they are to our contemporary preference for archaeological accuracy, for more than forty years after the publication of this work, purely Greek forms were unacceptable to the English taste and even Stuart, although he accurately reconstructed the Greek Doric temple shown in plate **9**, did not think of building consistently in that form himself. On his return to England, his general practise was simply to take appropriate motifs from his research, adapt them where necessary and fit them into conventional Palladian-proportioned façades.

As well as being a piece of academic research, the *Antiquities of Athens* was also, for Stuart, a form of exclusive and distinguished advertising to attract patrons to his style of architecture in the hope they would employ him. The young Robert Adam, for very similar professional reasons also felt obliged to produce a learned and diverting book to catch the attention of the fashionable world. During his Grand Tour from 1754–58 he surveyed with his mentor, Charles-Louis Clérisseau, the Emperor Diocletian's palace at Split in Dalmatia, the results of which were published under the title, *Ruins of Spalatro* in 1764.

Plates **10**, **11** and **12** show details from Stuart and Revett's *Antiquities of Athens*. Plate **10** shows a form of composite capital and entablature. It was an extremely novel design when published and was too bizarre to be immediately acceptable. It was not commonly used until the early 19th century when, for example, Nash used it to decorate his Strand improvements. Plate **11** must have been even more unpallatable to the Palladians of the day. Based on none of the established orders it has instead of volutes, palm leaves and then acanthus. It was taken from the ruins of the Tower of the Winds. But this pattern was picked up by Adam, becoming in fact one of his standard motifs, and by the end of the 18th century it had found its way into the repertoire of workmen throughout the country.

Plate **12** shows a more recognisable Ionic capital. The proportions of the volutes are large and the Greek anthemion motif around the neck of the column, a motif so beloved by the Neo-Classicists, is very finely recorded. As one would expect, the publishers of these architecturally blasphemous designs enraged the Palladians, but fashion was ready for a change, and rich patrons, intrigued by the published snippets offered by Stuart and Adam,

6 A handsome delineation of the Five Orders from Isaac Ware's *A Complete Body of Architecture* published in 1756

7, 8 Plates from Robert Wood's *Ruins of Balbec* published in 1757

made sure that money and commissions were forthcoming to produce buildings in the new style. Furthermore, having to be fashion conscious to survive, modest craftsmen and builders were more or less compelled to familiarise themselves with the new designs no matter to what extent the architectural establishment decried them, and thus Neo-Classicism found its way into even the back streets of East London.

The Palladians were, however, too officially entrenched to be immediately overthrown and although Neo-Classicism with its humane lightness and airy wit caught the favour of the fashionable world. Palladianism still kept control of the official architectural sphere, which readily characterised itself in the person of Sir William Chambers. Chambers, the leading late Palladian and declared enemy of Adam's brand of Neo-Classicism, had been tutor to the Prince of Wales and was architect for the new government offices built on the site of Somerset House. He had published as long before as 1759 his *Treatise on Civil Architecture* which had rapidly become an influential standard text, and when this classic work was reprinted in 1791 he took the opportunity to add some acid comments on the new architectural developments promoted by his younger contemporaries. After his descriptions of the interior of Kent's Holkham Hall, for example, which Chambers had discussed in 1759, he added in 1791.

"Since writing the above thirty years have elapsed, and a very different stile of decoration has been introduced . . . The executive powers of our workmen are certainly improved, yet, it is far from certain, that the taste is better now, than it was then. That stile, though somewhat heavy, was great; calculated to strike at the instant . . . They were easily perceptible without a microscope, and could not be mistaken for filigree toy work. Content with the stones, which the refined ages of antiquity had left them, the architects of the day ransacked not the works of barbarous times; nor the portfolios of whimsical composers; for boyish conceits and trifling complicated ornaments."

Plainly, Chambers was attacking Adam and, also plainly, he did not like Greek architecture for even that produced during the golden age of Athens he called barbarous. His concept of what classical architecture was, and should be, had crystallised some time before and it

9, 10, 11, 12 The elegant fruits of the Grand Tour taken from James Stuart's and N. Revett's *Antiquities of Athens* published in 1762

Fig. 2.

Fig. 1.

Chap:III.Pl:VII.

Fig:2.

Fig:3.

J. Basire sculp.

Vol. II Chap. II Pl. VIII

Fig. 3.

Fig. 4.

Fig. 2.

Fig. 1.

13

14

was impossible for him to aesthetically assimilate the new appreciation of Greek architecture.

In this 1791 edition he also wrote, "Since therefore the Grecian structures are neither the most considerable, most varied, nor the most perfect, it follows that our knowledge ought not to be collected from them; but from some purer, more abundant force, which can be no other than the Roman antiquity yet remaining." He went on, "... their gauty columns, their narrow intercaluminations, their disproportionate architraves, their temples, which they knew not how to cover."

Chambers was an old man when he railed against Neo-Classicism but N. Reveley in a later edition of *The Antiquities of Athens,* answered him slyly by reminding the public that Chamber's own Palladianism was not so orthodox that he had jibbed at building the celebrated Pagoda at Kew between 1757–62 when chinoiserie was all the vogue, "Sir William seems to insinuate in his opinion upon the subject that the Pantheon would gain considerably with respect of beauty, by the addition of a steeple. A judicious observer of the fine arts would scarcely be more surprised were he to propose to effect this improvement by adding to it a Chinese pagoda."

While the highly conservative Chambers was gradually fossilising, his arch rival, Robert Adam, was interpreting and building, to great acclaim, in the new style. By the mid-1770s Adam felt he had done enough good work to justify the publication of the *Works in Architecture of Robert and James Adam.* The first volume was published in 1773 (the second and third volumes following in 1779 and 1822 respectively) and was both a record of the brothers' achievements and a base from which Robert Adam could argue and analyse his architecture and style, and of course in the process, drum up more business.

In his preface, Robert Adam proudly wrote, "We have not trod on the path of others, nor derived aid from their labours ... The skilful will easily perceive within these few years a remarkable improvement in the form, convenience, arrangements, and reliefing of apartments, a greater movement and variety in the outside composition, and in the decoration of the inside an almost total change. The massive entablature, the ponderous compartment ceiling, the tabernacle frame, almost the only species of ornament formerly known in this country, are now universally exploded, and in their place we have adopted a beautiful variety of light mouldings, gracefully formed, delicately enriched, and arranged with propriety and skill."

To justify this self praise Adam, in a little sniping at the established forms, and perhaps at Sir William in particular, remarked, "Nothing can be ... more sterile and disgustful, than to see for ever the dull repetition of Doric, Ionic, and Corinthian entablatures in their usual proportions, reigning round every apartment."

Plate **13** is taken from the Adams' *Works in Architecture*

13 Plate encapsulating Robert Adam's most frequently recurring decorative motifs from the *Works in Architecture of Robert and James Adam* which the brothers published in three volumes between 1773 and 1822

and the details it contains are typical of Robert Adam's style. On the right the capital has large Greek Ionic volutes and the frieze contains Adam's anthemion designs. The impost, attached to the column shaft, has flutes. The column on the left has a capital derived from Stuart and Revett's *Antiquities of Athens.* Palm leaves replace acanthus and there are no volutes. The frieze is fluted and contains patera and the shaft of the pilaster is panelled (like Wood's Balbec example on page 8) and contains anthemions. The key pattern motif which came into new popularity during the Neo-Classical period is featured in a section of frieze as is the wave or Vitruvian scroll pattern.

These plates and quotations encapsulate the main stream of architectural fashion during the 18th century and also predict its course during the first few decades of the 19th century. Pure Greek forms and details gradually became more and more acceptable until by 1810–20 nothing else would do and temple fronts as pure as that illustrated by Stuart and Revett in 1762 (see page 10), were being built up and down the land in front of halls, churches, banks and mansions.

But as always there were more frivolous exceptions to the rule and subsidiary stylistic channels did run parallel with the mainstream of development. Sir William Chambers' celebrated Pagoda at Kew showed one course already well under way, that of chinoiserie, and although these frequently Europeanised evocations of Chinese art reached their greatest height of popularity during the 18th century the craze continued to linger on into the next, gaining yet another spurt of vitality from the Brighton Pavilion built between 1802–21.

Another constant subsidiary stream to the major flood of architectural debate was the Gothic style, which had never died out in the work of old-fashioned craftsmen working on small or out-of-the-way buildings. During the late 18th century the Gothic Revival gave a new and mannered impetus to the use of Gothic and since both the old-fashioned Gothic and the new sophisticated form of it overlap, the art historian is frequently confronted with distinguishing between the Gothic Survival and the Gothic Revival. Horace Walpole's Strawberry Hill built between 1750–70 is one of the most celebrated fragile and whimsical monuments of the new sophisticated, artificial Gothic in 18th-century England, but before work commenced on this building the London builder–architect Batty Langley in his spurious way, had already caught the drift of the new fashion for Gothicising and typically kept his options open by relating the new fashion to his own peculiar brand of 'classicism'. Langley's book entitled *Gothic Architecture Restored and Improved* was published in 1741 and, ludicrously, attempted to 'improve' Gothic by making it conform to classical orders and discipline. In many cases, as in the example shown here, Langley simply took classical motifs, made them suitably pointed, elongated and generally deformed, and rammed them together as Gothic. Plate **14** shows this eccentric approach in a classical entablature with cornice, frieze—containing pointed trygliphs and metopes —and architrave. The shafts are elongated Doric columns.

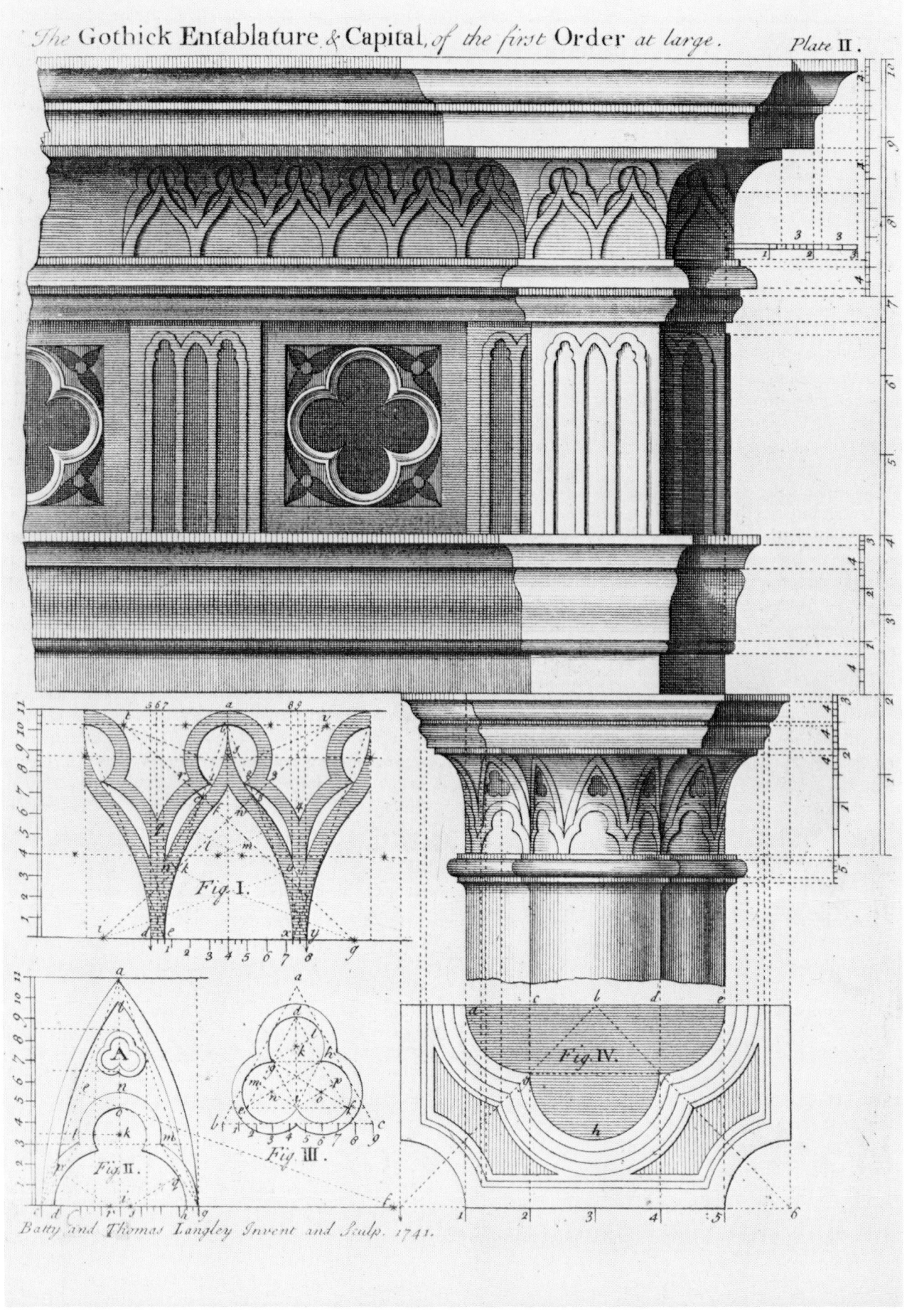

The Gothick Entablature & Capital, of the first Order at large. Plate II.

Fig. I.
Fig. II.
Fig. III.
Fig. IV.

Batty and Thomas Langley Invent and Sculp. 1741.

This was not taken seriously, especially by such thoroughgoing aesthetes as Horace Walpole who made a point of jeering at Langley and his optimistically opportune attempt.

Any brief examination of the publications in which the Georgians act out the cut and thrust of the contemporary aesthetic debates which ultimately affected all buildings from the greatest to the least celebrated, leads us inevitably to consider how two centuries or so later we ourselves evaluate their building achievements, not only technically or aesthetically, but as basic environmental assets. This book is a record of a wide range of modest Georgian buildings which existed in the summers of 1973 and 1974, but already some have been demolished and still more are threatened and derelict (see plate **15**). This situation reflects a sad paradox. While the modest works of the Georgian period are generally recognised as the highlights of English domestic architecture and indeed, perhaps England's most consistent contribution to European architecture, in our great cities they are being continually destroyed and often for no very good reason other than the cruel distortion of urban economics which makes the land a Georgian house stands on infinitely more valuable than the house itself, despite its craftsmanship, age and beauty.

Despite the complex system of legislation in Britain to preserve and protect historic buildings which has been devised since 1947, if a local authority is unwilling to take ultimate responsibility for a building listed as being of architectural or historic interest, there is no way of saving it, even if it is wantonly neglected by its owner. The owner can only be made to repair and restore his property if the local authority serves a Repairs Notice and once such a Notice is served, the council is obliged, if no repairs begin, to compulsorily purchase the building. Unfortunately, councils have generally proved themselves unwilling to take the chance of becoming responsible for decaying and expensive historic buildings and they prefer to negotiate with the owner to the extent that he can delay long enough to have the building declared a Dangerous Structure by the District Surveyor. Ironically, the motive for permitting minor Georgian buildings to rot beyond redemption is the same as that which originally caused them to be built—the raw exigencies of speculation, although the high standards in individual craftsmanship and design which characterised the works of Georgian speculative builders cannot be paralleled today in the new buildings which ultimately appear on the graves of the old.

The ultimate purpose of *London: The Art of Georgian Building* is therefore to show by new and painstaking measured drawings and by 18th-century plates and quotations how the Georgian terrace house works and the aesthetic and technical logic which informed it, in the hope that although such buildings will never be classified among the greatest monuments of 18th-century architecture they will be regarded afresh as objects of modest dignity and beauty which very necessarily, indeed vitally, lend a sense of cultural continuity and grace to the increasingly ravaged wastes of Britain's cities. In the preparation of this book many scenes of dereliction and desolation were surveyed and since these ravages occur daily and increasingly, they ultimately lead one to visualise what sense of place and time London will offer both inhabitants and visitors by the end of the 20th century. Inevitably, without a new commitment to protect the networks of minor Georgian terraces and squares, the extent and variety of which currently distinguish London from any other city in the world, it is safe to say that London will no longer be London, nor worthy of the name of the Augustans' city.

14 Shotgun marriage of Classicism and Gothic from Batty Langley's *Gothic Architecture Restored and Improved* published in 1741

15 Millman Place, Bloomsbury, built in 1721 and demolished in 1971

PART I FAÇADES

Introduction

"In Architecture, there seems to be two opposite affections uniformity and variety; yet these seeming opposites may be very well reconciled; as we may observe in our bodies, the great pattern of nature, which is very uniform in the whole figuration, each side agreeing with the other, both in number, quantity, and measure of parts; And yet some are round as the arms, others flat as the hands, some prominent, and others indented or retir'd; so the limbs of a noble fabrick may be correspondent enough, tho' they be various, provided we no not run out into extravagant fancies."

Richard Neve, *The City and Country Purchaser* 1703

The impact of the Georgian façade was due primarily to the careful blending and contrasting of its details, for although each detail, such as the doorcase, the cornice and the windows, expressed the essential qualities of Georgian design, it was only when they were framed in a well-proportioned façade that a synthesis was achieved in which the whole added up to an aesthetic effect infinitely greater than the parts. The balance and emphasis of this sum total of related details fluctuated almost year by year as each detail and proportion was revised in accordance with the latest fashion or the latest Building Act, and the purpose of Part I is to trace such subtle development in façade design beginning in 1680 and ending in 1830. (A detailed, illustrated chronological development is given in pages 40–81.)

The proportioning of the façade in which details were disposed was achieved according to an 'invisible' vertical and horizontal grid that crossed the surface of the façade (see plate **21**, page 39). Throughout the Georgian period the proportioning of this imaginary grid was based on a concept inherited from Italian Renaissance architects who in turn had drawn it from the Ancients' principle of proportioning the classical columns and entablature of the temple front. But the Renaissance architects also combined this regard for ancient proportion with a decision which was a reflection of con-

1 Plate from Sebastiano Serlio's *Tutte l'Opere d' Architettura* published in 1584

temporary social requirements in Italy, to make the first floor of a house or palace the primary floor: the *piano nobile*. The rooms in the *piano nobile* were the loftiest in the building and since windows were proportioned to room height, the windows of this first floor were the tallest windows in the façade. The *piano nobile* and the proportionally shallower floor above it, called the chamber floor, took up the portion of the façade which corresponded to the capital and shaft of the classical temple front. Above the chamber floor would be a cornice and any window above that, having to conform to the proportions of the attic, would therefore be squat and would be usually square. This proportioning, apart from being based on sound classical principles, looked har-

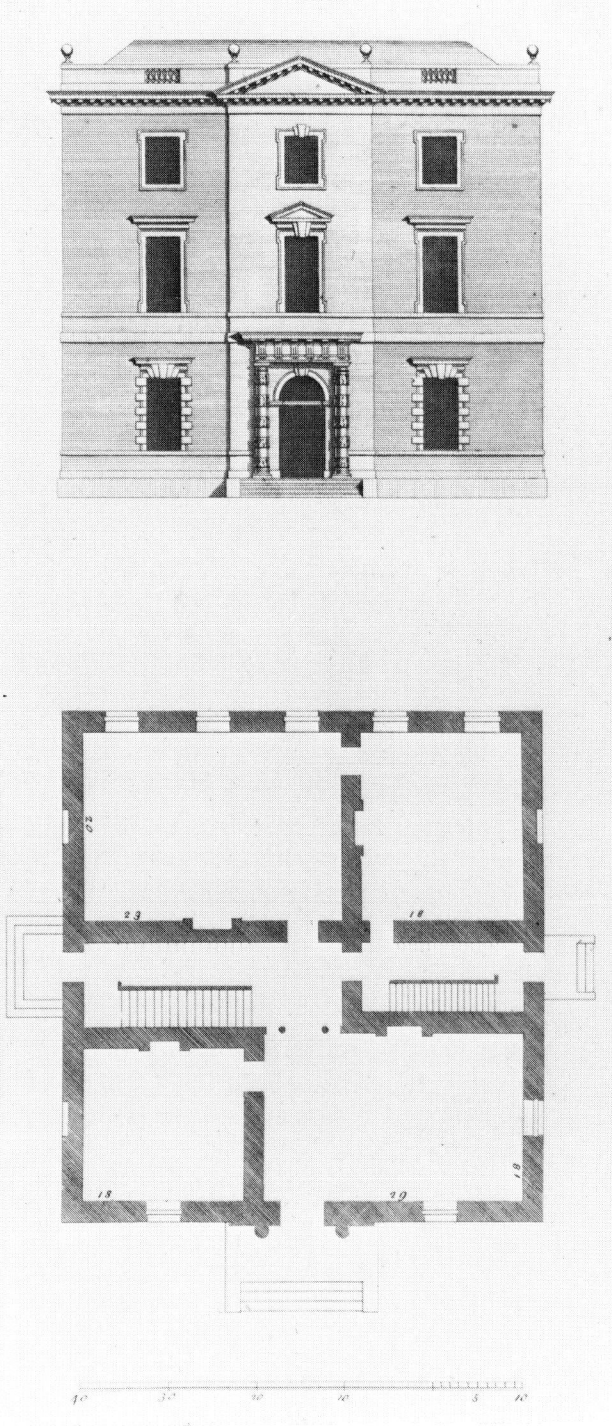

2, 3 Ideal elevations and plans from *A Collection of Designs in Architecture* published by the carpenter and joiner Abraham Swan in 1757. They show how completely the proportions of the 18th-century façade were based on the Italian tradition of the *piano nobile* and the concept of 'invisible' applied Orders

monious and balanced because the windows became shallower as they got higher. Furthermore, since the bottom of the tall first-floor windows corresponded to the base of a column, the ground floor itself corresponded with the plinth of a column, or the basement of a classical temple. Here again the windows would be sturdier, usually about the same proportion as those on the

Chamber Plan   Parlour Plan

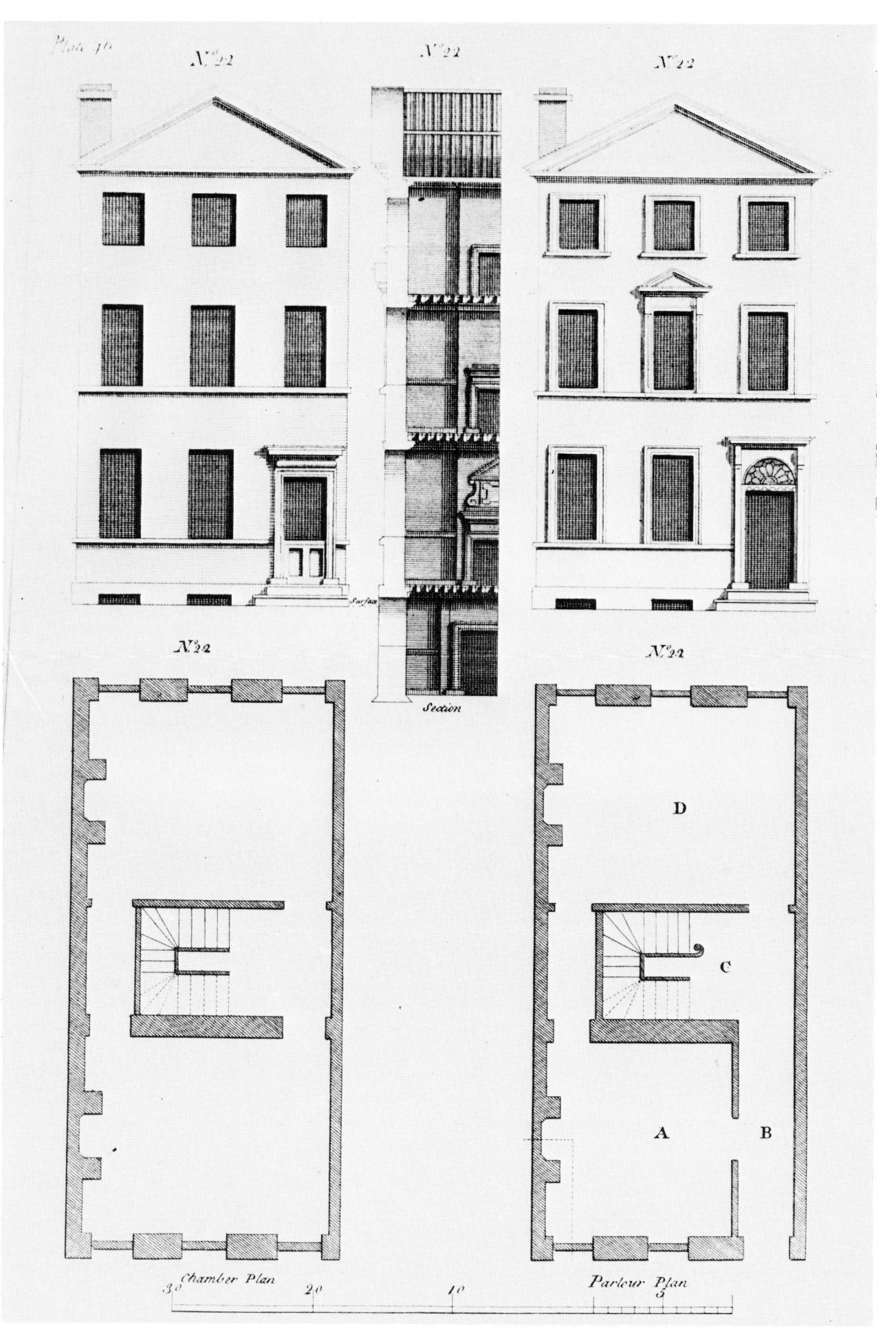

chamber floor, and possibly the surface of the ground-floor façade would be rusticated to give an additional impression of stability.

At first, the relationship of the column and its related parts to the façade was literal, for the façade would be dressed with columns and pilasters (see plate **28**, page 68). This meant that as well as the vertical grid, the columns also determined the horizontal grid because the placing of the windows on the same floor was dictated by the intercolumnation of the particular Order chosen to decorate the façade. When the actual columns themselves were dispensed with, the façade became a rigid chequer of void and solid and, if nicely proportioned, the solids above the window could also do much to enhance the total proportion of the façade.

When uniform terrace housing first came to London in the 1630s with Inigo Jones' Covent Garden Piazza it was, in the Renaissance manner, dressed with a classical Order which encompassed the first and second floors, whilst the ground floor was treated as a rusticated basement. After a transitional period in which the place of columns or pilasters was taken by a simple pilaster strip which articulated the façade in and out (see plates **5** and **8**, pages 43, 46) practically any obvious hint of a column or entablature had been dropped by the beginning of the Georgian period. The tradition had been established however, and windows continued to be placed as if they were fitting in between columns, entablature and basement. In fact the only clue to this disposition of voids was the cornice (this feature had decorated the façade until banished in 1707 and again reappeared between 1740–60 when it presented less of a fire hazard in stone) and the various string courses which, as well as structurally binding the façade, marked the various divisions of the classical front.

In the late 17th and very early 18th centuries, despite the influence of Wren and his school, the average speculative terrace house did not much display the principle of the *piano nobile* and as often as not all the windows would be practically the same height as would be the solids between windows. This was the period of the English Baroque and the Orders were used primarily as decorative two-dimensional motifs (see plate **3**, page 42) with no structural or proportional implications. A pilaster, elongated to the whim of the designer in accordance with Baroque verticality, might freely be used without it determining the positioning and proportions of the windows. But after the establishment of Palladian taste in the 1720s, the development and use of the *piano nobile* became one of the key features of the Georgian façade. By 1750 its use was very pronounced and a subtle and sophisticated method had been developed for relating the proportions of the window voids to the solids between them.

4 Elevations and plans for a terrace house from William Halfpenny's *The Modern Builder's Assistant* published in 1742 and 1757. Halfpenny, who was also known as Michael Hoare, produced well over a dozen such influential architectural manuals for country gentlemen and builders, some in conjunction with his son John Halfpenny

The Neo-Classical revolution of the 1770s did nothing to alter the basic proportion and structure of houses, only their decoration and by 1800 the *piano nobile* principle was so firmly established that when terraces were being mass produced all over London the *piano nobile* proportion was being used as a standard formula. Peter Nicholson writing in his *Practical Builder* in 1823 reflects the way the classical column was still totally accepted as the proportioning tool. "For in them," he said, "originate most of the forms used in decoration: they regulate most of the proportions." Concerning the way in which these Orders were occasionally misused, he continued, "The suppression of parts of the ancient Orders, with a view to produce novelty, has, of late years, been much practised among us, but with very little success."

Plates **2**, **3**, **4** and **5** published during the second half of the 18th century as ideal patterns for façades, show how completely the proportions were based on the *piano nobile* and the concept of 'invisible' applied Orders. Each example has a heavy horizontal emphasis from the strings and cornices that mark where the different elements of the 'invisible' Orders begin and end.

The 18th-century English Palladian totally accepted this Renaissance–Roman interpretation and categorisation of the Orders, of which there were five. The plainest and most squat was the Tuscan, followed by the Doric, Ionic, Corinthian and Composite which became progressively more decorated and elongated. The proportioning of the constituent parts of each Order was very precisely laid down and all one had to do was to determine a single dimension and all the other dimensions were worked out from that. Plate **6** shows the Five Orders as engraved for Edward Hoppus in his *The Gentleman's Repository, or Architecture Displayed* published in 1738. He describes them all in detail and of the Ionic Order for example he says,

"Any Height whatever being given for this whole Order, divide it into ten Parts, allowing two to the Pedestal, and divide the remaining eight into six, giving one to the Entablature, and five to the Length of the Column, inclusive of the Capital and Base. The said Length being divided into nine Parts, will be the Diameter of the Column, which must be found to regulate some of the smaller Members following.

The Height of the Entablature is divided into six, allowing two to the Architrave, one and an half to the Freeze, and two and an half to the Cornice. The Architrave projects one-fourth of its Height, and the Cornice equal to its Height. The Height of the Pedestal is divided into seven Parts, allowing two to the Base and Plinth, four to the Dado, and one to the Cap.

The Column is diminished one-sixth of the Diameter, from one-third of the Length of the Shaft, in the same Manner as the last Order was, and the Base of the Column projects the same, which gives likewise the Breadth of the Dado of the Pedestal.

The Base of the Pedestal is one-third of the two Parts given for the Base and Plinth, and the Projection thereof equal to the Height, and the Cap projects three-fourths of its Height."

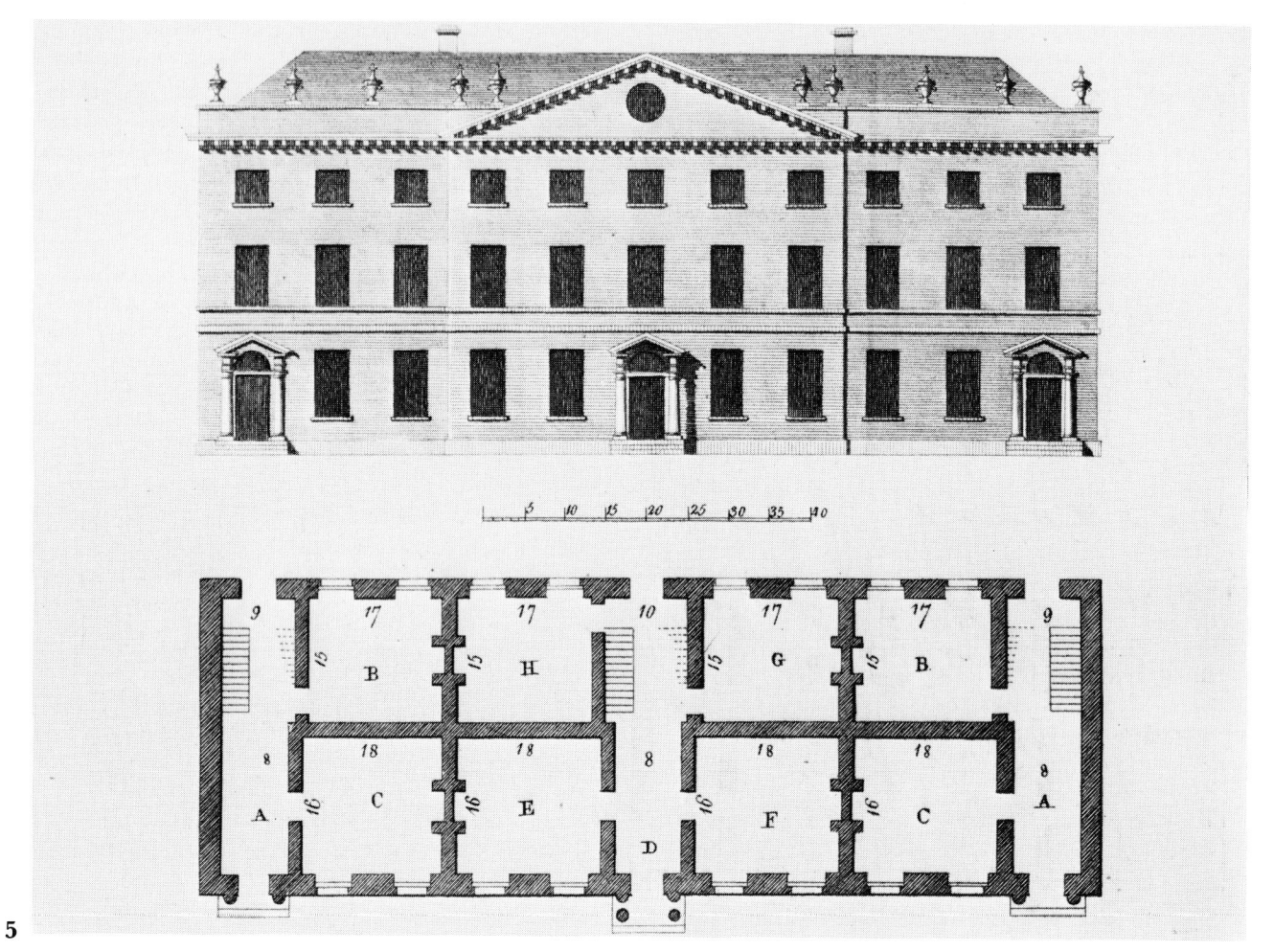

Briefly, these are the aesthetic disciplines which together determined the development of the Georgian façade, but it is important to realise to what degree these fashions were controlled and stimulated by structural and legal specifications and a comparison of the dates and requirements of the various Building Acts with the rise and fall of architectural fashions shows just how important to contemporary Georgian builders they were. More subtly, however, it must also be remembered that to some degree the Acts also reflected the general trends of taste itself. For example in the Act of 1774 the clauses which affected façades enforced a bold simplicity that was totally in keeping with the aesthetic trends of the time.

In the early 17th-century London was undergoing a revolution both in material and design as it was being transformed from a vernacular timber city to a classical one of brick and stone. James I actively encouraged this change from wood to brick and in 1619 a Building Act was issued that controlled the use of brick by relating thickness of wall to height of building, " . . . if the said building does not exceed two stories in height, then the walls thereof shall be of the thickness of one bricke and halfe a bricks length from the ground unto the uppermost part of the said walle."

This ratio remained fairly constant throughout the Georgian period until the very cheap speculation of the 1820s and 1830s when it was common for two- and three-storey buildings to have façades only 9 inches thick.

The first definitive Building Act to deal with the

5 Plate from John Crunden's *Convenient and Ornamental Architecture, consisting of Original Designs for Plans, Elevations and Sections from the Farm House to the most grand and magnificent Villa* which was dedicated to the Duke of Newcastle and first published in 1768. Crunden is thought to have been the pupil of Henry Holland the Elder and became District Surveyor to the parishes of Paddington, St. Pancras, and St. Luke, Chelsea

relationship between types and heights of buildings and their wall thickness was the Act of 1667. This Act was intended to control the rebuilding of the City of London and only applied there. The width of roads determined the heights and types of the buildings that lined them and primarily, the Act was therefore intended to prevent the City from being rebuilt to its former chaotic street pattern. Charles II in a proclamation of September 13th, 1667 summed up what the Act was essentially intended to do in saying that the ". . . City (should) have less lanes (and) fair new frontages to the River."

Apart from its townscape qualities, the Act also very much determined the development of façade design and decoration. Firstly, to ensure a handsome uniformity, the Act stated, "Be it enacted—that there should be only four sorts of buildings and no more, and that all manner of houses to be erected shall be of one of these four sorts of buildings and no other". Any offender, the Act said, ". . . shall be committed in the common jail of the said city, there to remain without bail or main prize, till he shall have abated or demolished or otherwise amended the same".

The four types of houses were:

"**A.** The first, or least sort of house fronting by-streets, and lanes. (It was to be two stories high with basement and attic. The basement and ground floor walls were to be 2 bricks thick, the first floor 1½ bricks thick, and the parapet only 1 brick thick. The basement was to be 6½ feet high, the first and second floors 9 feet high).

B. The second sort fronting streets and lanes of note and the Thames. (It was to be of basement, three stories and attic. Basement and ground-floor walls 2½ brick thick, first-floor walls, 2 bricks thick, second-floor walls 1½ brick thick, and the parapet 1 brick thick. The ground and first-floors were both to be 10 feet high and the second 9 feet high, so, by this Act, the *piano nobile* was, for medium houses, made illegal.)

6 Plate delineating the comparative proportions of the Five Orders from *The Gentleman's Repository, or Architecture Displayed* published by Edward Hoppus in 1738. This book was also known as *Architectura Civilis*

C. The third sort fronting high and principal streets. (It was four stories, basement and attic. Basement and ground-floor walls were to be 2½ bricks, first, second and third-floor walls 1½ brick thick, and the parapet 1 brick thick, and for this type of house the Act proposed a *piano nobile* proportion. The ground floor was to be 10 feet high, the first floor 10½ feet high, the second 9 feet and the third 8½ feet high.)

D. The fourth and largest sort, of mansion house for citizens or other persons of extra-ordinary quality not fronting either of the three former ways." (For this type the wall thickness and room heights were left to the builder's discretion, but the house could not be taller than four stories). Also, the Act specified that, "The roof of . . . the first, second, and third sorts of houses respectively shall be uniform".

Apart from the thickness of the walls being of brick, the Act also insisted that the outside of all buildings were to be, "Of brick or stone, or brick and stone, except doorcases, window-frames, breastsummers and other parts of the first storey to the front, between the piers, which are to be left to the discretion of the builder to use substantial oaken timber instead of brick or stone for conveniency of shops".

All through this Act there was great emphasis on the idea that brick was the material to build with—both for structural security and fire prevention and for aesthtic reasons. It said, for example, that the doors, window-frames and breastsummers were to be, "discharged of the burden" of carrying the load above by "arch work of brick or stone either straight or circular", so the structural use of brick arches was recommended. However, from the decorative point of view, the Act also said, "It is ordered that the surveyors take special care that the breastsummers of all houses do range of an equal height house with house, so far as it shall be convenient and there to make breaks by their directions, and that they do exchange and give directions to all builders for ornaments sake, that the ornaments and projections of the front building be of rubbed bricks; and that all the naked parts of the walls may be done of rough bricks neatly wrought, or all rubbed at the discretion of the builders".

Apart from all the directions that controlled the construction and aesthetic of the façade, the Act also contained many specifications to do with structural framing. It said for example,
"No timber to be laid within 12 inches of the fire side of chimney jambs.
No joists to be laid more than 12 inches apart.
No joists to bear length more than 10 feet.
No single rafter more than 9 feet in length. All roofs and window frames to be of oak. No girder in brick building to be over head of doors or windows.
No girder to be let less than 10 inches into brickwork."

The preoccupation of this 1667 Act with sound construction and the use of brick was a natural reaction to the Great Fire that had swept through the jumbled, wooden city the year before. But forty years later the fear of fire still determined the nature of the Building Act of 1707. The Act explained itself as, "an Act for the better, preventing mischiefs that may happen by fire" and like the 1667 Act also concerned itself with wall thickness and related design features.

"New houses shall have party walls wholly of brick or stone—2 bricks thick in cellar and ground storey, 13 inches thick upwards through all storeys to 18 inches above the roof." This "18 inches above the roof" meant that a parapet 18 inches high should divide the roofs of each house in a terrace. But the major effect this Act had on the design of façades was contained in the statement that, "No . . . mundillion or cornish of timber or wood under the eaves," which meant that the characteristic carved eaves cornice, along which flames could spread so easily from house to house, was banished from the façade. Since this Act only applied once again to the Cities of London and Westminster, houses with wooden cornices could still be built in the suburbs. In place of the cornice, the Act suggested parapets and it further laid down that front and rear walls were to be built of brick or stone and were to continue 2 feet 6 inches above the garret floor with no beams or rafters built into the brickwork of gable ends.

Two years later in 1709 another Act was issued to supplement the 1707 Act. It legislated further for the security of structures by stating that no brickwork or stonework in the front, party, or partition walls of any house should be supported, depend or otherwise bear upon any sort of timber or woodwork with the exception of piles or planks where they were absolutely necessary for foundations in marshy and unsound ground.

The influence this Act had on façade design was simple but profound. It required that door frames and window frames of wood be let 4 inches (or 1 brick-width depth) into the wall. Again this was to prevent fire spreading easily up a façade. Like the 1707 Act, this Act only applied in the Cities of London and Westminster, but, quite extraordinarily for various reasons it was not compl ed with so that until the late 1720s, even in the very heart of the fashionable West End, it was usual to fit windows out in box sashes flush with the façade.

These were the last major Building Acts for nearly 70 years, but attached to other Acts there were often clauses relating to building and some of these clauses affected the design of façade. In 1724 a clause in an Act required that down pipes be fixed to take water from roofs. This encouraged the highly functional use of one of the elements so characteristic of Georgian façades: the down pipe, which visually divided the continuous terrace

7, 8, 9, 10 Elevations and plans for First, Second, Third and Fourth Rate houses from Peter Nicholson's *The New and Improved Practical Builder and Workman's Companion* published in 1823. Nicholson was deeply interested in the application of scientific methods to building practise and apart from his improvements to the construction of hand-railing for which the Society of Arts awarded him its Gold Medal in 1814, he is believed to be the first author to have written on the construction of hinges and the hanging of doors

FIRST-RATE HOUSE.

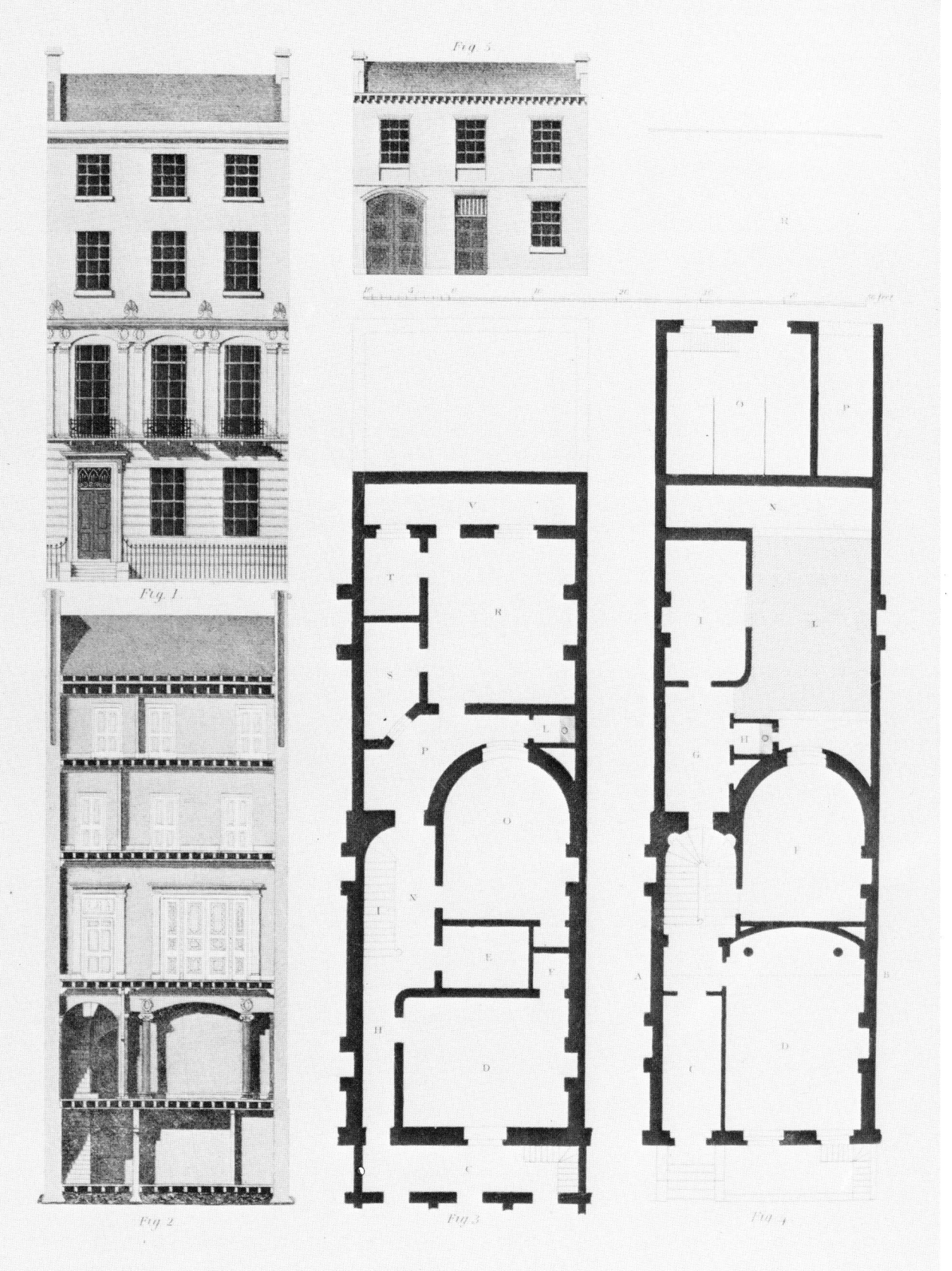

SECOND RATE HOUSE.

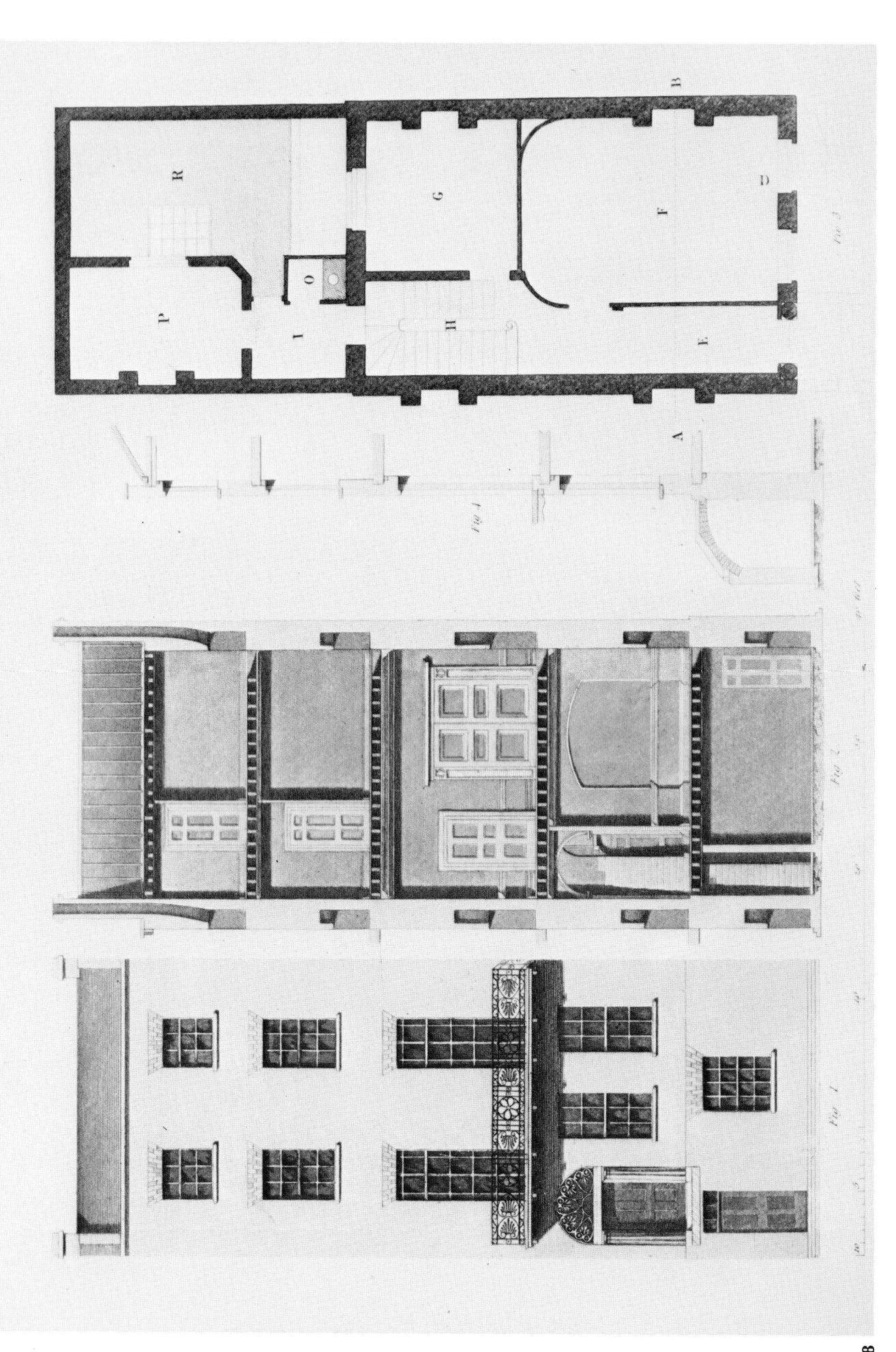

THIRD-RATE HOUSE.

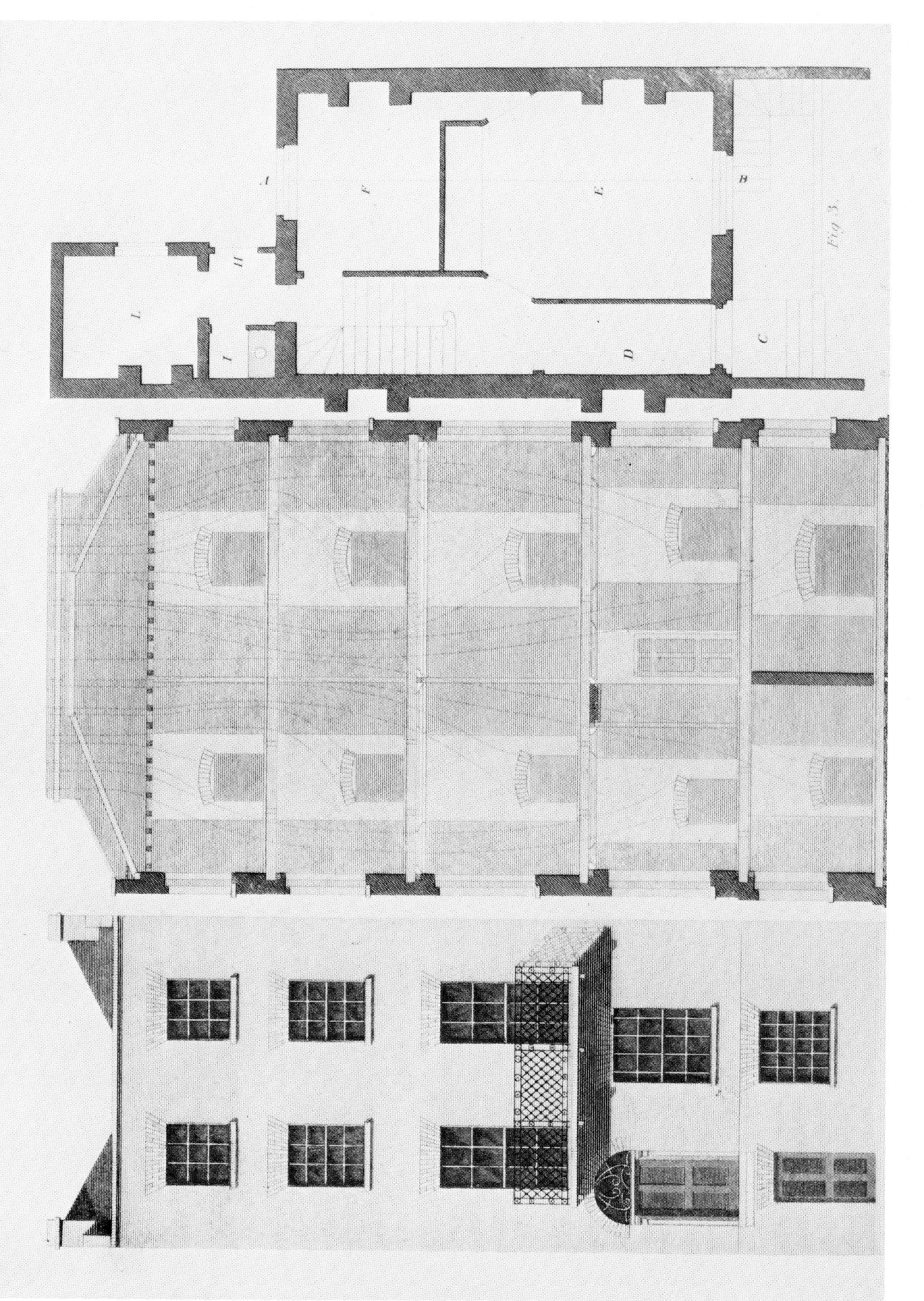

FOURTH-RATE HOUSE.

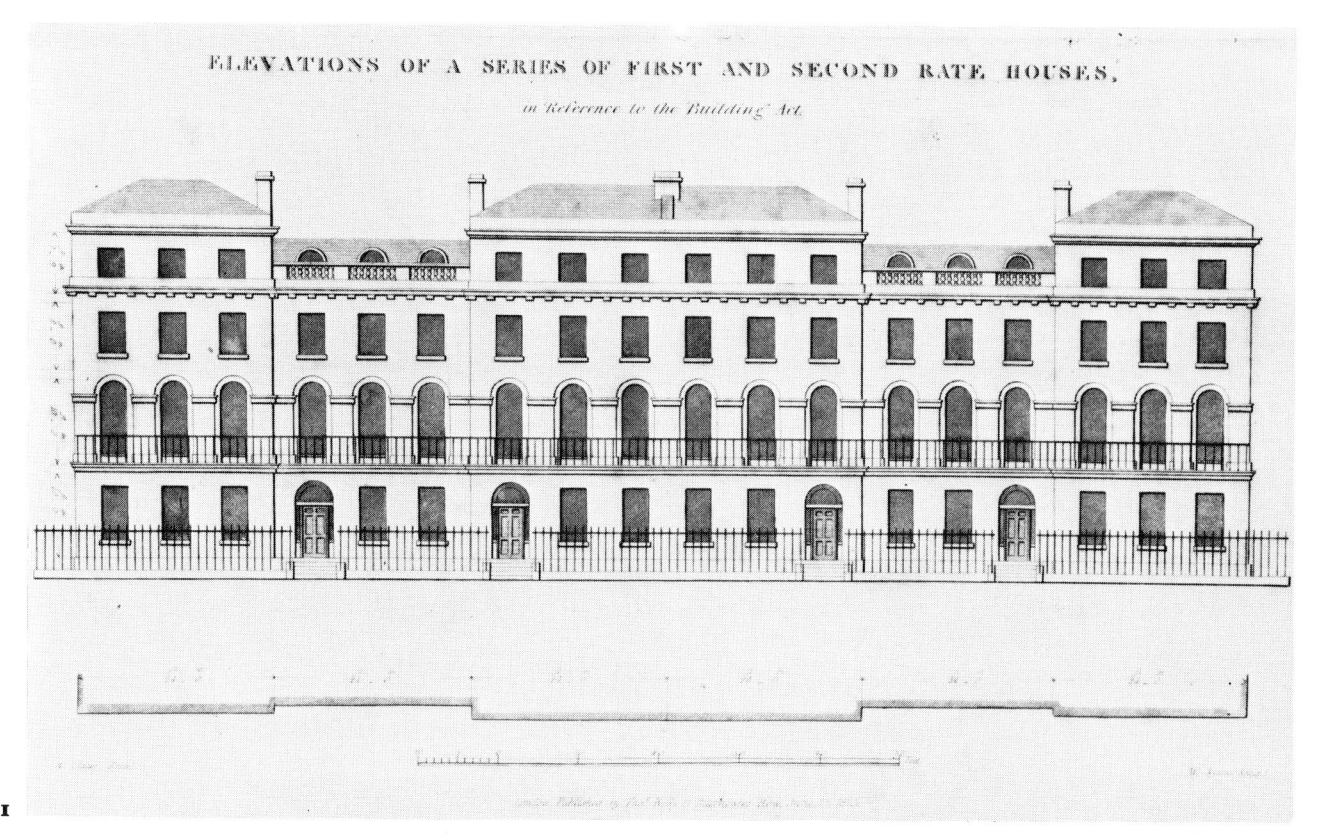

11 Elevation of a 'palace-front' terrace from Richard Elsam's *The Practical Builder's Perpetual Price-Book* published in 1825

front into many vertical and individual units. This played one of the major rôles in the subtle relationships between vertical and horizontal lines that kept the harmonious and austere Georgian façade from becoming merely dull and repetitive.

In 1760 a clause in an Act said that cellars should have walls 2½ bricks thick, and in 1764 party walls were to be 2½ bricks thick in the cellar, and 2 bricks to the garret with 1½ bricks at least 18 inches high above the eaves. This same Act of 1764 also said that, "All houses should be created and built of stone or good sound, hard, well-burnt bricks and none other built in the front and back walls and likewise the pantry walls and that no breast-summer shall be provided higher than the first floor".

In an Act of 1765 the use of bond timber in walls, except for short lengths to act as spreaders under the ends of heavy timber, was prohibited.

In 1770 an Act was passed for, ". . . continuing and amending several acts for preventing abuses in making bricks and tiles". This Act fixed dimensions and prices of bricks and, to a degree, specified their manufacture and sizes. The Building Act of 1774 was an enormous affair, and was intended to be comprehensive and, once and for all, to tidy up all the loose ends and define concisely all aspects of construction and, to a large degree, determine decoration.

The oath the surveyor for the Act swore explains very well the aims and areas of jurisidiction of this Act, "for the further and better regulations of buildings and party walls; and for more effectively preventing mischief by fire within the Cities of London and Westminster, and the liberties thereof, and the other parishes, precincts, and places within the weekly bills of mortality, the parishes of Saint Mary-le-bone, Paddington, Saint Pancras and Saint Luke of Chelsea, in the county of Middlesex."

As far as it affected façades, the main interest of the 1774 Act was that it divided buildings into seven different classes or Rates according to their volume, expense of construction, use and position. It also very rigidly controlled the amount of decoration on façades, especially wooden ornament. Unlike the 1667 Act which this Act repealed and superseded, it did not relate size of buildings to width of streets and after 1774 mansions could legally be built in alleys, a fact which from the townscape point of view made this Act retrograde. The seven Rates of building in the 1774 Act were as follows:

First Class buildings included such structures as churches, manufactures, warehouses and large dwellings worth at least £850. Dwellings to come within this class had to exceed 9 squares in areas (a square was 100 square feet—see page 3) and all other buildings had either to comprise at least four storeys above the ground or exceed 31 feet in height measured from the pavement to the top of the front wall (see plates **7** and **11**).

To qualify for the Second Class buildings had to be at least three storeys above the ground in height and be worth not more than £850 (see plate **8**).

Third Class buildings had to be at least two storeys above the ground (see plate **9**) while Fourth Class structures were to be one storey above the ground and worth no more than £150 (see plates **10** and **12**).

The Fifth and Sixth Classes referred to isolated buildings. Those isolated buildings erected 4 feet from

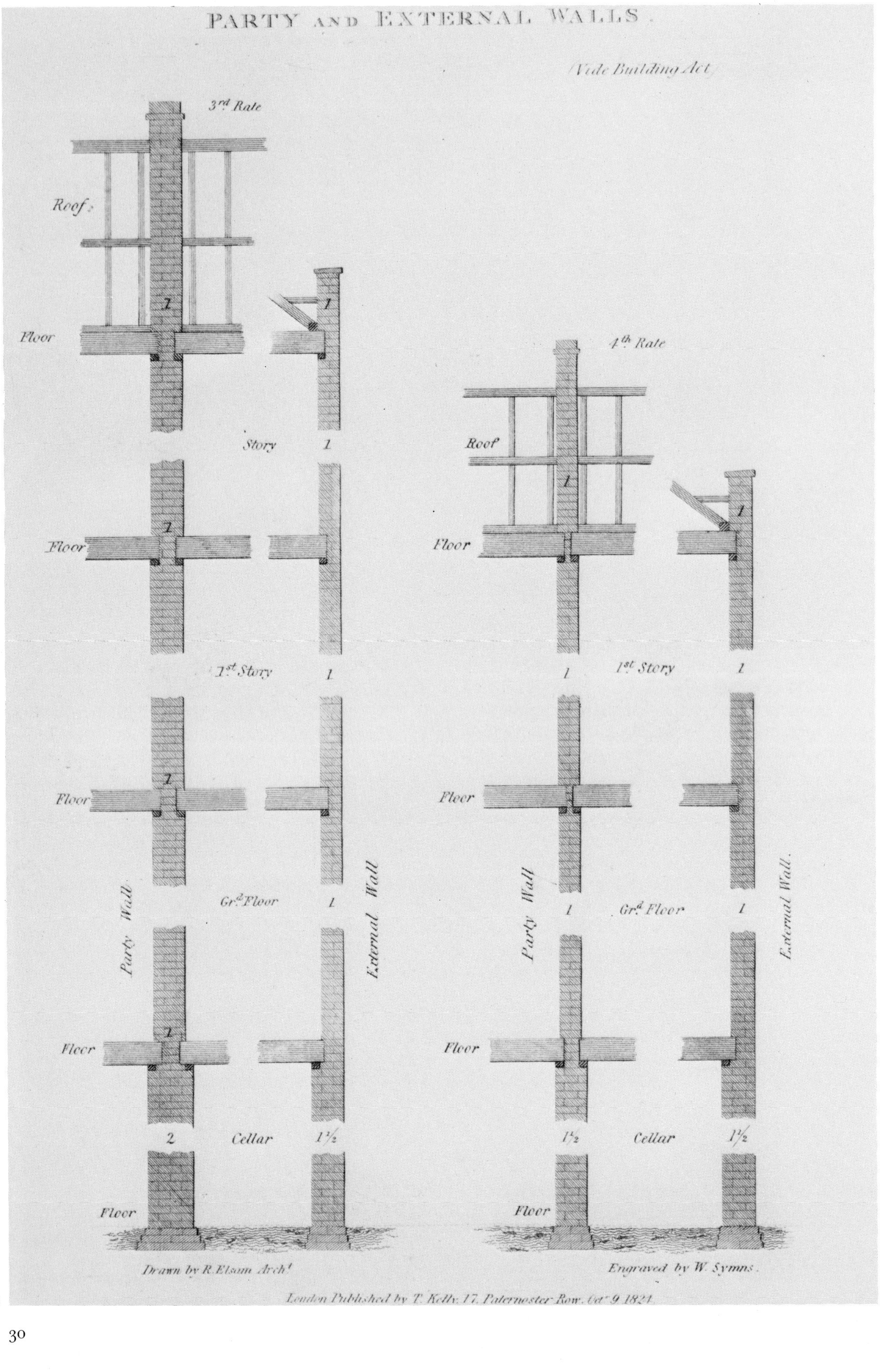
PARTY AND EXTERNAL WALLS.
(Vide Building Act)
3rd Rate
Roof
Floor
Story
1
1
Floor
1st Story
1
Floor
Gr.d Floor
1
Party Wall
External Wall
Floor
2
Cellar
1½
Floor
4th Rate
Roof
1
1
Floor
1
1st Story
1
Floor
Party Wall
1
Gr.d Floor
1
External Wall.
Floor
1½
Cellar
1½
Floor
Drawn by R. Elsam Arch.t
Engraved by W. Symns.
London Published by T. Kelly, 17, Paternoster Row, Oct.r 9. 1821.

12

any public road and 16 feet from any other building could be built to any dimension. Those 8 feet from any public road and 30 feet from the nearest building could be built to any dimension and also in any material.

The Seventh Class dealt with special structures such as crane houses, windmills, watermills and workshops which could "... be built to any dimension whatsoever".

The 1774 Building Act specified the thickness for party and external walls for each Class. All external walls were to be 2½ bricks thick at the bottom and then diminish. Furthermore, for Classes One to Five, the Act laid down that the external walls were to be built of "brick, stone, artificial stone, lead, copper, tin, slate, tile or iron, or of brick, stone and such artificial stone, lead, copper, tin, slate, tile and iron together, except the necessary piling, bridging and planking for the foundations of the same and also except the necessary template, chains, bond-timbers, and also except the doors, sashes, window-shutters and door and window frames to such buildings". For the purpose of fire prevention, but with the result of controlling and simplifying external decoration, the Act ruled that the bow window should not be built to extend beyond the line other than the cornice to door and window, of the iron area railings. Shop windows in streets 30 feet wide and more, could not project more than 10 inches and in streets less than 30 feet wide could not project more than 5 inches. Nor could cornices in streets 30 feet wide, project more than 18 inches, nor more than 13 inches in streets less than 30 feet wide. No external decoration was to be of wood except cornices on dressings to shop windows, and frontispieces to doorways.

An important and characteristic change to windows and doors occurred in the statement, "all which ... shall be set in reveals, and (recessed) at least 4 inches from the front of the building in which they are fixed." No longer was it good enough to merely recess the vulnerable box sash: after 1774 it had to be completely kept out of the way of flames by being tucked into and behind the brick of the window void.

Work not executed in accordance with the 1774 Act could be demolished or amended and workmen liable to a fine of 50 shillings for executing work contrary to the Act. They could also "... be committed to the house of correction, there to remain without bail or main prize, for any time not exceeding three months or less than one month unless the penalty be sooner paid".

In 1810 an amendment was passed to the 1774 Act. It allowed the use of a bitumen-type material for covering any flat roofs and gutters, etc. It was an extraordinary amendment, and read rather like an advertisement, referring to Ambrose Bowder who in 1806 had, a "... newly invented composition called John's Patient Tessera composed of limestone or any other stone powdered, or road stuff, where stone is made use of for repairing roads, and other articles of a stoney, sandy or calcareous nature, with a sufficient addition of tar or other bituminous

12 The construction of Third and Fourth Rate party and external walls from Peter Nicholson's *The New and Improved Practical Builder and Workman's Companion*

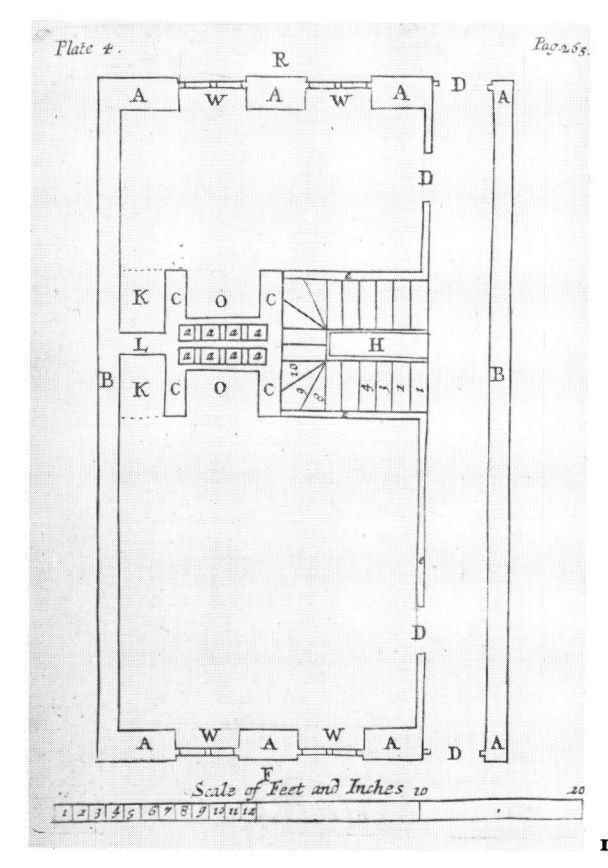

13 Ground-floor plan of a post-1667 Building Act terrace house from Joseph Moxon's *Mechanick Exercises* published in 1703. Key: "*A* Piers of brick, *B* Flank walls, *C* Jambs of chimneys, *D* Doorcase of timber, *E* Timber partitions, *F* Front, *H* Open Nuel to give light to stairs, *K* Closets, *L* A brick and a half between closets, *O* Chimneys, *R* Rear front, *W* Windows of timber, *a* funnels of chimney, *1, 2, 3, 4* Steps of stairs called fliers, *8, 9, 10* Steps of stairs called winders"

substance mixed together by the application of considerable heat and powerful machinery, and afterwards pressed together and rolled into sheets ... to be used in the covering of buildings".

So much for the Building Acts as they affected façade design. The 1774 Act, like the 1667 Act provided a great deal of important legislation that ensured the firm construction of the interior of buildings, and since London brick-faced houses were, until the late 18th century, generally only brick shells filled with timber and plaster, the Act got deeply involved with the nature and quality of timber-framing within brick external and party walls. For example, the 1774 Act said, "No timber hereafter to be laid in any party arch, nor in any party wall, except for bond to same, nor any bond timber, within 9 inches of the opening of a chimney, nor within 5 inches of the flue ... All framed work of wood for chimney breast to be fastened to the said breast with iron work as holdfast, wall hooks, spikes, rails etc. .... No timber bearers to wooden stairs let into an old party wall, must come nearer than ... 4 inches to the internal finishings of the adjoining building".

Plate **13**, from Joseph Moxon's *Mechanicks Exercises* of

31

15

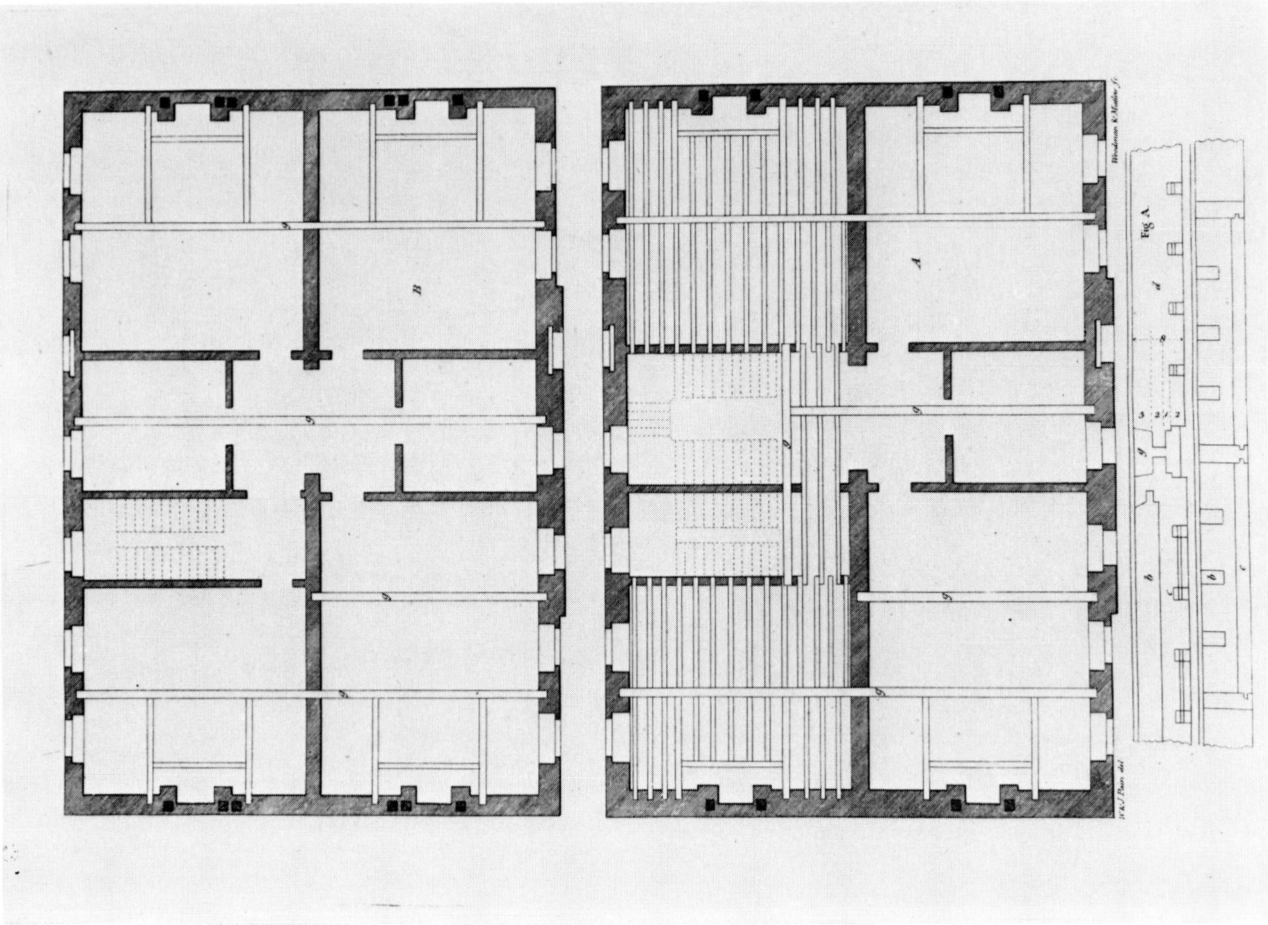

14

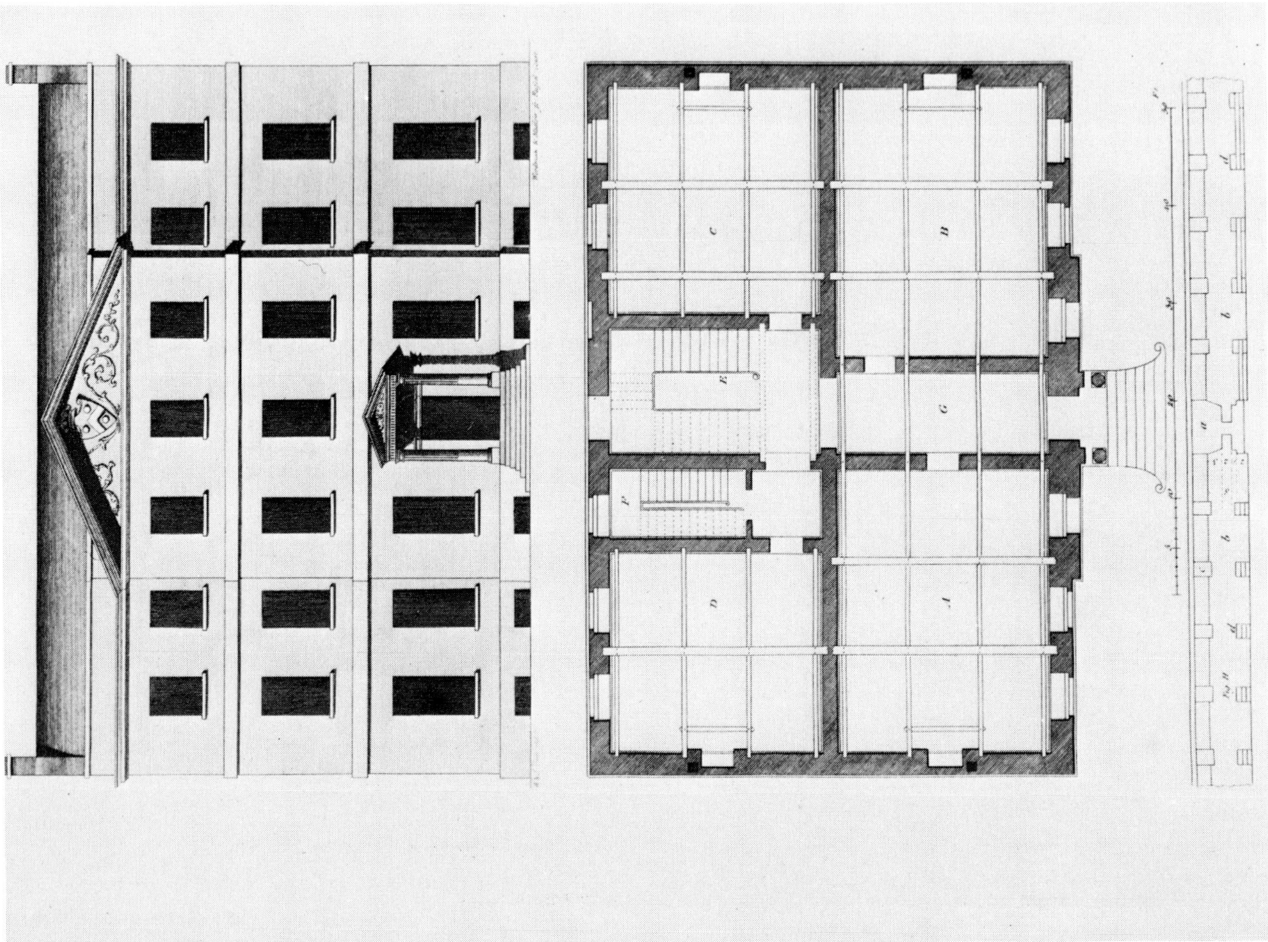

1703, shows the plan of a small terrace house after the 1667 Act. The plan is by no means that commonly used since the flues to the back and front rooms combine to form a central structural brick pier, one side of which supports the winders of the staircase and is itself unusual being in a central well rather than a dog-leg in one corner of the building. (Flues to chimneys were usually arranged so that the one in the front room stood in the middle of the wall and so formed a structural pier with the flue of the adjacent house—an essentially mirror plan.)

This could only happen if the same builder was responsible for both houses and this was often the case for it was proportionally cheaper to build a pair of houses rather than one. In the backroom it was common, throughout the Georgian period, to put the flue into the angle of the wall, usually the far corner. Again it would form a structural pier uniting with the adjacent paired house.

Plates **14, 15** from William Paine's *Builder's General Assistant* of 1786, shows a very large terrace house as it would have been constructed after the 1774 Act. Again uncommon because of its size, this house is designed with a number of internal structural walls. Usually, until about 1740–50, the main internal structural element of a terrace house was its large square beam running from party wall to party wall (and sometimes from façade to back elevation), with all the secondary joists running from these to the piers between the window of the external wall. In the second half of the century, it became usual to replace this timber structure with a brick internal spine wall running parallel to the external walls.

Plate **16** is from Peter Nicholson's *Practical Builder* of 1823 and shows the more usual joisting for a small post-1774 Building Act house.

14, 15 Post-1774 Building Act house from *British Palladio; or Builder's General Assistant; all the rules of Architecture; designs for Houses etc, with prices* published in 1786 by the architect and joiner William Paine. Although this was a very large house, it was designed with only two fronts and was presumably meant to be part of a terrace. Although the plates are dated 1785, the design is very archaic for that period, with a solidly Palladian façade of a kind that was being designed by fashionable architects from the 1740s to about 1760. Such details as the rococo enriched pediment, the cornice, heavy string courses and pedimented Doric porch, contain no trace of the Neo-Classical movement which by 1785, was already 20 years old.

Paine published a very detailed description of these plates and should the terms he uses be unfamiliar they are explained in brackets

14 "The length of the girders on this floor is 23 feet (these are the thickest main beams running at right angles to the façade and fixed between the piers between the windows and the internal spine wall parallel to the external walls); the clear between the walls 21 feet 6 inches (this means that each end of a girder goes into the brickwork to a depth of 9 inches); the scantlings 13 by 12 inches, the clear bearing at the binding joist about 10 feet (this refers to the smaller timbers running at right angles to and linking the girders), the scantling 9 inches by $4\frac{1}{2}$ inches, and they must be formed about $\frac{1}{2}$ inch below the underside of the girder and the girder pared down for the lathing, otherwise the ceiling will crack at the girder, which will spoil the beauty. The scantling of the bridging joist, 5 inches by 3 inches, to be used about a foot apart, the ceiling 3 inches by $2\frac{1}{2}$ inches, the distances for framing the binding joist from 4 feet to 6, or 6 feet 6 inches as they will best come in. The distance for the trimmers from the chimney breast 1 foot 6 inches or not to exceed 1 foot 9 inches (trimmers were small joists placed parallel to the wall immediately in front of fireplaces to receive the joists which would otherwise run into the party wall. The object of trimmers was to avoid the passage of structural joists too near the fireplace). Wall hold for girders to lie on the wall, from 9 inches to 12 inches; ditto for binding joist 6 inches. Oft is necessary to run arches over the end of girders; for, if any settlement should happen, that will prevent the wall from breaking"

15 This plate shows more joists connecting main girders to party walls and the pattern clearly shows how the trimmers in front of the chimneybreast worked. The floor boards would then be placed on these joists and so would run parallel to the girders.

The stairs on this plan run up between continuous structural brick walls, but in smaller terrace houses an oblique beam ran from the girder of one floor into the party wall or girder of another and the stairs were fixed into this. Usually, therefore, stairs were fixed in one corner of the house so that the other end of the treads—those not in the oblique beam—could be cantilevered out of the party or external wall.

Paine's plan also illustrates the disadvantages as well as the advantages of internal brick walls. These walls had to be bonded to the piers of the external walls and this could have awkward results. Once the positioning of the internal walls had been established to suit the requirements of the ground-floor front, the logic had to be continued upwards and the inflexibility could lead to the blocking up of two windows on each floor. In fact, Paine does not follow his own logic in this plan because, of the two walls that create the entrance hall, only one forms a foundation for the walls above it. On the other side of the building it would appear that the structural walls stand on nothing but floor boards and joists.

Paine's description of this plate reads, "*A* the one-pair floor, *B* the attic floor. The one-pair is divided into five bedrooms, the attic into six. Figure A (at the bottom of the plate) is the section of the floors for the one-pair and attics, drawn half an inch to the foot. The principal joists to this floor are about half an inch deeper than the girders, to prevent the ceiling from cracking; and they are framed at such a distance as will admit of two or three immediate joists between them, as shown in the section. The ceiling joist is framed into the principal joists, as in the section. *B* the intermediate joist; *C* the ceiling joist; *D* the principal joist; *G* the girders"

PLANS OF FLOORS TO A FIRST RATE HOUSE.

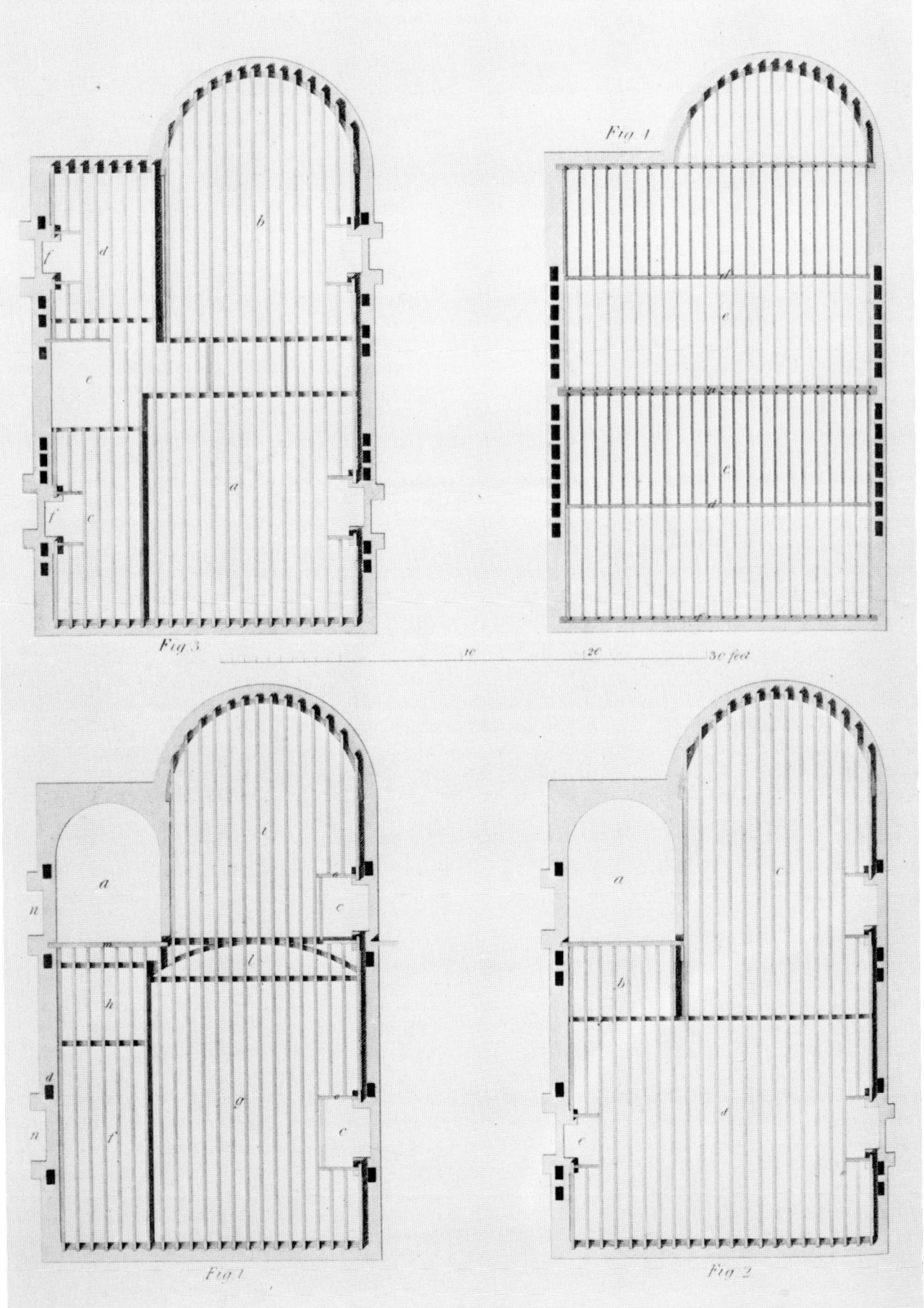

Fig. 3

Fig. 1

Fig. 1

Fig. 2

By the early 18th century, in terms of façade design and the proportion of voids and volumes, the Palladians had firmly established the principle of relating the interior and exterior of buildings. The façade was to be designed according to the size of the rooms, while the choice of surface decoration for the façade was generally dictated by the use of the building and the general concept that it should complement the interior designs. A characteristic of Palladian architecture is the contrast between the well-proportioned, austere façade and the rich, almost rococo interiors. This Palladian approach is very concisely recorded by Isaac Ware in his *Complete Body of Architecture* of 1756 (see plates **17** and **18**). Since 18th-century terrace houses were, structurally, merely traditional timber-framed structures hiding within fashionably dressed brick façades, it becomes clear that the relationship between interiors and exteriors in structural terms was very tenuous.

This relationship was weakened further by the demands of economy. In speculative building the fashionable and well-wrought brick façade was only half a brick deep, the bulk of the brick piers being cheap place bricks, and

16 Floor plans of a First Rate house from *The New and Improved Practical Builder and Workman's Companion* by Peter Nicholson, published in 1823

17, 18 Pages from the 1756 edition of Isaac Ware's *The Complete Body of Architecture* which, first published in 1735, became one of the most widely read 18th-century architectural text books. A youthful study of façades seems to have been unusually fortuitous for Ware since he is reputed to have been a chimney-sweeper's boy who was discovered by Lord Burlington whilst drawing an elevation of Inigo Jones' Banqueting Hall in chalk

these two skins were not bonded together nor even to the party walls which they passed across. Within this shell, the floors and walls would be framed in timber because wood was cheaper than brick.

Structurally therefore, the mass of Georgian architecture in the form of the speculative terrace house, was conceived very much as a stage set and the interior was only related to the exterior by the use of similar surface decoration. The 18th-century acceptance of superficial effects made this curious relationship possible, in the same way that it was socially acceptable to cover an ageing face and bosom with white lead-based paint or to wear heavy, rich Spitalfields embroidery and velvet over dirty linen. To a degree the dubious relationship between interior and exterior was a symptom of the continuing change from traditional building practice in London to new foreign influences. It is significant that this same superficiality manifested itself even in the treatment of different façades of one building. At Meard Street, Soho for example (shown in plate **19**) the pedestrian can see the front façade of some buildings as easily as the sides and back of others, yet in its visual effect the treatment of each elevation becomes progressively meaner and cheaper.

Even in the 18th century this contrast in the treatment of elevations was marked by the discerning architectural critic. John Gwynne in his *London and Westminster Improved* wrote in 1766, ". . . another great absurdity has been practised, which is that of erecting single brick edifices with stone fronts of a regular design, the sides and backs of which being entirely exposed present nothing but absurdity and contradiction, as motly compositions of stone and brick walls perforated with holes in order to admit light."

The sites on which such façades and their guts stood also received this same superficial treatment. Soil analysis and the preparation of foundations were barely understood sciences at the beginning of the Georgian period and had advanced only a little further by the end. Despite the plethora of books on building which were published between 1703 and 1825, those written towards the end of the period still put forward the same stock solutions practically word for word. Joseph Moxon in his *Mechanick Exercises* of 1703 wrote, "Try ground, that it be all over an equal firmness, that when the weight of the building is set upon it, it may not sink in any part." To achieve this he continued, "If ground is hollow or weaker in any place, he strengthens it, sometimes by well ramming it down, and levelling again with good earth, lime, core rubbish, or sometimes with ramming in stones, or sometimes with well planking it over; or most securely by driving in piles." Moxon also suggested that any faults should be "dug out" by extending the foundation until good ground was reached. In 1703 he also edited a book entitled *Theory and Practice of Architecture or Vitruvius and Vignola Abridged* in which Vitruvius' solution for good foundations was given. Vitruvius' recommendations were that the foundations for a building should be excavated to a level where solid earth could be reached, at which point the soil should be levelled or rammed down. If solid earth could not be reached, piles of elder, oak or olive were to be driven into it and the gaps filled up with coal. Evidently therefore, the treatment of foundations had not changed much in the preceding 1500 years either.

In 1756 Isaac Ware, in his *Complete Body of Architecture* wrote of foundations, "It is the first thing to be regarded in the erection of a house, and so much depends upon it that it can never be considered too thoroughly. In some places the ground is naturally firm enough for supporting the building . . . in others the ground wants this natural firmness, and must be assisted by art . . . The best ground for a foundation is that which consists of gravel or stone . . . We have advised the digging for wells and sewers first, and have cautioned him (the architect) to observe exactly what is thrown up; he will thus know what is beneath that uppermost bed, which promises in itself so much strength and solidity. There is often unsound matter underneath, and in that case the strength and firmness of the superficial strata is but a decoy . . . Foundations laid on the solid earth are always the most secure where that is hardest, and it is a very good sign when every shower of rain does not melt it into dirt. We have earth so hard that the tools will scarce penetrate them; these, when they have a sufficient support below, are the best of all". And as regards solution to difficult earth, Ware suggested, "Piling is the method in case of . . . boggy earth, and where there is a uniform sand, and this is one of the securist foundations when properly executed".

Ware also mentioned sewers and wells and later in his book he stressed the importance of providing proper sewers and drains when the foundations were being dug, for any omission or mistake then would take much time and money to correct later. "A private house", he said, "must have its principal drain for receiving from all the rest, and this, as it is the most essential article, is to be the architect's first care".

Nearly 60 years later in 1825 Peter Nicholson wrote in his *Mechanic's Companion* that, "Having dug the trenches for the foundation, the ground must be tried with an iron crow, or with a rammer, and if found to shake it must be pierced with a borer, such as is used by well diggers, then if the ground proves to be generally firm, the loose or soft parts, if not very deep, must be excavated until a solid bed appears . . . If the ground proves soft in several places to a great depth under apertures, and firm upon the sides on which the piers between the window of the superstructure are to be erected, the better way is to turn inverted arches under the apertures."

Nicholson in his *New Practical Builder*, published two years earlier, also pointed out an important link between foundations and the layout of streets. He wrote, "If a projected building is to have cellers, or under ground kitchens, there will commonly be sufficient bottom, without any extra process, for a good solid foundation. When this is not the case, the remedies are to dig deep, or to drive in large stones with the rammer, or by laying in thick pieces of oak . . . the ground having been previously well rammed under them". In writing about cellars or underground kitchens acting as foundations, Nicholson showed how the excavation for buildings could relate to, and determine, certain patterns of urban layout. The very word 'terrace' gives an understanding of the nature of the foundation. Before building a house the site had to be levelled—built up or excavated and in fact a level terrace created. In the early 18th century, for economic reasons and for reasons of land ownership, most London houses, although built in rows, were developed on individual or paired sites, and often building took place years apart.

Because of this unavoidable lack of co-ordination, the natural level of the site was taken as the basis for terracing

19 The 18th-century acceptance of superficial effects manifests itself in these terrace houses in Meard Street, Soho, London W 1, where, although three elevations are equally visible, the architectural treatment of them becomes progressively meaner

19

and usually all basements were completely excavated unless the nature of the terrain permitted different treatment. Later in the 18th century, however, when such great estates as the Bedford and the Portman Estates were being developed, a different kind of terracing was possible. As these estates were developed on the initiative of a few people and were generally under the entire control of one individual, development within the environs of the estate took place simultaneously and the use of built basements as foundations became a feasible practice. The section of a typical late 18th-century terrace house and road would show that the basement, say approximately 8 feet deep, would only be half excavated and 4 feet of earth would be thrown over the retaining wall of the coal vault, which ended at the pavement edge. This would mean that road would be built up about 4 feet above natural level, with the soil from the excavated basement of the house on each side. This rise, plus the 4 feet excavation, would give the basement its depth and the only place where the natural level survived would be in the back yard which would be approximately half way between the ground floor and the basement. This change of level is striking when, walking along a made-up road, the pedestrian reaches a mews or a side street and within the end depth of one house, the road surface falls down abruptly to the natural level.

20 These two houses in Britton Street, Clerkenwell, London EC 1, dramatically illustrate the chronological extremes of Georgian domestic design. No. 55, shown on the left of the photograph, is a perfect example of design in the 1820s, while its neighbour, equally perfect, dates from the 1720s. The arch motifs and imposts on the first floor of the former house only became really fashionable in the 1820s. Within the arch the window frames are recessed and the box let into the brick joists. The brick of the façade, both facing and cut, are pale marls.

The earlier house has a fine cantilevered doorcase and its bricks are warm, while the windows are dressed with fine red bricks. The sashes are flush with the façade and the boxes exposed

21 Geometry for the construction of an early 19th-century façade. The proportioning module for this construction was a square, usually 3 feet 6 inches, which determined both the width of a window and the horizontal and vertical distances between windows. By being logically extended this module also determined the depth of windows. Plate **29** on page 68 shows a house proportioned by this method

Road level

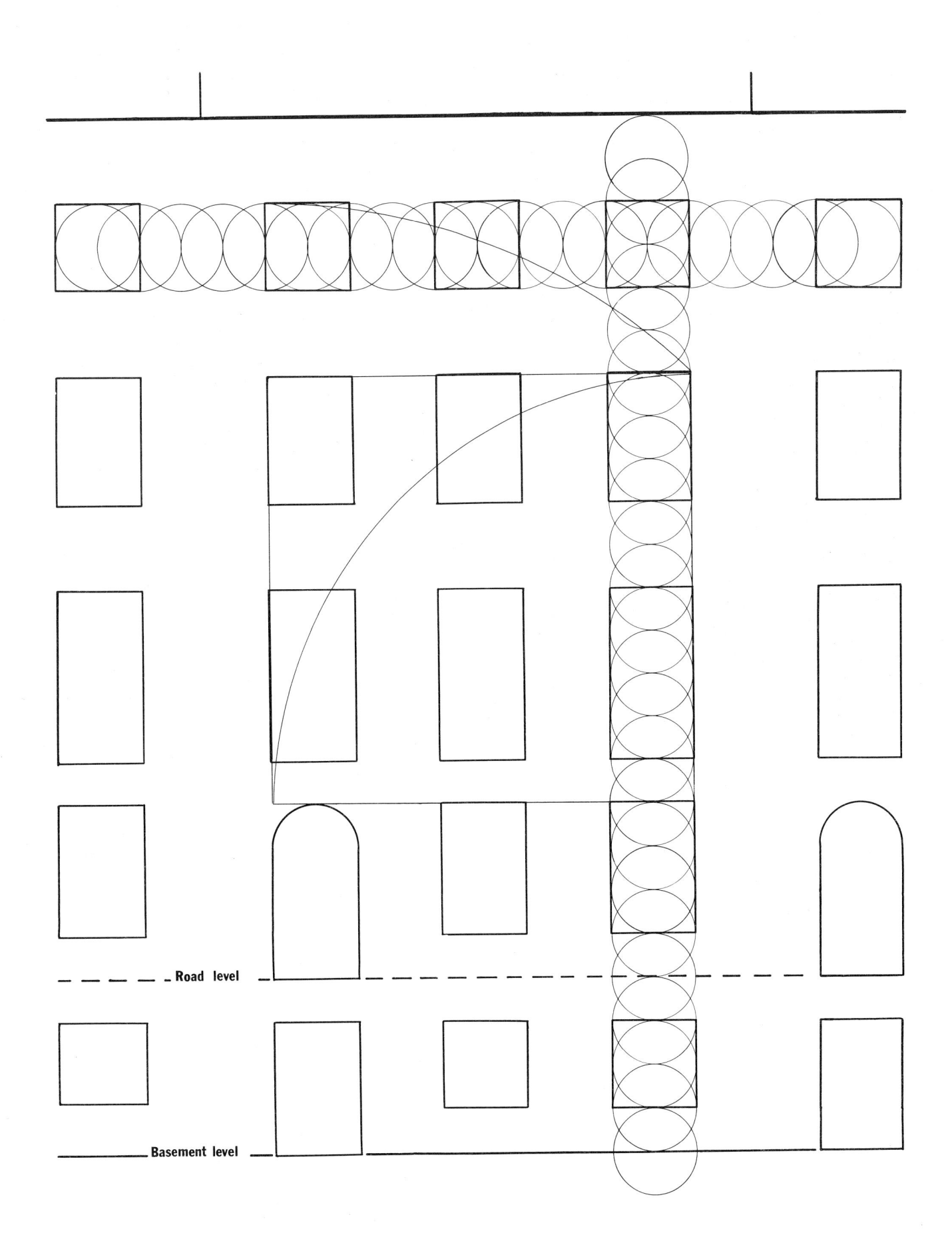

Basement level

21

Illustrated development

1 This much mutilated and decaying group of houses in Denmark Street, London WC 2, is very important as it is amongst the few surviving works of Nicholas Barbon, the prolific, speculative builder-architect of the late 17th century. Built in the 1680s, these houses are typical of Barbon's superficially sophisticated, highly fashionable, and almost mass-produced designs and they indicate the direction that speculative building in London was to take for the next 150 years.

The windows on the first floor of the centre house have been dropped and the subtle *piano nobile* of the left-hand house has more of Barbon's style. The string-courses and keystones are architectural devices used by Barbon to give his houses a bit of class and originally they would also have had wooden eaves cornices. The centre doorcase definitely dates from the 18th century, the left-hand doorcase probably does. The houses would have been built with casement windows but have been restored, in this drawing, with early 18th-century box sashes

2 This group of three houses in Old Town, Clapham, London SW 4, built *circa* 1705, contains many of the features and quality common in houses built before the 1707 and 1709 Building Acts. Buildings of this period are striking because of the incomplete synthesis between English vernacular building and foreign classical design and this may be seen here in the use of a heavy traditional pitched roof and dormer and the finely formed classical doorcases in one composition.

Elements of this façade which would later be controlled by the Building Acts are the cornice and the windows. For reasons of fire prevention the wooden eaves cornice was made illegal in the Cities of London and Westminster in 1707 and flush box sashes were ordered to be set back in 1709.

The windows are decorated with red brick dressings and, a common feature in the very early 18th century, the soffits of the first-floor window arches have been cut into serpentine shapes. Although built at that time in the country, this group of houses was conceived as a terraced urban unit and this was very likely due to economy of construction. The two houses on the right have a mirror plan and share a wide doorcase, while the house on the left is very much a separate composition. The double doorcase is shown in detail in plate **73**, page 126

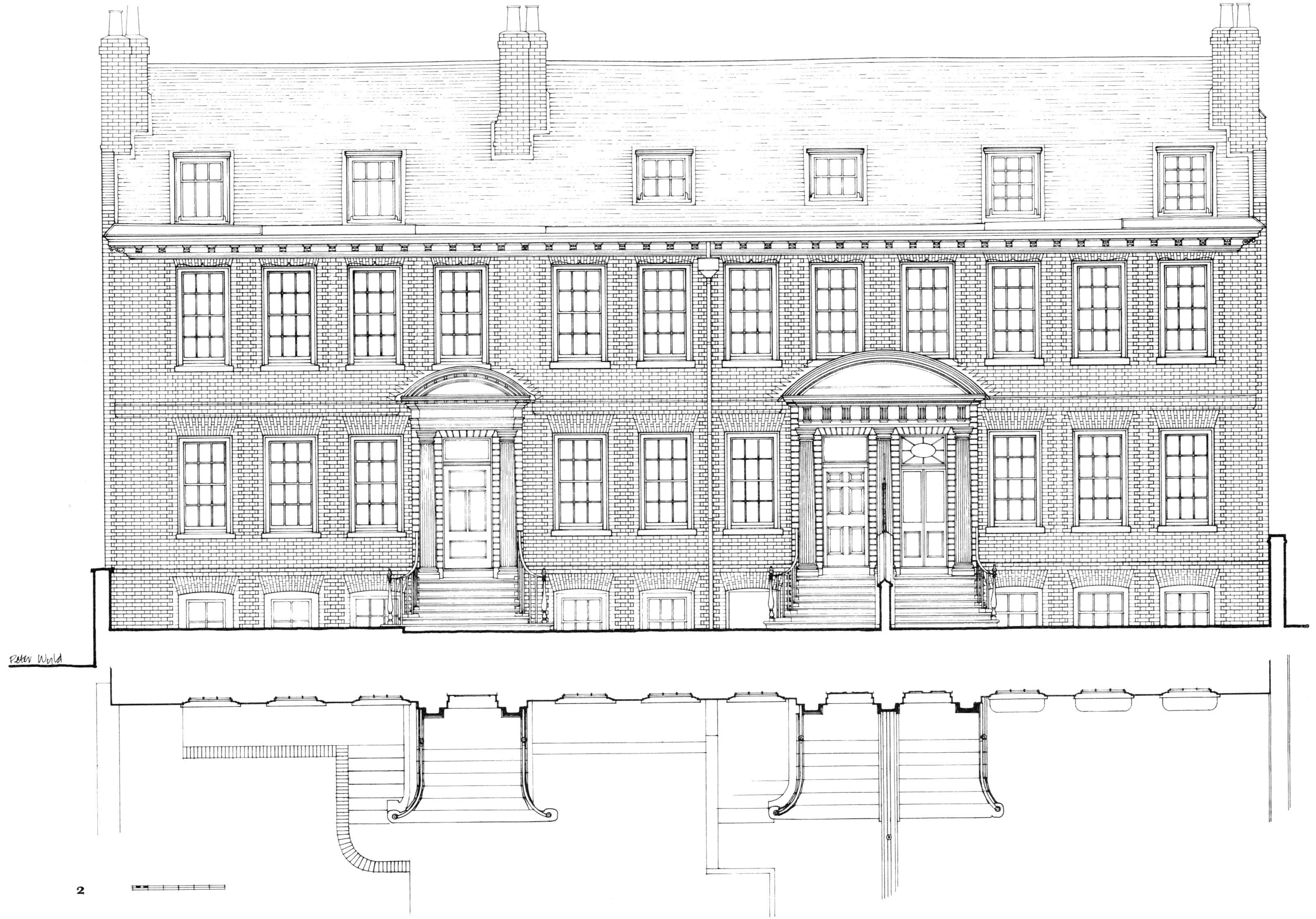

2

3, 4 The façade of Bradmore House, Broadway, Hammersmith, London W 6, thought to have been designed by Thomas Archer *circa* 1710, originally formed the garden front of a manor house. In the early 20th century the house was demolished and this façade was removed and rebuilt to form the front of Hammersmith Bus Station, during which rebuilding the façade was heightened by being elevated on a plinth. Since then, the façade has been mutilated and is now standing under threat of demolition once again. In this drawing the façade has been restored to as close an approximation as possible of its original appearance.

This example is one of the richest Baroque façades in London and the brickwork, although rebuilt, is very fine with red dressing bricks outnumbering the regular yellow stocks. The stone Composite elongated pilasters and the ramped-up central feature make this design worthy of the authorship of Thomas Archer. The photograph shows the façade of Bradmore House in its present sorry condition

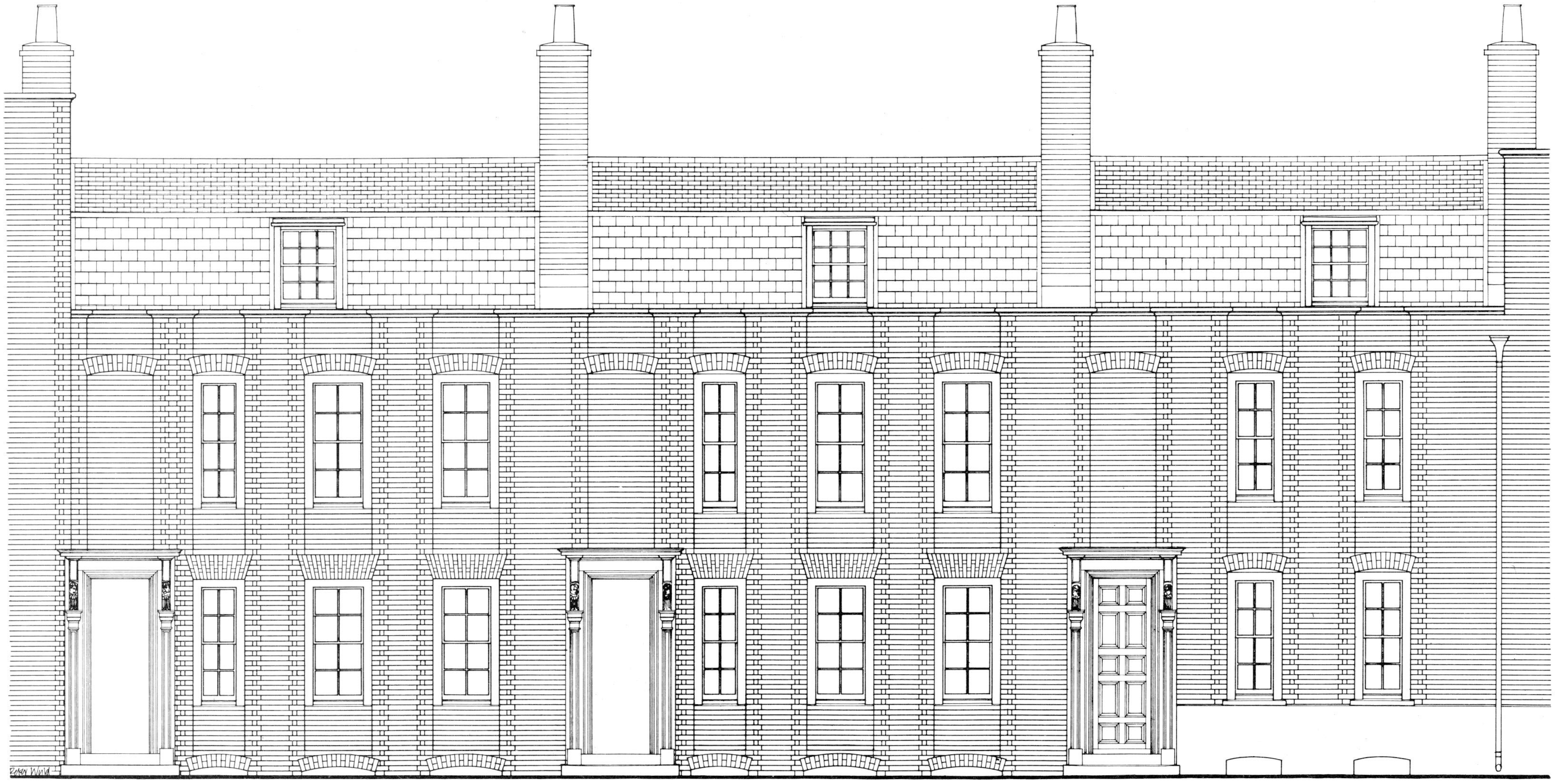

5

6

7

8

5 Part of a terrace of houses built between 1709–20 in Albury Street, Deptford, London SE 8. This street has been greatly altered and many of the façades cheaply rebuilt. In this drawing a group of three houses has been reconstructed to illustrate the special features this terrace once possessed.

Albury Street was developed by William Lucas, a master builder and friend of both Thomas Archer the architect of St. Paul, Deptford and Nicholas Hawksmoor who had built the nearby St. Alphege, Greenwich. Whether these architects were involved in the design of Albury Street is not certain, but the façades of these houses quite clearly display the strong Baroque motifs which were highly fashionable in the first decade of the 18th century. The whole terrace was given a strongly vertical and unified appearance by being divided into vertical bays. Like pilaster strips, these bays always break forwards (the window voids always being set in the recesses) and they give the design both vertical movement and continuity. The discipline of this grid was very flexible for it could incorporate houses of different widths, from 5 to 3 bays, and even differing window widths or no windows at all. In this group the houses are of differing widths, with two of $3\frac{1}{2}$ bays and one of 3 bays and variety is also present in the width of the windows. In contrast to the discipline of the façade may be set the individuality of the carved door surrounds for each example in the street is differently, well and deeply carved (see plate **21**, page 95). Equally, this individuality was also probably true of roof design in this street, some being simply pitched and others mansards containing garrets

6 This example of façade design in Eastern Avenue, Wanstead, London E 11, typifies the way in which Baroque ideas were adapted and applied to English domestic architecture in the early 18th century. The wide façade is framed between two blatantly non-structural Corinthian pilasters and the windows are linked vertically by blind panels. Predictably, the door is enriched with a Corinthian pilastered surround

7 This house in Mare Street, Hackney, London E 8, was built *circa* 1715 as a country house on the road connecting the ancient village of Hackney with London. The horizontality of this example is very typical of domestic design in the late 17th and early 18th centuries and its brick arches and string courses are also typical of the period. The window arches are not constructed in gauged brick but are modestly built with stock bricks in a simple 1:2:1 bond. The fine Doric doorcase dates from 1750–80 and can be seen in detail in plate **66**, page 122

8 No. 187 Stoke Newington High Street, London N 16, a magnificent house built *circa* 1715 which now stands derelict. This house is a very fine example of a type of façade design common in the late 17th century, in which windows were linked by blind panels, giving the façade a Baroque sense of movement and verticality

9 Built *circa* 1717, this house in Hanover Square, London

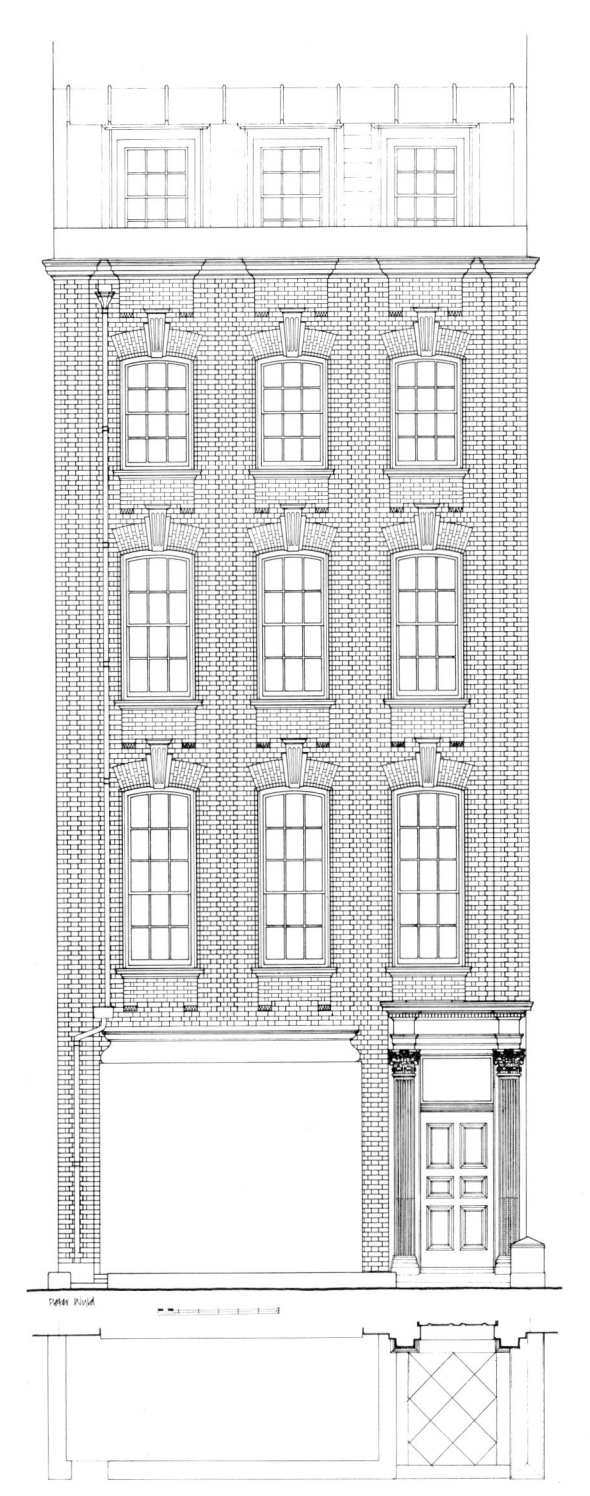

9

W 1, has extremely ornate and decorative brickwork. The red, rubbed dressed bricks of the window arches and jambs and of the quoins and aprons, far outnumber the plain yellowish-grey stocks of the façade. Although of an early date, this design conforms exactly to the Building Acts of 1707 and 1709 as the cornice is of stone and the box sashes of the window jambs are recessed 4 inches into the façade. The well-developed *piano nobile* is also unusual at so early a date. The Corinthian doorcase, however, truly reflects the Baroque taste that dominated English domestic architecture in the first two decades of the 18th century, as does the vertical emphasis given to the façade by the linking of the windows by their dressings and aprons and the narrow piers which frame the façade. A further Baroque touch may be seen in the fluted keystones and guttae which decorate the aprons

10 Built between 1715–25, this pair of semi-detached houses at nos. 808–10 Tottenham High Road, London N 17, contains several very interesting and beautiful features. The grouping itself is unusual so early in the 18th century for the houses have mirror plans with coach houses attached at each end. The fenestration of the shared façade is treated in such a way as to suggest that the two houses are in fact one large one. The two end windows for example are slightly narrower, an unusual and effective way of punctuating a façade, while the centre window as a result of the party wall, is blank.

The façade is very neatly embellished. The windows, which have aprons below and whose jambs are dressed with red bricks, have high segmental arches and stone keystones. The parapet, above a rubbed brick cornice, is panelled. The doorways have entablatures with architraves that loop up through a frieze to join cornices that are cantilevered out. In this drawing the houses have been restored by the removal of a later shop front from the ground floor of no. 810 and the addition of glazing bars and box sashes to the window voids

11 Rugby Street, London WC 1, was built in 1721, possibly by the master carpenter William Pain and the subtle way these houses relate to each other is a feature of particular interest. The centre and left-hand houses which share a chimney stack were built as a pair, with the same floor levels yet the window arches are different. The right-hand house is as high as its neighbours, yet it has lower floor levels and its door case crashes into that of no. 10. The ironwork is original, and in this drawing the glazing bars have been restored

11

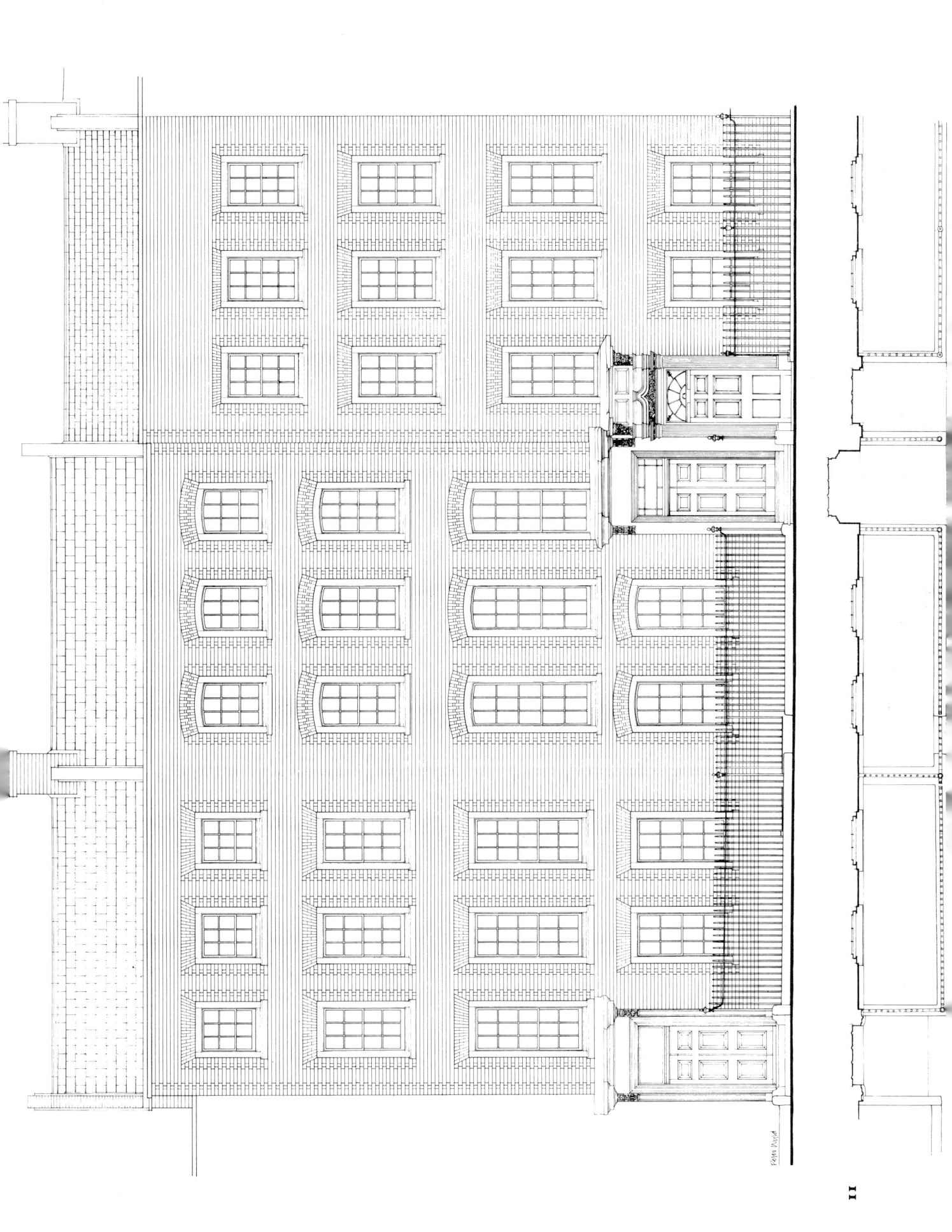

12 This pair of houses in Wilkes Street, Spitalfields, London E 1, dates from 1723 and although their façades are fashionable for the period they contain two elements particularly common in Spitalfields. The first of these is the roof in which the tall windows were particularly necessary to light work at the loom and the second is the motif used on the doorway. This motif, consisting of rustic pilasters supporing a flat entablature is a design with a good classical precedent, but is relatively uncommon in the rest of London

13 This pair of houses built during the 1720s in Took's Court, Chancery Lane, City of London EC 4, is particularly interesting for its use of decorative pilasters and the rusticated doorcase. The use of pilasters for decorative, non-structural effects was a common Baroque architectural device and here it is carried out to perfection. The shafts of the pilasters have been given an entasis and are constructed of rubbed and gauged fine red bricks. The Ionic capitals are made of carved and rubbed bricks, while the dentil cornice is built up of specially cut and laid red bricks. The windows which are without dressings, have fine segmental arches and are proportioned in the common *piano nobile* form. The house on the right of the drawing retains its, presumably original, excellent mansard roof

13

14

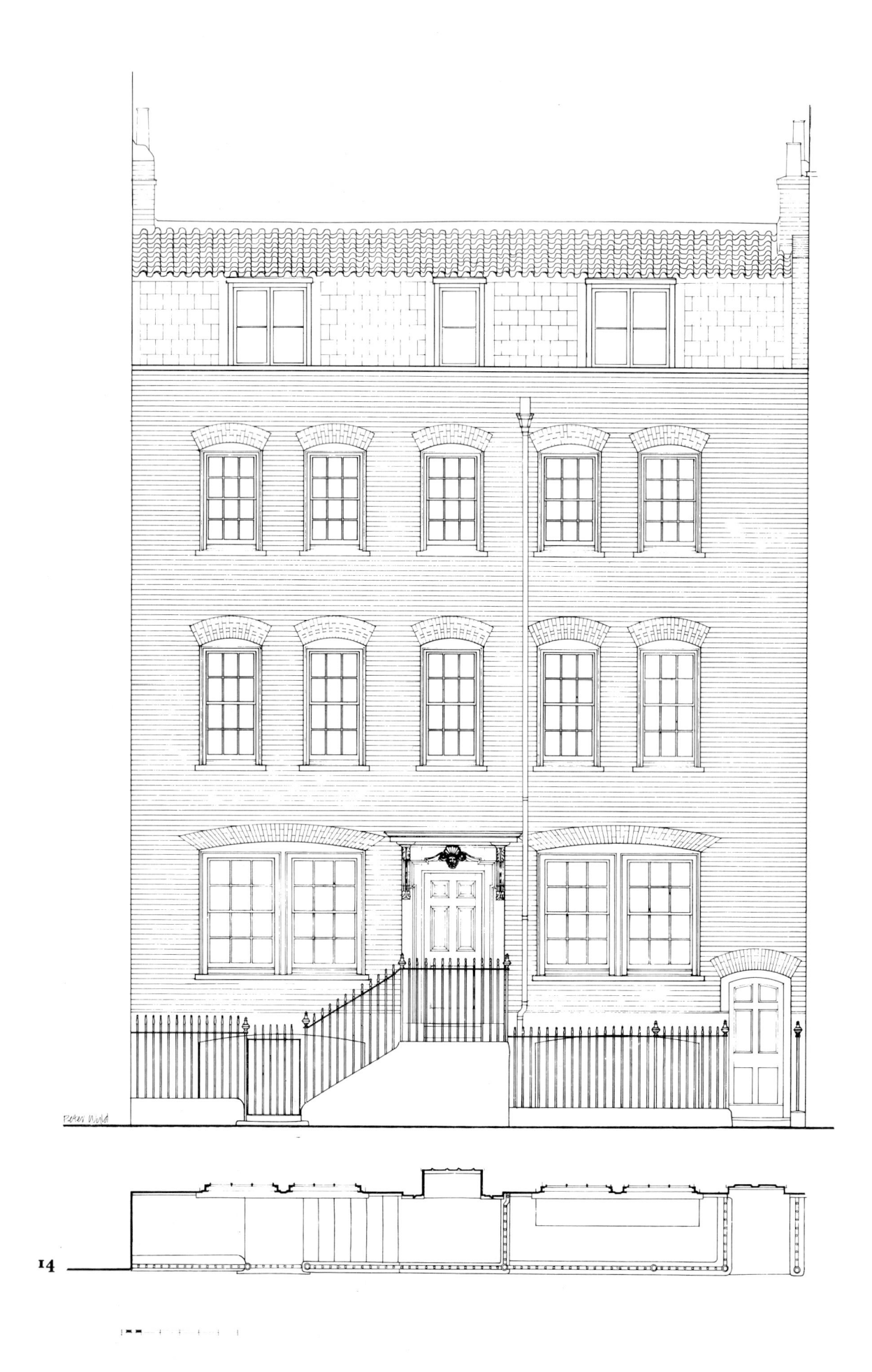

14 Built during the mid 1720s, this building in White's Row, Spitalfields, London E 1, is a fine example of a house designed with both function and fashion in mind. With the exception of its doorcase, taken from a James Gibbs pattern of 1728, the façade is unusually severe. The window jambs have no dressing and the ground-floor and basement windows are particularly interesting for their unusual width suggests that the house may have been associated with the Spitalfield's weaving industry, an idea reinforced by the large and well-lighted attic

15 Although built in the 1720s in a thoroughly urban setting and what is more, in a rather unfashionable part of London, this house in Charles Square, Hoxton, London N 1, was designed as a small free-standing country house. It is more horizontal in appearance than the usual terrace house and originally must have had an even greater horizontal emphasis as it was built with two flanking wings which broke forward of the main façade. The window proportioning is very fine, with square attic windows appearing above the gauged brick cornice and the *piano nobile* being demoted to the ground floor. The entire façade is constructed of red bricks, a practice uncommon during the 1720s

16

16 Built in 1725 this façade at NO. 2 Wilkes Street, Spitalfields, London E 1, is both typical of its period and of surrounding houses then being developed in Spitalfields. Although appearing fashionably spacious from the exterior, it is in fact cramped, being one-room deep, and archaic inside. The central blind windows are not, as is often thought, the result of the window tax, but were built in that manner. The staircase rises against the inside of the blank windows, so they could never have been 'sighted'. Simply, to maintain the rhythm of the façade, the designer preferred to build in window-shaped recesses than blank wall. Like many of its neighbours in Spitalfields this house has been rotting for half a century and is currently used as a storage space by market men. It will not survive much longer unless positive action is taken soon to restore Wilkes Street and nearby Fournier and Princelet Streets

17 Richmond Buildings, Soho, London W 1, built in 1732 and demolished in 1971 as slums. The design of this façade was more fashionable and up-to-date than that of nearby Meard Street (see plate **18**, page 56). The bricks were pale and the windows, without brick dressings, were recessed 4 inches into the façade. The doorcases were bold and simple designs of plaster or stone

18

57

18 Meard Street, Soho, London W 1, was developed in 1732 by Mr Meard, a local builder, businessman, politician and friend of Batty Langley. He had bought a court off Wardour Street and by 1722 had replaced it with a new cul-de-sac development of modest three-storey brick terraces. Ten years later he bought a court off Dean Street and having built on the site of this as well, connected up with his earlier development, forming the present Meard Street.

Although grander in conception than the earlier terraces, the houses built in 1732 are in the same architectural style and to a degree this was intentional, for where the two developments joined up, he built a house in the same style and scale as those of 1722. This is shown to the right of the drawing and was occupied by Batty Langley. For its date, Meard Street is therefore extremely archaic in style. The four houses of 1732 shown here were developed as two pairs with mirror plans and shared chimney stacks and although the *piano nobile* of each is pronounced, the windows still have flush box sashes, red brick dressings and heavily carved consoled doors (see plates **24** and **25**, pages 96–97) Meard Street also provides a fine example of the way in which equally visible elevations were treated differently according to their status. The formal front elevation of the four houses contains all necessary decorative elements and details; the side elevation (of a contemporary house in Dean Street) has few decorations but is regular, whilst the back elevations were merely thrown together (see also plate **19**, page 37)

19 Nos. 9 and 10 St. James's Square, London SW 1 designed by Henry Flitcroft and built by Benjamin Timbrell, form a good example of a highly fashionable house of 1734. Built of pinky-grey bricks, this building has a pronounced *piano nobile* (the balcony and the consequent lowering of the first-floor windows of NO. 10 is an early 19th-century alteration) and the façade is divided horizontally by a string course and a stone, moulded cornice. The plain consoled doorcases are also made of stone and the sashes of the undressed windows are recessed 4 inches into the façade

20 This gatehouse in Arlington Street, St. James's, London SW 1, was probably designed by James Gibbs during the 1730s as part of Lord North's House and is a fine example of Palladian concept of architectural form appropriately fitting function. Being a gatehouse and a thing of utility rather than decoration, its embellishments are bold and simple. The entrance is surrounded by vermiculated rustic stone blocks and the windows are set in deep reveals which give the façade an extraordinarily sturdy appearance

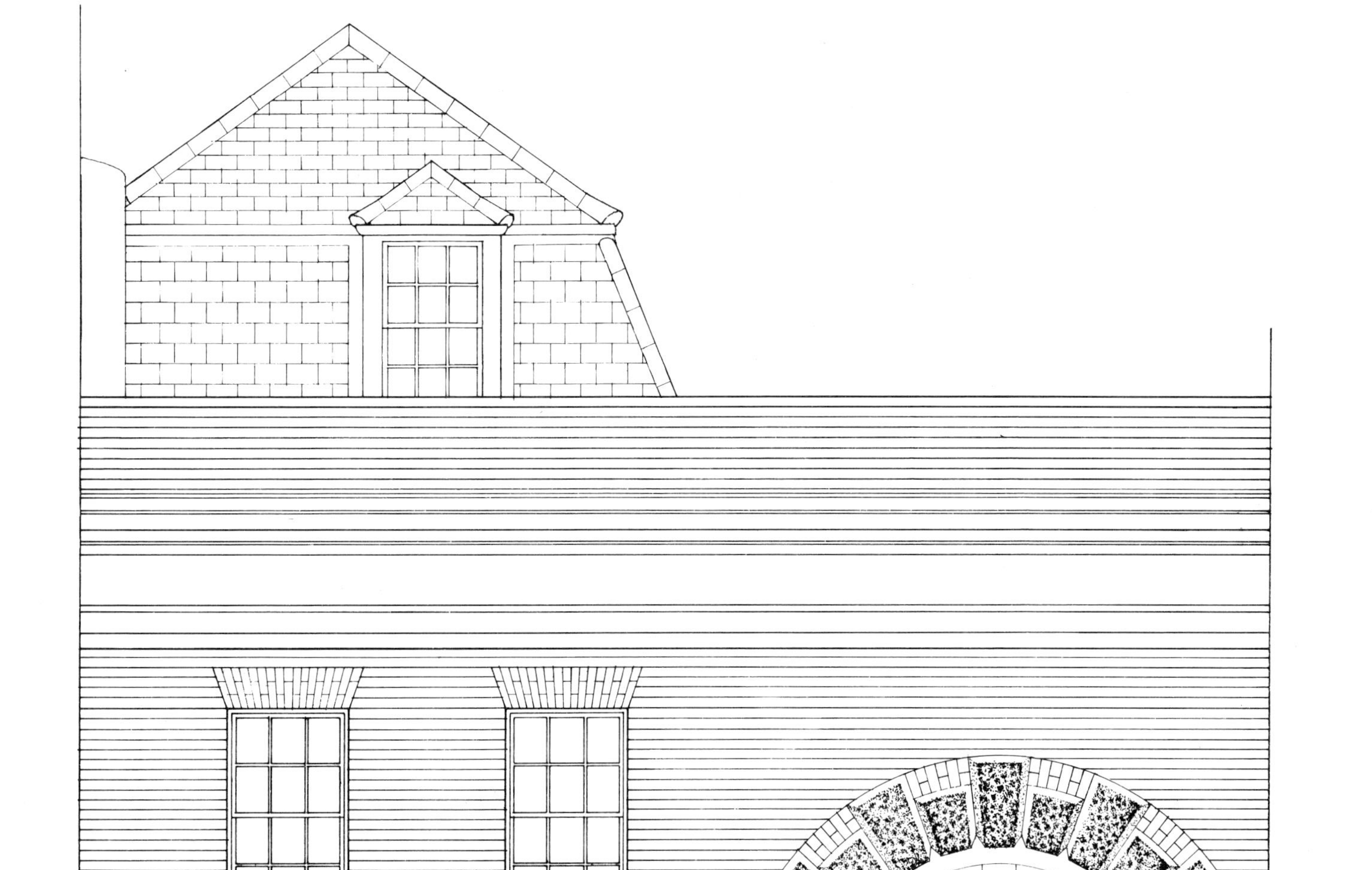

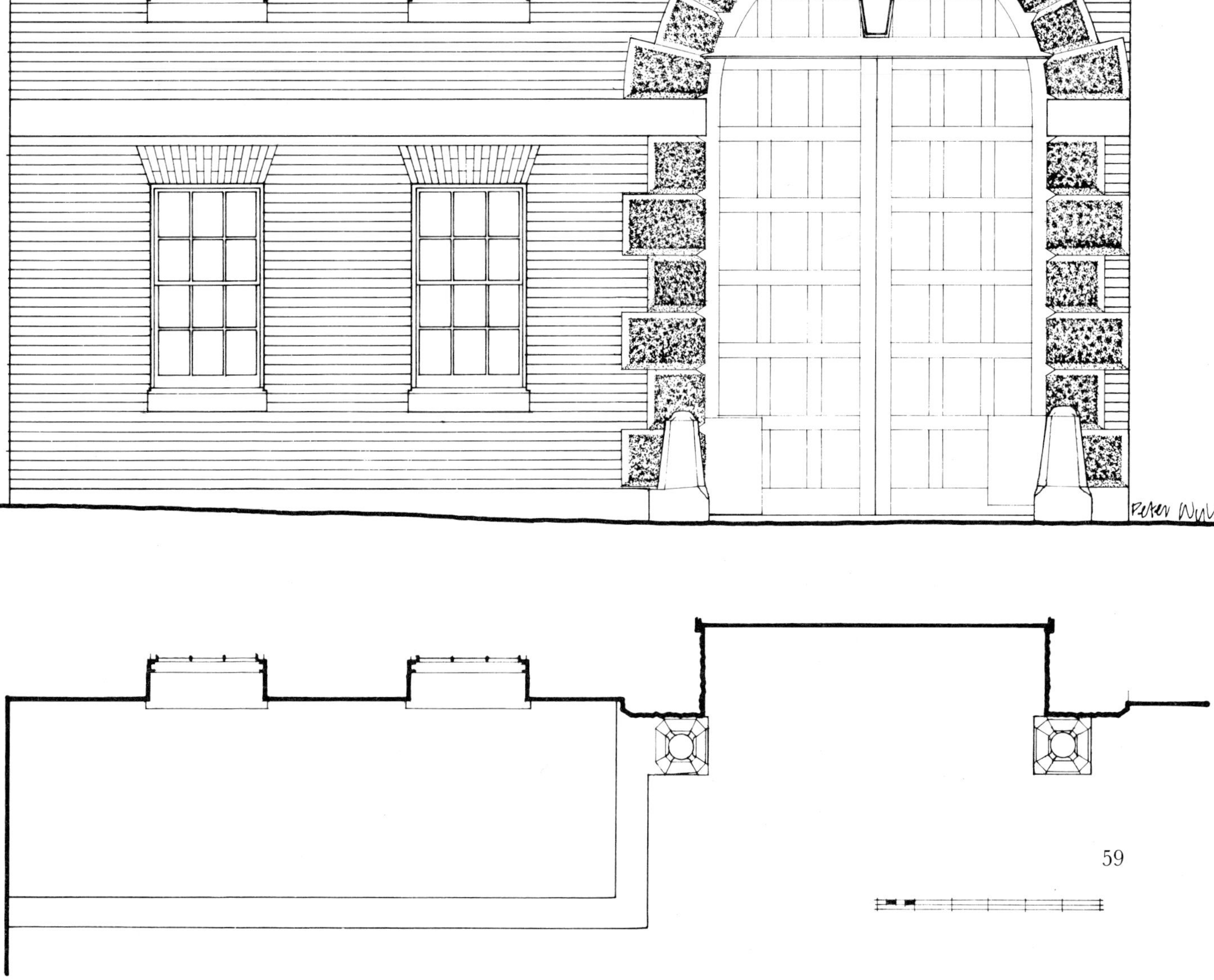

59

21 This house in Bloomsbury Way, London WC 1, was built during the 1740s and traditionally is attributed either to Isaac Ware or Henry Flitcroft. This house is one of four which form the south-west corner of Bloomsbury Square and as a group they provide a fine example of mid 18th-century Palladian domestic design. The *piano nobile* is strong yet the relationship between the window void and solid is more subtle than it was later to become. The broad string course above the ground floor marks the base of the proportioning column while the block cornice marks its top. The windows of the first and second floors are placed within the area taken up by height of this 'invisible' column and their horizontal positioning is dictated by intercolumnation. There is, in this house, no attic but a blocking course and a range of pedimented dormers in the mansard roof.

The door of the right-hand house forms the base of a formal and symmetrical composition which, having gone through a series of elements each made up of three elements, terminates in a pediment. The first floor contains a form of spaced-out and plain Venetian window motif which is held together by a continuous sill band. On the second floor is a Diocletian window, also known as a thermal window because of its use in the Thermae of Diocletian, Rome, which was a device beloved by the Palladians and often used by them beneath pediments and over Venetian windows

22 This example at NO. 43 Parliament Street, Westminster, London SW 1, built in 1753, contains all the architectural characteristics of a fashionable house belonging to the decade 1750–60. The façade is constructed of very regularly laid greyish-purple stocks and although the window arches are composed of the same stocks, they are of rubbed, finer quality firsts and present a subtle difference in colour and texture. The wooden doorcase is a perfect Doric pedimented porch and is shown in greater detail in plate **63**, page 120. Capping the façade is a cyma recta block cornice, a ubiquitous architectural feature during the 1750s. The proportioning of the façade is very fine and true to its Palladian inspiration, the *piano nobile* is pronounced. The two horizontal bands dividing the ground floor from the first floor are formalised reminders that both the vertical and horizontal proportions of a façade are based on the proportioning of a column, its base and entablature. This house is to be demolished to make way for government offices

22

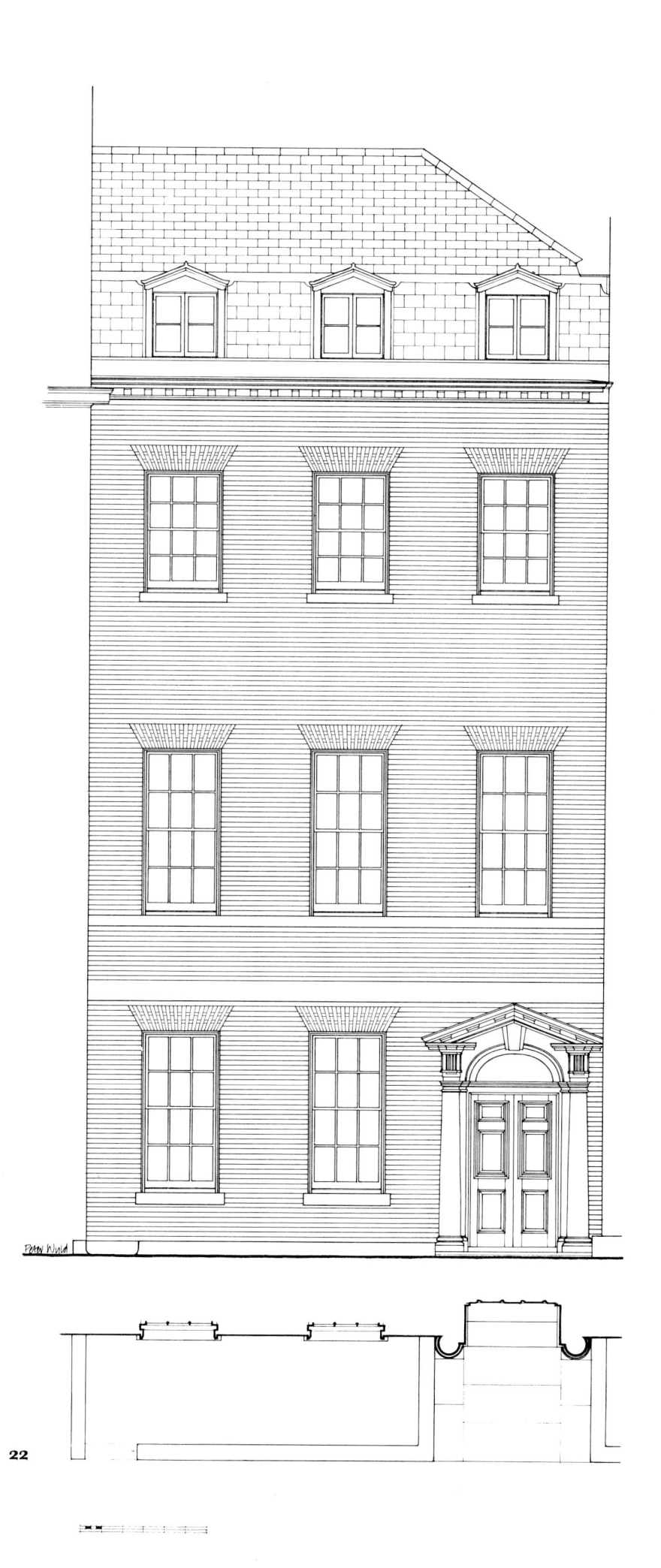

23 This house in Harpur Street, London WC 1, forms the return front of a terrace of houses belonging to the 1760s in Dombey Street, Bloomsbury, but the unusual window arrangement and the wooden architraves surrounding the windows, suggest that the façade was altered some time in the 1830s. The door and ironwork however, appear to date from the 1760s. Empty since 1971, this house continued to rot while its owner, the Harpur Estate, and the council disputed its future. Now restoration work has begun

23

24

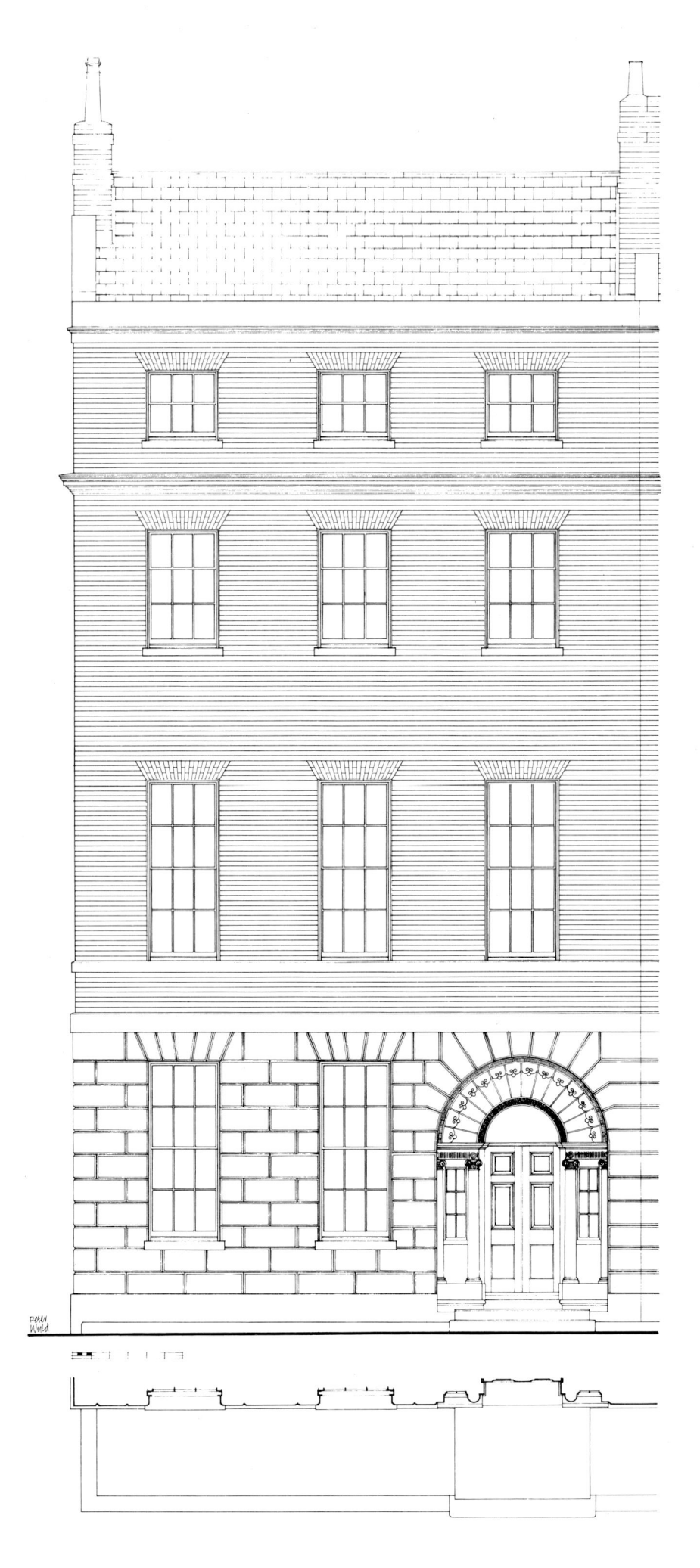

24 Mansfield Street, London, W1 designed by James Adam in the early 1770s as part of the Adams' Portland Place development, is a fine example of both a fashionable Georgian terrace and the Adams' domestic decorative style. The façade is purely Palladian in its proportions and in its use of string courses and cornice to relate these proportions to those of plinth, column and entablature. It is the ground floor with its heavy rustication and beautiful doorway which contains the decorative details peculiar to the Adam Brothers. A doorcase very similar to this example is shown in detail in plate **105**, page 144

25 No. 7 Adam Street, London WC2 designed by Robert Adam in the late 1760s is the sole surviving house of the Adelphi development to be dressed in the full Adam decorative finery. The pilasters which are designed without an entasis, fit comfortably between the standard fenestration of a well-proportioned terrace house, but they are too elongated to be classically 'correct'. Robert Adam in fact cared very little for conventional architectural 'correctness' and here he uses the pilasters simply as decorative panels to contain his favourite and ubiquitous anthemion leaf motif. The entablature, which divides the second floor from the attic windows, lacks an architrave while its frieze contains anthemions and pendants instead of the more usual triglyphs and metopes. The panels below the second-floor windows give the façade a chequer-board appearance because due to their presence the dark stock bricks which form the facade are only visible as square areas beside the windows. The doorway is a fine piece of Adam design and may be seen in greater detail in plate **4**, page 212. The splendid balconies may also be seen in closer detail in this plate

26 Brunswick House, Albert Embankment, London SE 11, was originally a riverside house. It now stands with a cold storage tower in its garden and dense traffic swirling around it, and its owner, British Rail, is currently toying with the idea of rebuilding it elsewhere.

Although built in the 1780s, Brunswick House has all the characteristics of the austere Palladian style typical of the 1750s. The façade is topped by a pediment and block cornice and a fat string course indicates the base of the proportioning column, while the central three bays, which break forward beneath the pediment, are given additional unity by another shallower cill band. The first-floor windows have been dropped through this at a later date and the porch, a fine piece of Neo-Classical design is of Coade stone (see also plate **120**, page 151)

27 An impressive expression of the discipline that could be achieved in late 18th-century speculative building. This terrace in Kennington Road, London SE 11 was constructed in the late 1780s by various builders and yet it has an architectural coherence comparable with the Nash Regent's Park terraces of 30 years later. A central pediment (albeit a rather deformed and awkward one) completes the composition and the ends of the terrace are emphasised by the use of round-headed rather than square-headed windows on the ground floors of the last two houses

27

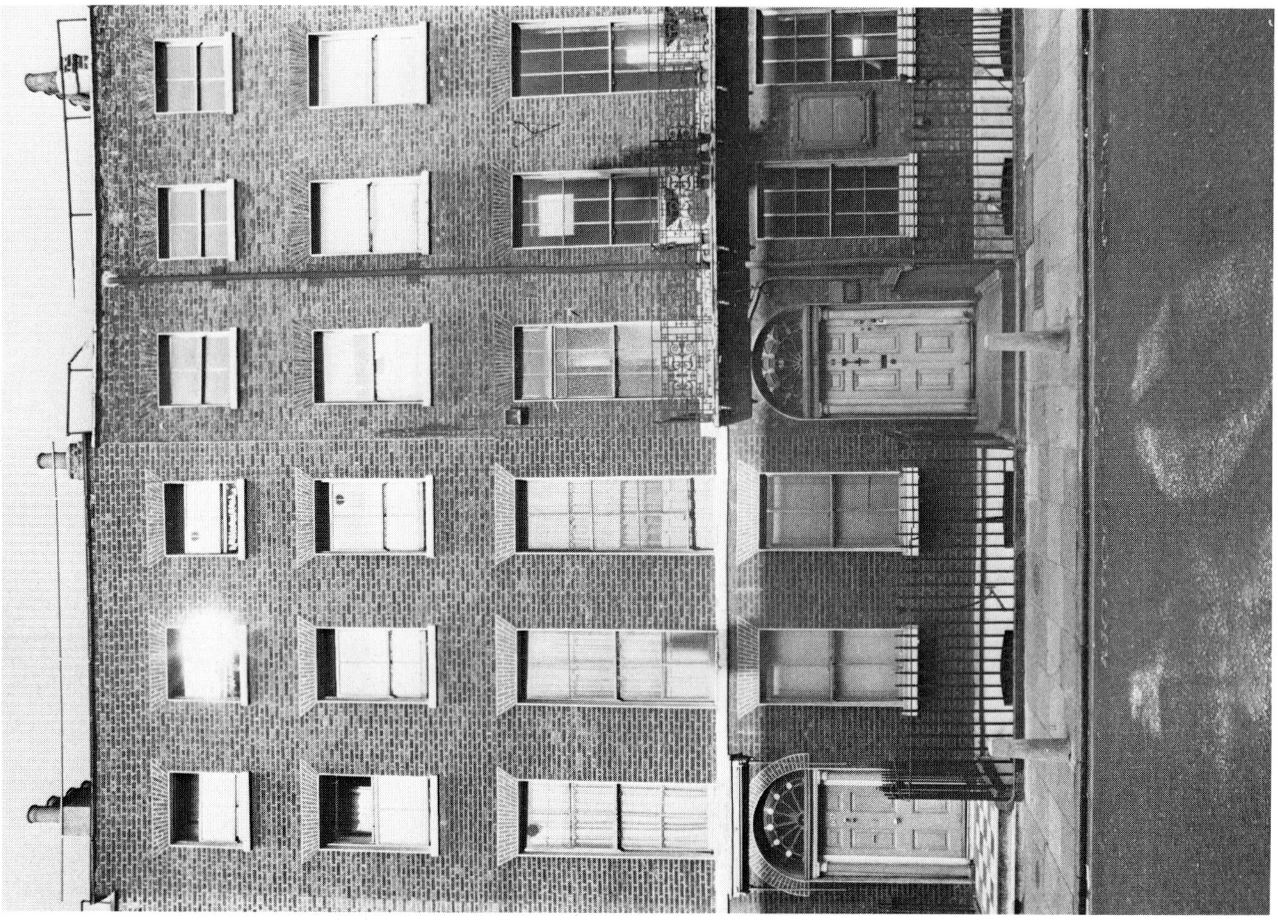

29

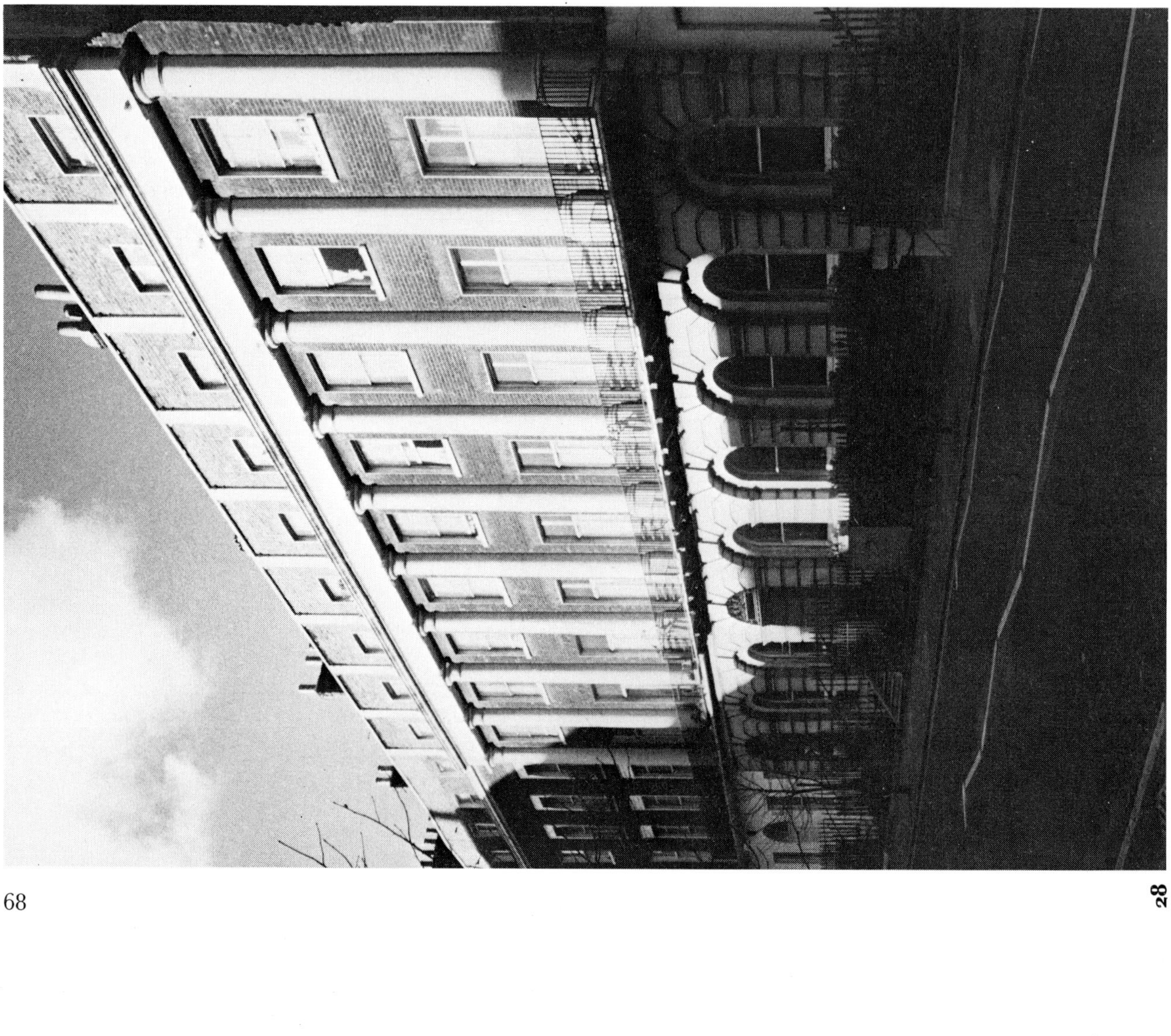

28

28 Guilford Street, Bloomsbury, London WC 1, was developed by the speculative builder James Burton during the first decade of the 19th century and although the houses shown here were run up to standard Burton proportions, because of their position in closing off the northern end of fashionable Queen Square, they were decorated with half-columns, entablature and attic. The result is interesting for it shows that even the early 19th-century speculative terrace house was still designed as if it were to be faced with an architectural Order. The ground floor is currently rusticated to provide the visual strength to support the columns above and the columns and entablature in their turn fit over the regular grid of the windows without compromising their own proportions or that of the fenestration

29 Built at the beginning of the 19th century, these houses at NOS. 58 and 60 Grafton Way, London W 1, epitomise the proportioning technique of late Georgian terrace design. The ground floor is divided off from the rest of the composition by a thin horizontal band which marks the base of the invisible proportioning column, the ground floor forming its plinth. Above this band the invisible column rises through the first and second floors, the 'capital' occurring just below the attic windows. By the early 19th century a more simple rule-of-thumb proportioning method had been devised out of this theory, based on a module whose measurement was determined by the width of the windows. Usually this was 3 feet 6 inches and the proportioning module for the façade would then be a 3 feet 6 inch square. Using this module and working downwards from the top of the building, the distance from the top of the parapet to the top of the attic window would be 3 feet 6 inches; the attic window itself would be 3 feet 6 inches square; the distance between all windows both horizontally and vertically would be 3 feet 6 inches and the depth of the windows would be proportions of the 3 feet 6 inch module; the second floor might be 1 module wide by $1\frac{1}{2}$ modules deep and the first floor a double square, 1 module wide by 2 modules deep. This mechanical proportioning was rescued from too boring a repetition by the fact that, as here, the ground-floor/first-floor relationship was varied, or the fact that more space could be left between houses than between windows. This incorporation of a wider vertical element every three bays or so introduced another slower rhythm into the spacing of windows in a long terrace

30 Coram Street, Bloomsbury, London WC 1, a more modest example of James Burton's speculative work, was built between 1800–10. Typical of Burton's style is the way in which the ground floor is stuccoed (although in this case not rusticated as well) and the way in which the sill band both links the attic windows into a horizontal composition whilst helping to discipline the proportions of the façade by defining the cornice level. These houses have now been demolished

31

32

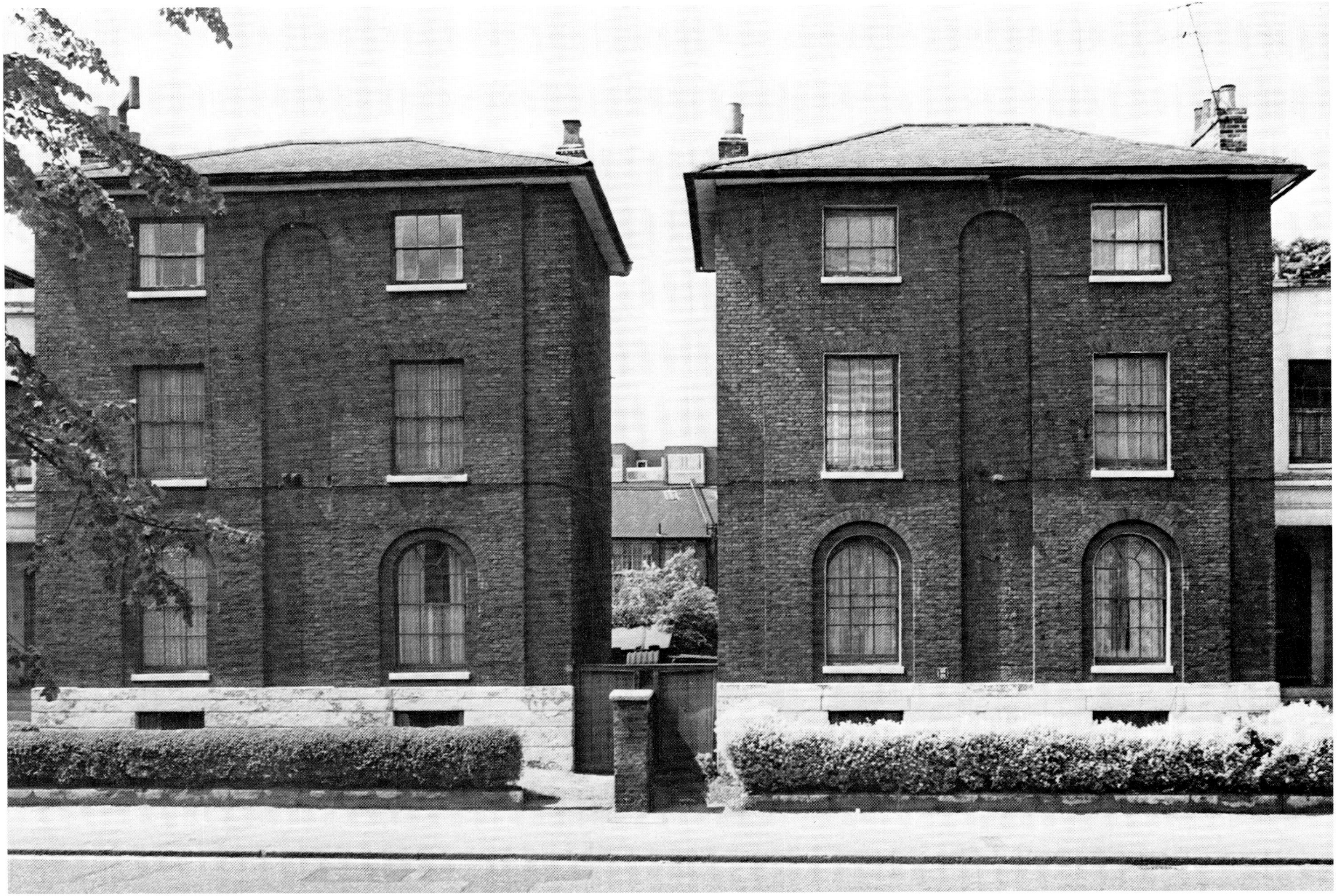

34

31 Montague Street, Bloomsbury, London WC 1, built during the decade 1800–10 by James Burton, is a splendid example of this architect's First Rate speculative housing and an equally fine example of an extensive, highly uniform, yet austere, terrace composition. The fact that space between individual houses is the same as that between windows makes the rhythm of this terrace particularly repetitious

32 Although dating from the same period as James Burton's Montague Street, Bloomsbury, due to the fall of the land and the independence of the builders, this terrace in City Road, Islington, London EC 1 has a more ragged face. Although this quality has been exaggerated by later mutilations, the rhythm of the terrace is still strong

33 These pairs of villas linked by entrances in Foxley Road, Camberwell, London SW 9, contain a fine mixture of standard early 19th-century speculative motifs together with unusual Neo-Classical motifs. In the former category might be included the semi-circular ground-floor windows set in concentric arches and the shallow-pitched villa roof with eaves. Particularly Soaneian are the elongated decorative blind arches that divide the façade into two elements

34 Built during the 1820s, this small house in Vassall Road, Camberwell, London SW 9, is a striking example of the dignity that could be evoked by the judicious use of a simple architectural motif. In this instance the motif is a semi-circular arch with stone imposts and it elevates this simple structure from the level of a brick box to a building of calculated austerity rather than involuntary economy

35 Built in 1820, this school in Wyndham Place, Marylebone, London W 1, is a fine example of the formalisation of light-hearted Regency design. This example is interesting because it is really the side elevation of a regular brick terrace and the designer has found a very neat solution. The concentric arches are a common early 19th-century motif

35

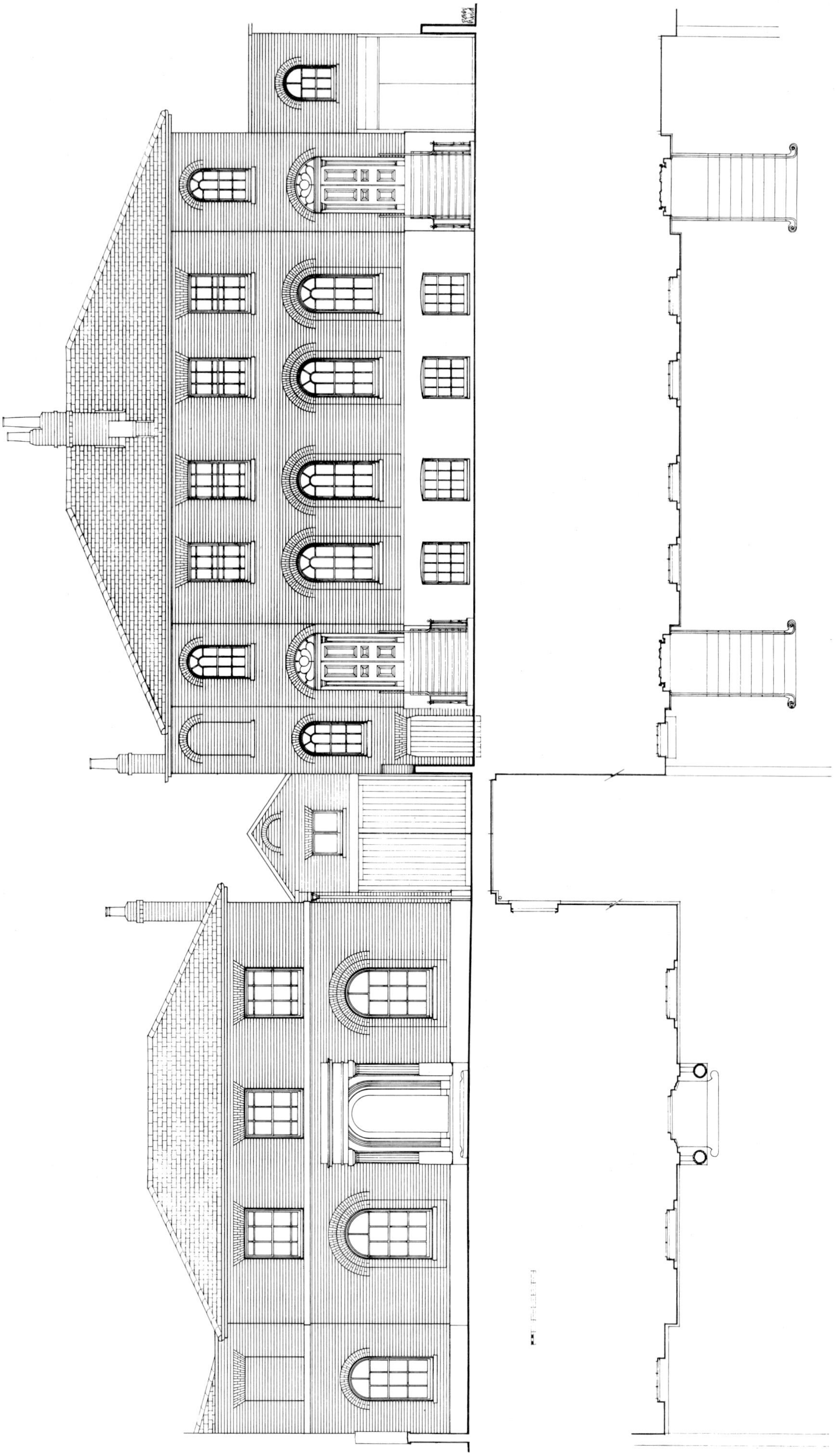

36

37

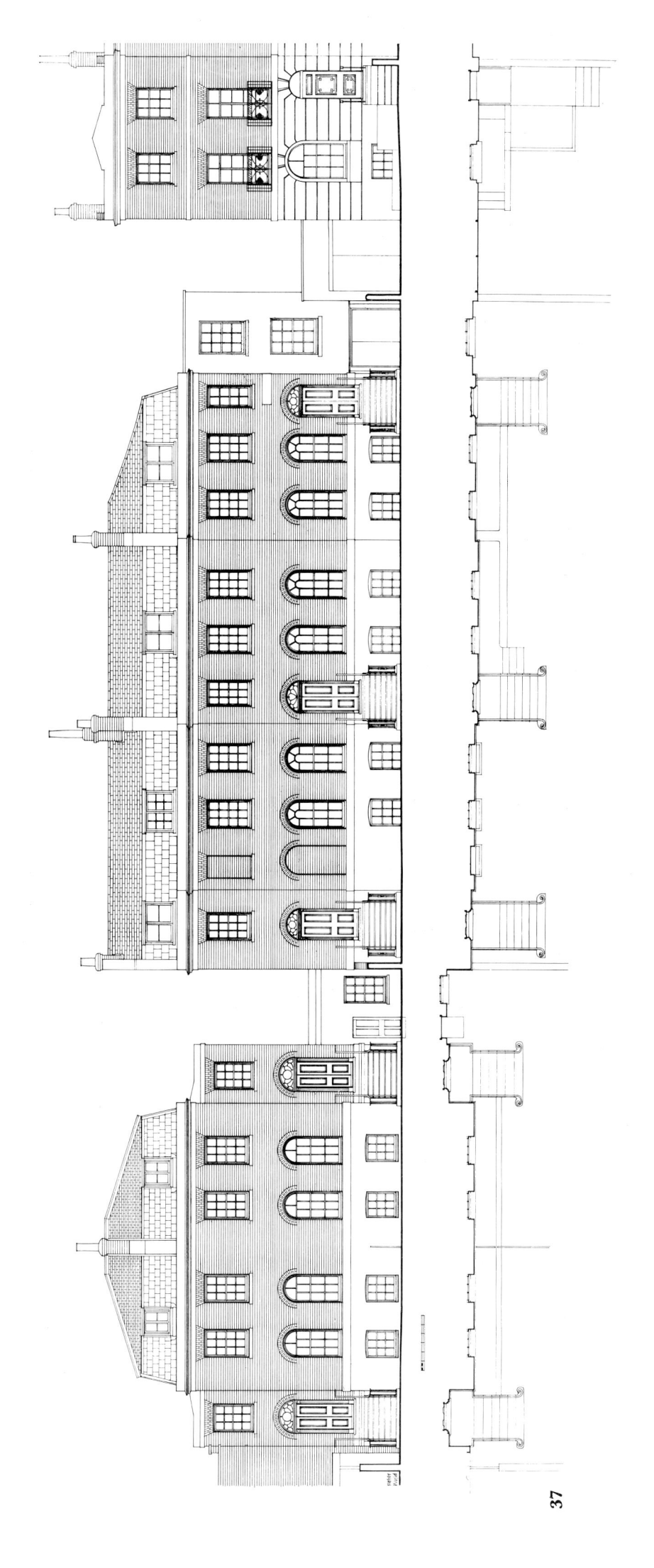

38

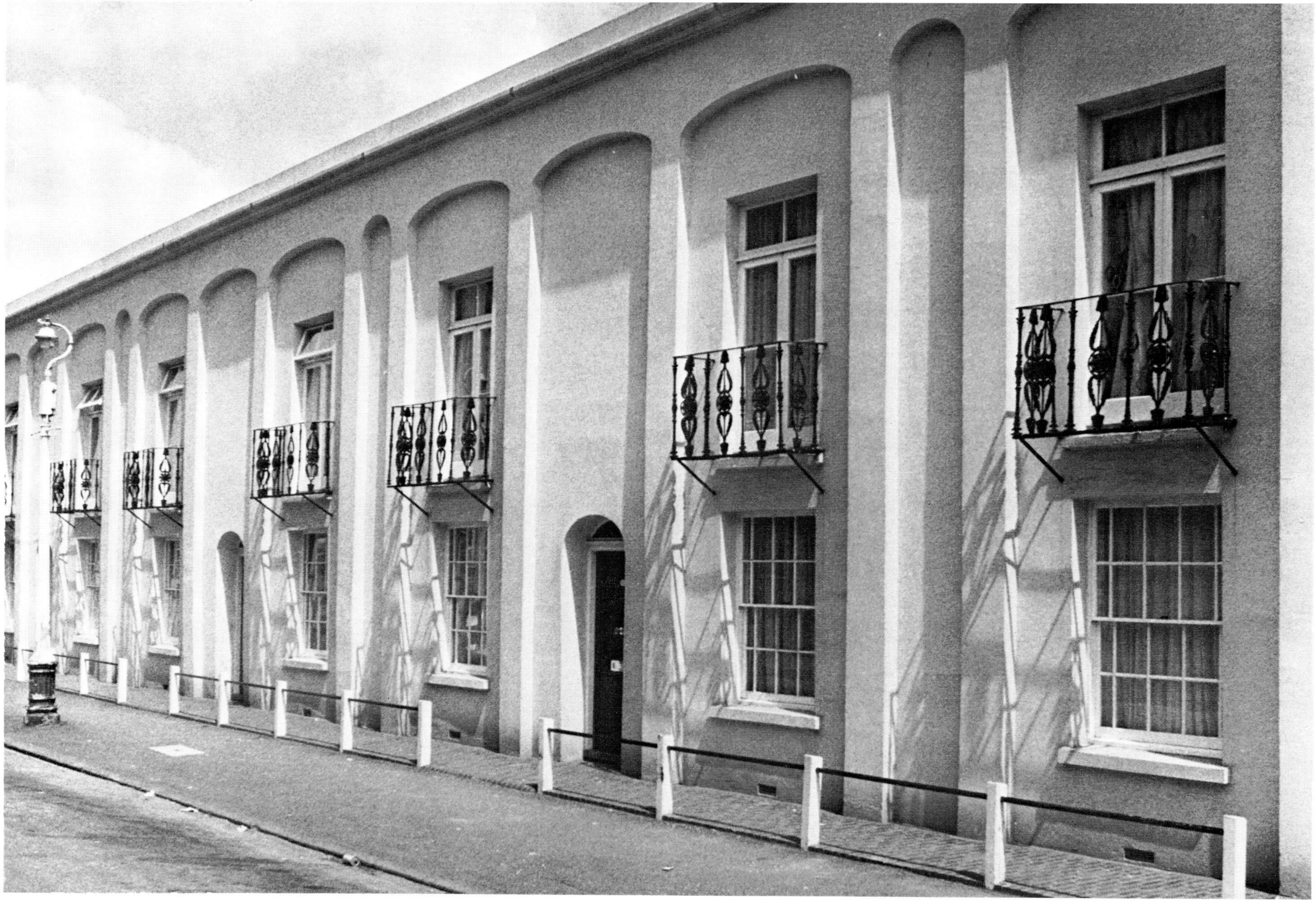

39

40

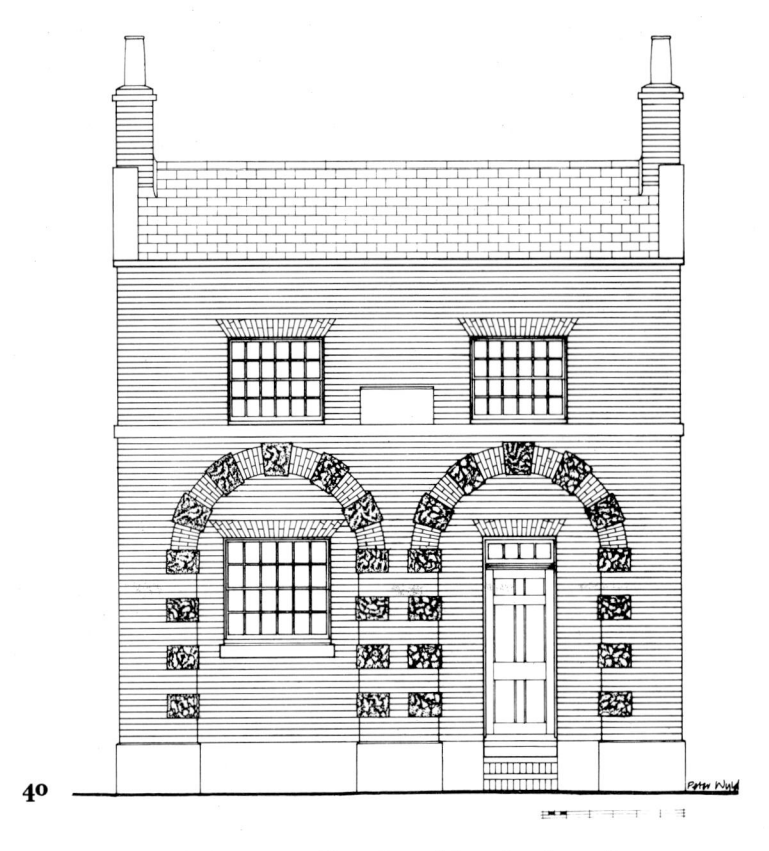

36 These three houses form part of the west side of Camberwell New Road, London SE 5, and the whole of this side is under threat of demolition for the purpose of Greater London Council road improvements. Laid out during the 1820s, this road is of particular architectural interest for the entire spectrum it contains of early 19th-century speculative building forms, ranging from terraces and linked terraces to semi-detached houses and villas.

The villa on the left of this drawing is already derelict and semi-demolished. It is a fine design with such characteristic elements of its date and type as a shallow pitched roof, a columned Grecian Doric porch and semi-circular-headed windows on the ground floor. The semi-detached houses on the right, linked to the villa by a coach house, are also very typical products of their period, with a ground floor raised on a high basement and round-headed windows set in concentric arches

37 This group of houses is also situated in Camberwell New Road, London SE 5 and consists of, from left to right, a semi-detached pair, a composition of three and the end house of a uniform terrace. The two groups of attached houses contain elements typical of the 1820s such as semi-circular windows, pretty attenuated fanlights and high basements. These architectural features reflect a definite break with urbanised house design for these examples were, after all, built on a new road in the country and are consequently more indulgently wasteful of space than if they had been built in central London.

However, there are some extremely 'urban' terraces lining this road too and the house on the right of the drawing is one of them. Its formality, when compared with the adjacent buildings in this drawing is astonishing. It is rusticated, decorated with cast-iron balconies of a standard design and being the end of a terrace, is topped with a simple pediment

38 This terrace in Sekforde Street, Clerkenwell, London EC 1, is unusual because of the horizontal proportions of the individual houses. Each is proportioned rather as if it were a free-standing cottage and the way in which the imposts of the first-floor windows are linked to form a continuous string course is particularly fine

39 Cowley Road, Camberwell, London SW 9, of 1824, a Neo-Classical terrace composition in which the alternation of three broad arches with one narrow arch, gives this terrace an abstract quality worthy of the works of Sir John Soane. Yet beneath this almost surreal façade of arches and stucco, the houses themselves are built to standard late-Georgian cottage proportions

40 Built during the 1820s, the Lodge to St. Matthew's Churchyard, Bethnal Green, London E 2, was intended to house a guard to protect graves from body-snatchers. Its protective function is reflected in a robust design in which the ground floor is decorated with large vermiculated Coade stone arches and the first-floor windows are small and square

41 The Paragon, Hackney, London E 9, an ambitious attempt at elevating a group of speculative semi-detached houses into a piece of interesting town planning. The elevating device is the simple Tuscan colonnade which screens the entrance door and links the semi-detacheds together. The fret pattern above the ground-floor windows is a motif common during the 1820s and 1830s. Hackney Council, which owns these houses, plans to demolish them as slums

41

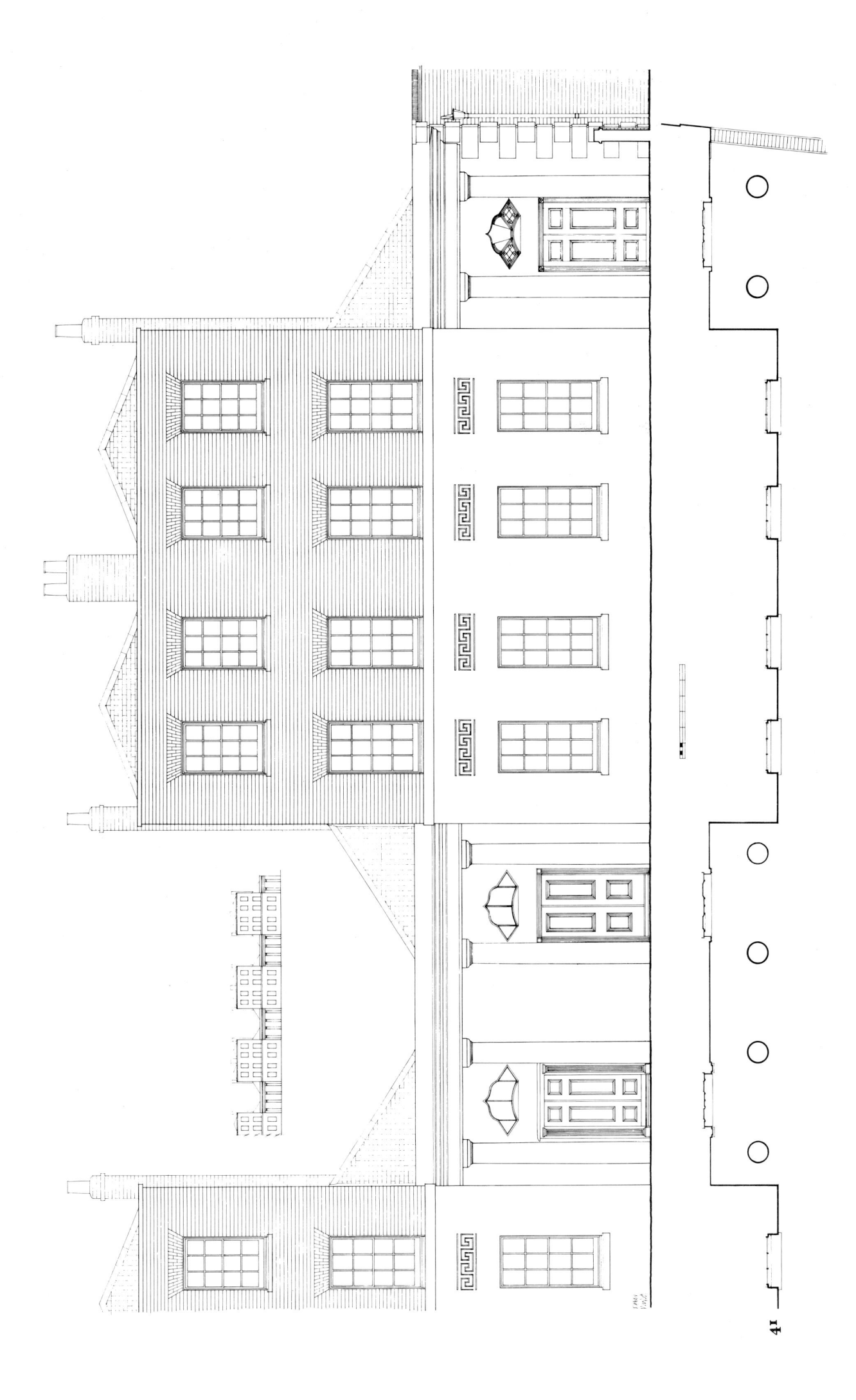

42 Carlton Cottages, part of a group of cottages in the Old Kent Road, London SE15, all belong to the late 1830s and all are decorated with pilasters supporting ammonite capitals. This motif, based on the fossil ammonite, is fairly common in some Sussex towns, particularly Brighton and Lewes, where the architect Amon Wilds (*circa* 1762–1833) virtually adopted it as his trademark. All these cottages in the Old Kent Road are due for demolition

43 Dated 1833, this cottage in Camberwell New Road, London SE5, points fittingly to the end of the Georgian period. Despite all the debauchery that architectural classicism and urban planning was undergoing during the 1830s, this cottage, date apart, still strongly evokes the best qualities of Georgian domestic design. The ornaments are correctly proportioned (the door is very similar to the pattern used for Hanover Square in 1717, shown in plate **88**, page 134) whilst the scale and horizontality of the whole make it entirely domestic

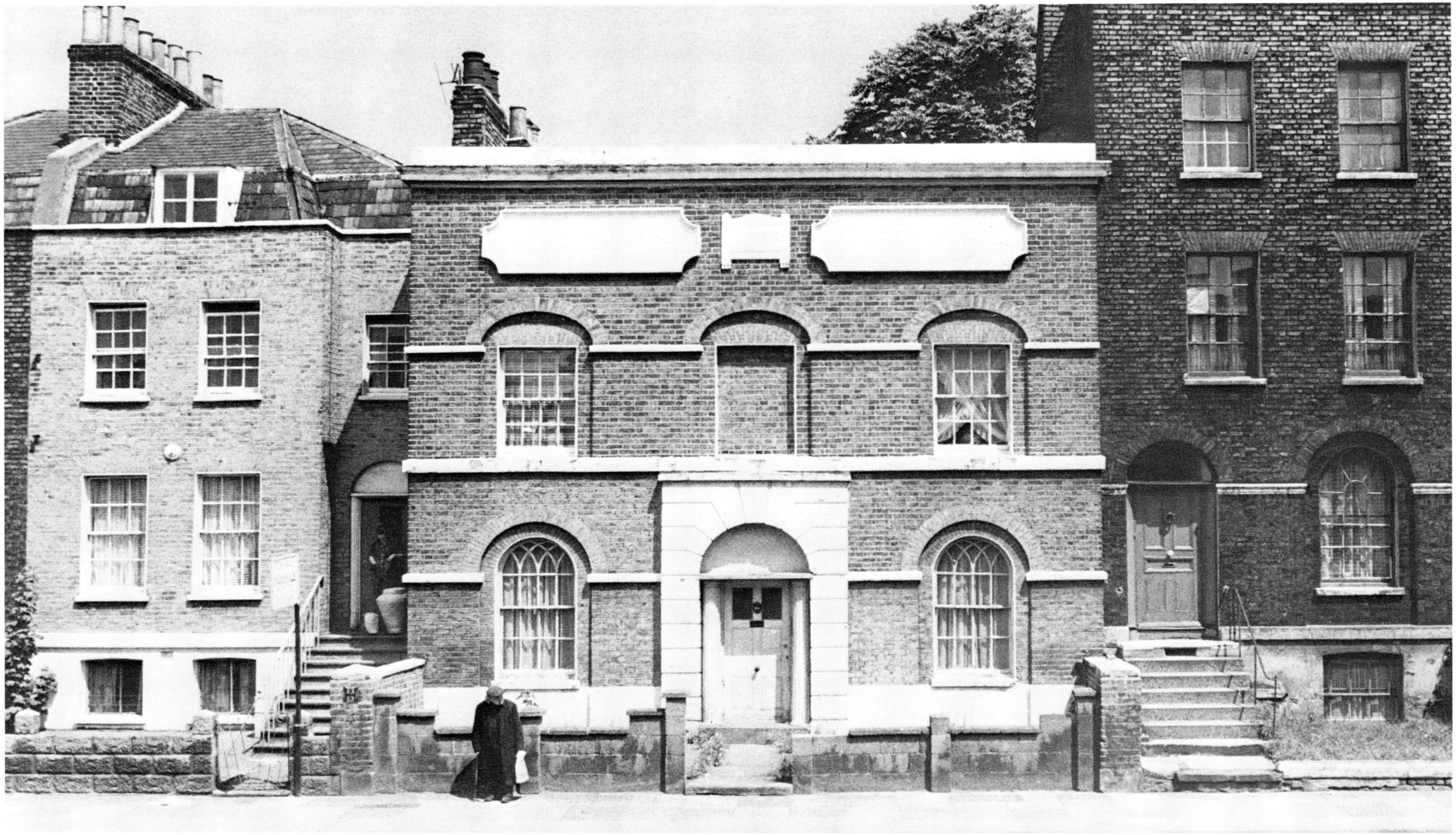

43

PART II ELEMENTS: DETAILS

Doors

If a façade could have only one ornament during the Georgian period, that ornament would generally be the doorway. No matter how economical the structure, nor how austere the design, it was practically inevitable that at least a little extravagance and a little freedom of design would be allowed for the door. The predilection of 18th-century architects and builders for enriching the doorway had its origins in the emphasis given to portals in Renaissance Italy. Although in pre-classical England the doorway, being the most dignified intermediary between man and building, had traditionally been an obvious element to enrich, it was Renaissance architects who developed the idea of surrounding the door with a miniature temple front consisting of pediment and columns.

Thus, from the beginning of the period covered by this book, the door became the one element in the façade on which decoration would be relatively lavish and during the Baroque influence of the early 18th century, this took the form of elaborately carved brackets supporting a flat, moulded hood or a shell-shaped concave niche. Such cantilevered and carved door surrounds were extraordinary pieces of craftsmanship and were used freely by Wren and his school. They were, however, based on no direct classical precedent, but were made up of motifs taken from the classical architectural repertoire: cornices, panelled soffits, scrolls and modillions, which were enlarged, distorted and mutilated to form a highly practical doorcase suited to the requirements of the English climate (the jutting-out cornice, for example, usefully kept the rain off as well). This curious distortion and combination of classical motifs was later made even stranger by being coupled with more standard features. It became usual, for example, for the small scroll which supported a large bracket to sit on top of a Doric pilaster. Obviously the pilaster could not support the scroll and bracket, other than visually, and even then it was of an illusory usefulness for generally the hood was supported by unseen pieces of old timber fixed within the panelling of the hood and then let into the brickwork. From the standpoint of the later Georgians who, as Palladians, believed that architectural function, form and decoration ought to be firmly related, these early works must have seemed ridiculous.

This type of door was very much the province of the carver. Before the restrictive Building Acts of 1707 and 1709 the carved door was complemented by a carved and modillioned eaves cornice, but when this feature was banished as a fire hazard, the door became the only element of a façade where the carver could display his skill. Limited only by the basic scroll shapes and the necessity to use certain motifs, the carver had licence to carve very much what he pleased. He could carve scrolls deeply or only scratch the surface of the wood, or he could give it an acanthus leaf flourish or a cherubic head to suggest only two variations. But for all this freedom of expression, door brackets have a certain 'regional' similarity in that brackets and scrolls in certain parts of London (where they survive in any reasonable quantity as in Fournier and Wilkes Street, Spitalfields; Rugby, Great Ormond and Great James Streets, Bloomsbury; Ormond Road and The Green, Richmond; Albury Street, Deptford and Church Row, Hampstead) have definite similarities in craftsmanship and design. Obviously in an astonishingly uniform street like Great James Street which was developed in 1722, one can assume that one carver and his apprentices were responsible, but even in places like Spitalfield where terrace houses were developed at different times and worked on by different carpenters, the brackets and scrolls form a recognisable and 'localised' set.

This type of door enrichment survived in some less fashionable parts of London until the early 1730s by which time it was elsewhere extinct. The doors in Meard Street, Soho, for example (see pages 96–97) built in 1732, are enriched with carved scrolls with acanthus leaves, supporting cornices. These are very late examples of a motif common some 30 years before and in many ways Meard Street was archaic in its own time. As the 18th century progressed the door became much more the province of the joiner than the carver, being a combination of glued-up columns and entablature with capitals of turned and applied moulding. All the carver had to do was to cut out the volute for an Ionic capital or occasionally cut a few acanthus leaves for a Corinthian capital. Later still, doors became the realm of the imitation stone merchant and the cast-iron founder who provided it with rustic blocks or grimacing key stones and huge fan lights. At the end of the 18th century it became the duty of the bricklayer to form the arch of the doorway in gauged bricks while the joiner filled the void with a panelled door and perhaps a couple of attenuated columns. Finally, by the end of the Georgian period, if a doorway had any enrichment beyond its panelled door and a withered keystone, it would certainly be made of stucco or cement.

All these changes in the treatment of doorway decoration of course reflected in miniature the changing fashions in architecture. As taste moved from the Baroque through Palladianism to Neo-Classicism, door decoration also moved from being heavy, personalised carving to more classically correct joinery and thence to slick and mass-produced decoration. What did not change, since doorways were also functional objects, was the basic size and proportion of the door void itself. As early as 1624 Sir Henry Wotton had written in his *Elements of Architecture*, "Leon Alberti (a learned searcher) who from the school of Pythagoras (where it was a fundamental maxim that the image of all things are latent in numbers) doth determine the comliest proportions between breadths and heights; namely the symmetry of two to three in their breadth and length, in others the double as two to four, these will indubitably result from either a graceful and harmonious contentment to the eye."

This logic continued and was laid down again and explained in 1756 by Isaac Ware when he spoke of doors in his *Complete Body of Architecture*, "Human stature is the mark for the least height that can be proper . . . This limits measure to 6 feet . . . the sides must be so distant that they must not crush the largest body . . . the smallest dimension therefore . . . is 3 feet and this being half of the given height has a very good effect in respect of general proportions . . . .

These are the rules laid down by nature . . . while we are near these we are sure not to err."

Ware goes on to explain that "there is Latitude . . . within which the fancy may rove, but which it must not pass," and then gives the directions in which architectural fancy could rove within these limitations. He explains that, for example, the more the door is raised above the level of the street, "the more the breadth should exceed the natural proportion with respect to height" and that it was an attractive idea to keep the proportion of a door to the same proportions as the house it was intended for: for example a tall house should have an elongated door and vice versa. But having said this, Ware solemnly warned that a "great variation from common proportions will always be wrong." Once again it is astonishing to think to what extent these men were confident that their aesthetic views were not transitory or arbitrary but concrete realities in tune with the truths of nature.

But these strong conventions about the size and proportion of doors that come from Ware and his contemporaries, were very much the result of their own preferences for, as Ware admitted, their great precursor Palladio had himself laid down no rigid procedure: "He gives no rule and he says none can be given; all he directs is that they be proportioned to the dignity of the inhabitants of the house."

But there were some among Ware's contemporaries who did not in his opinion very sensitively interpret Palladio's advice: "It is common," Ware recorded, "to see doors whose breadth occupies near one half of the extent in front: in Dover Street there is one whose top covers half the window placed over it in the upper storey."

This is a criticism of the proportion of doors to façades, not of the doorcase itself and in fact Ware, writing as he was in the mid-18th century, would have had to be a very severe critic indeed to have found much fault in the proportion and workmanship of the doors then being produced. To an amazing degree, the average door was an exquisite example of taste, proportion and skilful joinery. But also, to a distressing degree, the average door was truly average. All through London and indeed the country, the same variety of dignified, sound, Palladian doorway was taking over the streets and gone were the days, no doubt to Ware's relief, of the hand-wrought and individual cantilevered and canopied door surround (see pages 84–89).

This creeping sameness, profound as its effect was on Georgian building practice and on vernacular traditions, was the result of a very simple cause—the proliferation and spread of the pattern book.

Pattern books were themselves the result of another cause: the desire by workman to have for practical reference an understanding of classicism as it was practised both by currently celebrated architects and their venerated precursors and as it was demanded by fashionable patrons. Simply to satisfy the increasingly discriminating demands of their clients, the average builder had to have at his disposal a basic knowledge of the ancient canons of architecture plus an acquaintance with the prevailing fashion.

All through the 18th century London builders and architects flooded the country with books on architectural details and patterns for all the structural and decorative elements required in house building. Pattern books were of various types, ranging from the humble and practical instructions passed from one craftsman to another, to the more sophisticated books published by would-be architects to attract attention to themselves. Some were published by established architects like Sir William Chambers and James Gibbs to 'spread the word', whilst others were pompous attempts by architect–builders like Batty Langley to invent and sell new designs. Perhaps the most influential pattern books could not be strictly designated pattern books at all. These were the books of original research published by young architects who, returning from their Grand Tour, thought this a good way of advertising themselves and their erudition and of attracting discriminating clients (see pages 8–15). Some of these publications proved to be rich mines for novel detail when the Neo-Classical architect of the later 18th century began to dig into them. That these pattern books did have an influence on the designs of workmen is undeniable, as is the fact that they led towards correctness at the expense of originality, but it is also undeniable that as a body, pattern books represent the comic face of 18th-century classicism, being a peculiar mixture of the works of the pompous, the ignorant, the ambitious and the plagiarist as well as the shared experience of unpretentious craftsmen. The mongrel and generally charlatan nature of the majority of these books was marked by Ware, "If he looks into the common books of design he will find nothing but absurdity. There are in none of the parts of architecture monsters equal to those we find in these books intended for this purpose . . . from Francini to Batty Langley."

Langley tended towards the promotion of the Baroque whilst Ware was a rabid Palladian and perhaps he permitted personal antagonism to colour his criticism, but certainly many of these pattern books leave one with the impression that despite their superficially fashionable air, they were simply graveyards for old architectural plates. It is common for example to see in a pattern book published in the 1730s, designs that were fashionable 20 or 30 years before. Possibly it was just a question of using old plates for padding but with a detail so especially subject to the whims of fashion as doorways, it is strange to see in Batty Langley's *The City and Country Builder's and Workman's Treasury of Designs*, published in 1745, a set of designs which Langley monstrously claims as his own invention but which he had stolen from Gibbs' *Book of Architecture* which had been published in 1728 and then set a fashionable pace for the next decade.

Proportions
Despite the emphasis laid by Isaac Ware on the double-square proportion of 3 feet wide by 6 feet high, doors were very rarely of this exact proportion. If they were to be topped with a pediment and cornice and surmounted by an architrave, they would have looked too squat. The pattern from Edward Hoppus' *Gentleman's and Builder's Repository* of 1737 (see plate **17** page 93) is a perfect example of the double square type and how all the proportions were related in simple geometrical terms. Like the proportioning of the columns of the Orders, once a key dimension was fixed, and a few decisions taken about decoration, the doorway virtually designed itself. The door published by Batty Langley in 1745 (see plate **18**, page 94) which he had plagiarised from Gibbs, shows how, taking the basic double-square proportion, one could logically elongate it. (No matter how arbitrary this act might in fact be, as long as there *appeared* to be a regular logic the 18th-century mind was satisfied.) The diameter of one circle was divided into seven equal parts (this one-seventh of a diameter related to other key dimensions in the proportioning of the door's decoration) and one could continue adding one-sevenths to the height of the door until a pleasing proportion was reached. Plate **65** gives a breakdown of the proportions of a door.

So far discussion has centred on features which surround a door rather than that which fills the door void itself. Like its surround, the actual door itself also changed with fashion although about 1790 it was still common to see the heavy panelled doors common in the 1720s. In the early 19th century there was suddenly a greater freedom in door design. What had been the standard solution of numerous panels invariably being set in pairs so that the width of any door was always made up of two panels, was replaced by doors only one panel wide, or with doors displaying varying Regency motifs such as oval or round panels, reedings, rosettes and raised and fine mouldings.

Also common in the 1830s were doors made of only two thin panels running the whole length of the door and decorated in the Greek fashion with great curved and impressive bolts. This was just one step away from the true Greek Revival style in which doors tapered from top to bottom. A few churches and public buildings, for example St. Pancras Church of 1827, were furnished with these products of the classical-precedent mania, but features such as the tapered door never found their way into the vocabulary of the early 19th-century speculative builder. Certainly if Isaac Ware's mid-18th opinion that "a door narrower at the top than the bottom must have appeared a deformity in any building" still held sway, this omission is quite understandable.

Cantilevered hooded doorcases
The cantilevered and hooded doorcase was not unique to London but was common all over South East England. Due to its popularity with such influential architects as Wren it also found its way in lesser quantities into most parts of the provinces, although it was really only possible in its fully developed form in regions where wood was the traditional decorative material. The carved scroll and moulded canopy was too expensive a feature for a speculative builder to produce if it had to be made of stone. The essence of this type of door lies in its variety of detail and although this automatically involves the sphere of wood carving, this section deals only with the basic structure of the door surrounds and carving is discussed in Part III, pages 204–205.

There were two basic structural types of cantilevered hooded doors and plate **1** shows the simplest form, in which a piece of timber was let into the wall and supported a canopy on the cantilever principle. As the visible part of the post was then carved into a decorative scroll, in these cases the scroll is structural as well as decorative. In the second type this combination of function and decoration was not always the case. Plates **4**, **6–10**, pages 87–89, show the variety of doorcases which were made up of a bracket cantilevered off a scroll and supporting a flat cornice or concave hood. To enable the carver to work freely and carve deeply without concern about the weight of the load crushing his work a neat decision was taken. The supporting bracket and scroll were relieved of their actual supporting rôle and instead the hood was supporting by pieces of wood attached to it and then let into the wall.

Working with the simple motif of a bracket with its long side horizontal and appearing to support the hood, and a scroll with its long side vertical and appearing to support a longer bracket, the carver was able to achieve astonishing variety in this work. This freedom of invention was perhaps connected with the fact that this type of door decoration was not influenced by pattern books but was always the product of an individual craftman's fancy. Despite its fall from favour by the mid 18th century when ideas about architectural classicism had become more correct and less individually exuberant, this type of door did survive and the example from East London in plate **10** is surprisingly late, *circa* 1780.

1 Carved bracket from Redman's Row, Stepney, London E 1, dating from before 1720. The door surrounds in this group of buildings are much mutilated and some of the brackets look as if they were reused from elsewhere. Some of the brackets are exactly the right scale to have come from a modillioned eaves cornice and in fact the classical modillion eaves cornice must have supplied the inspiration for this type of doorway which is so much the result of an incorrect use of classical motifs. In many cases these bracketed doorcases are simply slices of giant modillioned eaves cornices. This group of houses in Redman's Row was derelict in March 1974 and due to be demolished by the council as slums. They were listed Grade II by the Department of the Environment

2 A pair of cantilevered doors from Drummond Street, Islington, London N 1, of about 1700. They are both simply scaled-up versions of modillions as used in Corinthian eaves cornices. As was typical with this type of doorway, the brackets are simply decorated and let into the wall: there was no attempt, as with the bracket and scroll type, to give the bracket the appearance of being supported by a pilaster

3 A very curious mixture from Tottenham High Street, London N 17. Here the standard early 18th-century cantilevered hood sits on an inserted early 19th-century door. Both are such good examples of their respective periods that it is quite astonishing to see how well they blend together. The fanlight and its surround are by no means a common design, while the reeded moulding framing the door, and the lion masks are to be found from Hackney to Bloomsbury

4 This pair of doorcases from Laurence Pulteney Hill, City of London, EC 4 are dated 1703. They are rich and finely made examples of a type once common. The concave scallop shell was a popular motif early in the century and lent itself well for use in enriched hooded doorways. The amount of carving in this pair is exceptional—even for the period and is, in fact, so rich that the different elements blend into each other. Unlike most examples of bracketed and scrolled doorways, on this pair the bracket (with the lion mask) is smaller than its supporting scroll

5 NOS. 4–6 Fournier Street, Spitalfields, London E 1. Built in the late 1720s this shows a well-controlled example of cantilevered door design. An architrave surrounds the door void and these are then surrounded by a plain fascia.

This fascia has two roles. Above the door it acts as a frieze, while beside the door it is panelled and acts as a visual support to the two carved brackets. The hood is the cornice of this composition and the whole design very neatly shows its derivation from a classical entablature

6 Doorcase built in the early 1720s for a house in Montpelier Row, Twickenham, Middlesex. It is unusual in that the cantilevered brackets are supported by very small scrolls

86

4

5

6

88

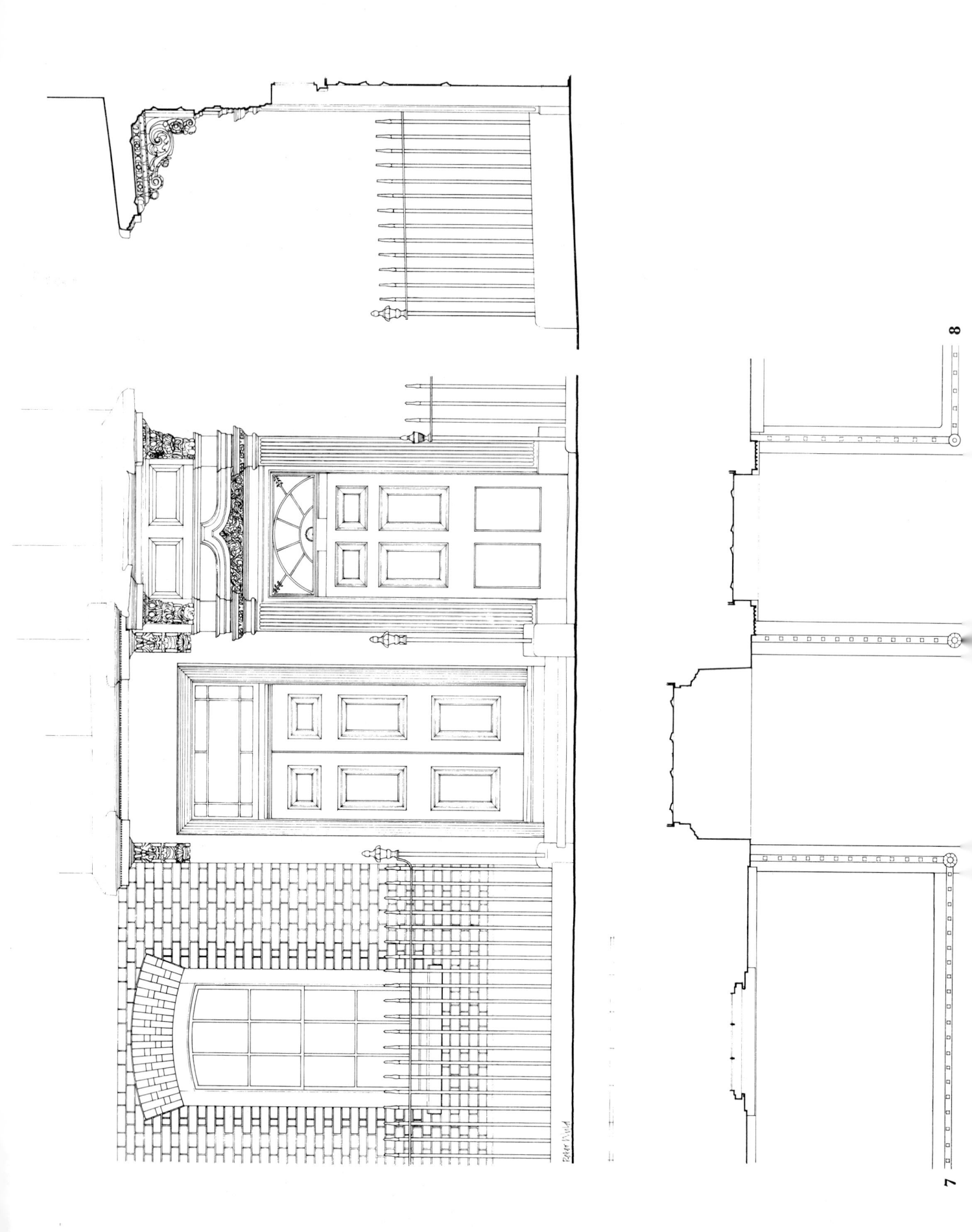

7, 8 Doorways from Rugby Street, Holborn, London WC 1. These houses stand on the Rugby Estate which was laid out in the 1680s by Nicholas Barbon, although actual building did not begin until 1702. Even then only a few houses were begun and there was a further delay until 1716 when building began in earnest. Most of the estate was built over the following 10 years. These particular houses date from the 1720s and were probably developed by William Pain, the father of William Pain who published pattern books in the later 18th century. No. 12 Rugby Street is extraordinary in being virtually two types of doorcase squeezed into one. It is a perfect Doric pilastered door surround topped by an equally perfect entablature with an architrave that sweeps (as was the fashion in the 1720s) up through the frieze to join the cornice. But where the cornice should be and the doorcase should end, a second doorcase begins, and this is the cantilevered and canopied type. The bracket and scroll relationship is a 'text book' example and even the motifs used by the carver are as standard as any carving can be. The little cherub's head which finishes off the scroll and stares at people going in and out of the door, is also found staring in Spitalfields and Hampstead.

All this perfection is rather disturbed by the relationship NO. 12 has with its neighbour. No. 14 was there first but when NO. 12 joined it a few years, or perhaps only a few months later, a jostling match was begun that goes on still. No. 14 is much plainer and loftier but its plainness is at least to a degree the result of later alteration. Both these houses retain their original heavy and fielded panelled doors. The flush bottom panels on the door of NO. 12 is a feature found throughout London during the 18th century as is NO. 12's fanlight. Almost identical mid-century fanlights exist around the corner in Great Ormond Street and in Wilkes Street, Spitalfields (see plate **12** page 50). The doorcases of NO. 10 of apparently the same date as NOS. 12 and 14 contains scroll and brackets of the same basic design yet being the product of individual carvers the actual details are different. On this door the hand of the 18th century rests heavier than on NOS. 12 or 14. The panelled door seems original work of the 1720s, but its surround of fine reeded architraves and lightly fluted lintel, with oval rosettes in the corners, is more likely to be *circa* 1790–1800

9 The front door of NOS. 4–6 Fournier Street, Spitalfields, London E 1. It is a fine composition being a combination of the peculiar cantilevered and well-pedigreed, rusticated door surrounds. (The rusticated door was fully explained to 18th-century designers in Sebastiano Serlio's 1584 edition of *Tutte l'Opere d'Architettura*.) Compared with those in Rugby Street this doorcase seems to have much solidity. Certainly the way the brackets embrace the door opening rather than sitting above it gives the elements an appearance of fitting together better. The scrolls and bracket look solid for they are broad and the carving only superficial. Again the scalop shell is used but here in miniature in the scroll. The door is original as is the ironwork. The semi-circle above the door would suggest that a fanlight was conceived in the original design, although this would be a very early date for a fanlight. Possibly the semi-circle was filled by the door being curved at the top as does a door in nearby Elder Street (see plate **48**)

10 Houses in Cannon Street Road, Stepney, London E 1. The principle of the door's construction is exactly those of the preceding early 18th century example, but this one must have been put together during the 1780s. But in place of the rich carving, enervated standard Neo-Classical design were used

Consoled doorcases
At first glance the early examples of consoled doorcases are similar to the bracket and scroll varieties for, like them, the consoles were enriched with carving and acanthus leaves. Unlike the cantilevered type, however, the consoled doorcase was based on sound classical precedents. The basic consoled types, taken from Sebastiano Serlio's *Tutte l'Opere d'Architettura* published in 1584, are illustrated in plates 11 and 12, opposite. Having such a respectable pedigree, consoled doorcases survived the changes of taste from Baroque freedom to Palladian correctness, even through to Neo-Classicism, and became one of the standard doorcase types.

The consoled doorcase was a very adaptable form and could be designed to support various types of pediment or only a cornice. It could be decorated to suit any order (see page 94), so that during the 1740–1760 period it was as much used to decorate façades of Roman austerity as it had been during the 1700s, to enrich elevations of 'hot' red bricks and richly carved cornices.

11, 12 The basic consoled door surrounds which influenced the English builder of the 17th and 18th centuries. Both come from Sebastiano Serlio's *Tutte l'Opere d'Architettura* published in 1584

13 A console detail published in a 1686 reprint of Sir Henry Wotton's *Ground Rules of Architecture*. Compare with plate 14

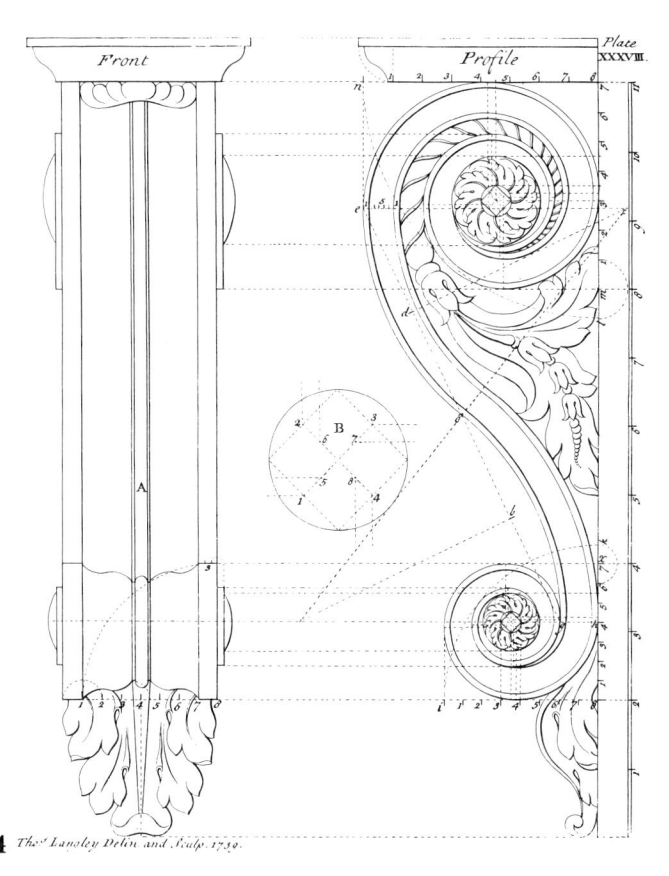

14 Console from Batty Langley's *The City and Country Builder and Workman's Treasury of Designs* published in 1745. It is a standard type and was drawn in 1739

15 Plate from James Gibbs' influential *Book of Architecture*. Published in 1728 one of its designs is said to have inspired the White House, Washington. These designs were based very much on Renaissance precedents and became standard types, due to Gibbs' promotion, during the first half of the 18th century. Although Gibbs started work in London as a Baroque architect, presumably in deference to the taste of his Roman Catholic, Scottish benefactors, he soon changed to a Palladian manner of working. By 1728 his work, being a fluid mixture of imaginative Baroque and fashionable, correct Palladianism, was calculated to appeal to the taste of the average builder

16

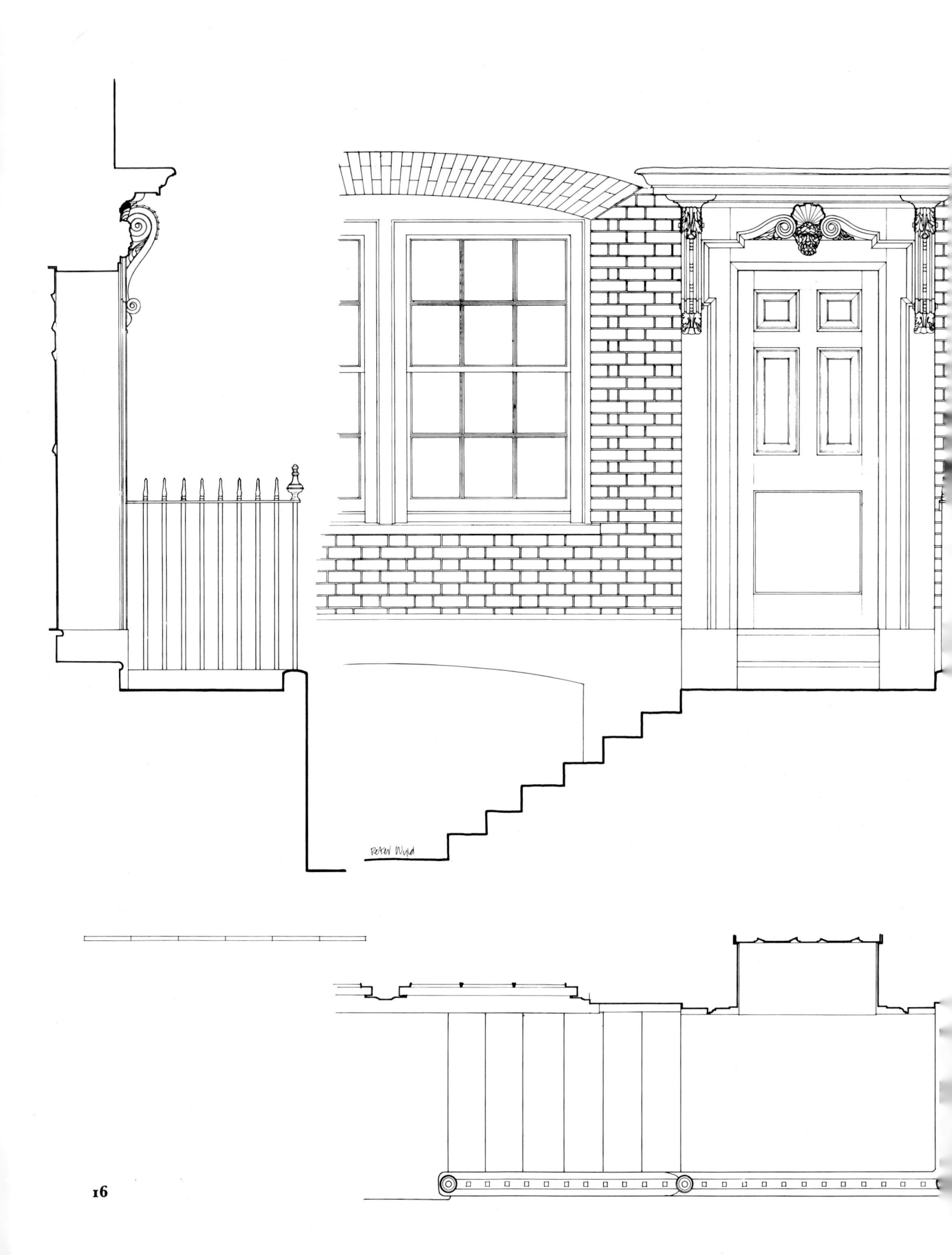

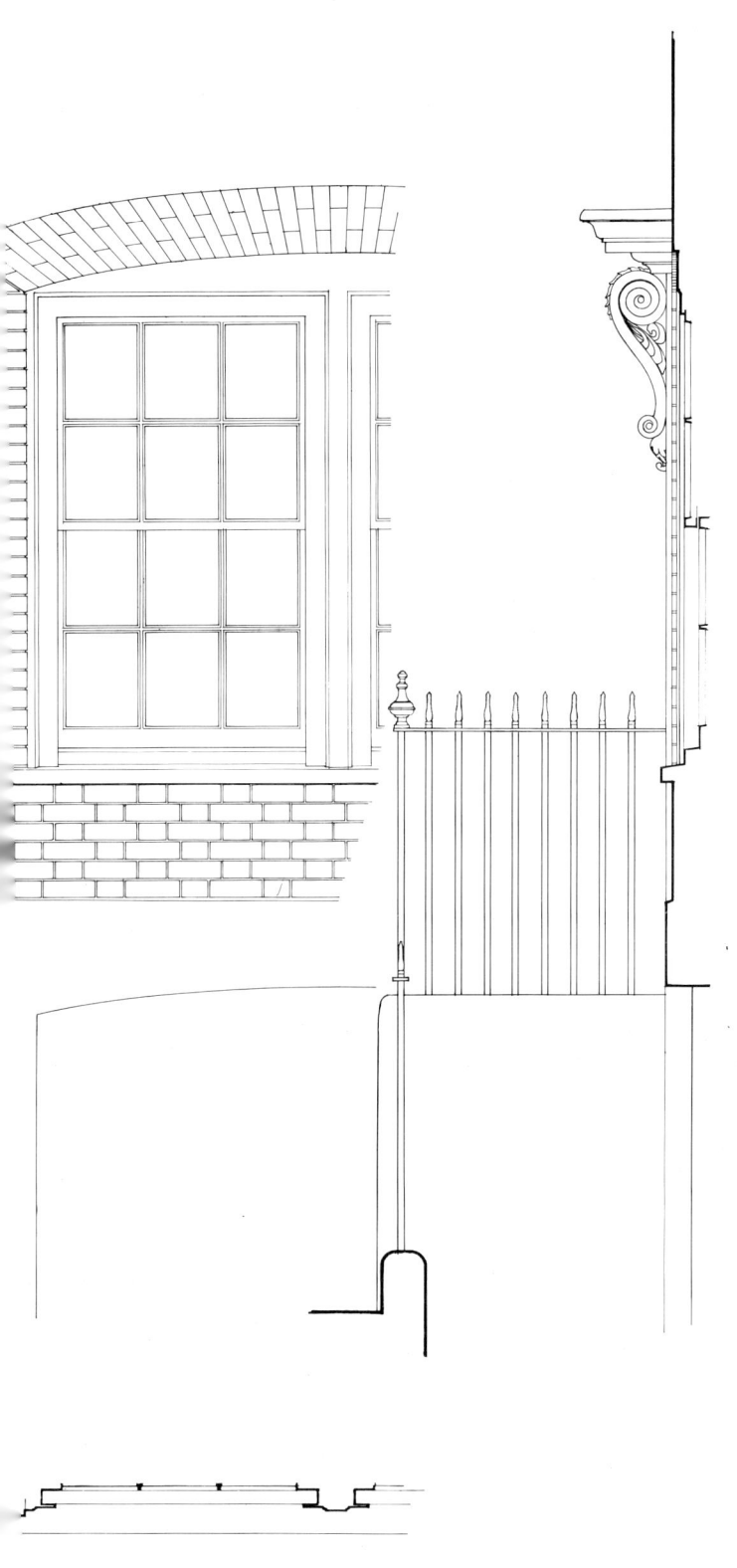

16 A built example based on a Gibbs design. The proportions of the door void, and certain of its parts, was changed but the joiner, in principle, kept very close to Gibbs' original. This door stood in White's Row, Spitalfields, London E 1, and was put together during the 1720s

17 A pattern from Edward Hoppus' *Gentleman's and Builders' Repository* of 1737. It is clearly based on the basic Serlio type and is an excellent specimen of the removal of arbitrary elements from the proportioning of a doorcase after the original arbitrary decision about its basic size had been taken. (This was not entirely arbitrary if the builder followed Isaac Ware's advice to base it on the double-square proportion of 6 feet by 3 feet.) Basically, the proportions were determined by the fixed relationship between the parts of the doorcase. In this example the void is in fact a double square and the centre of the top circle forms the centre of the entire composition. The drawing is in fact self-explanatory and, to a classical mind seeking order and rules, very satisfying in its apparent achievement of perfection by excluding any unmeasurable factors. For this very reason a whole street of such purity would be very impressive, but surely rather dull. Fortunately, the nature of the method by which Georgian London was developed did not allow for this type of repetition. Until the late 18th century, most of the streets were developed by many individuals who, although conforming in their basic understanding of classicism and its fashionable interpretations, would always differ in their choice of such detail of doorcases. An interesting variety of detail within a general conformity was therefore assured

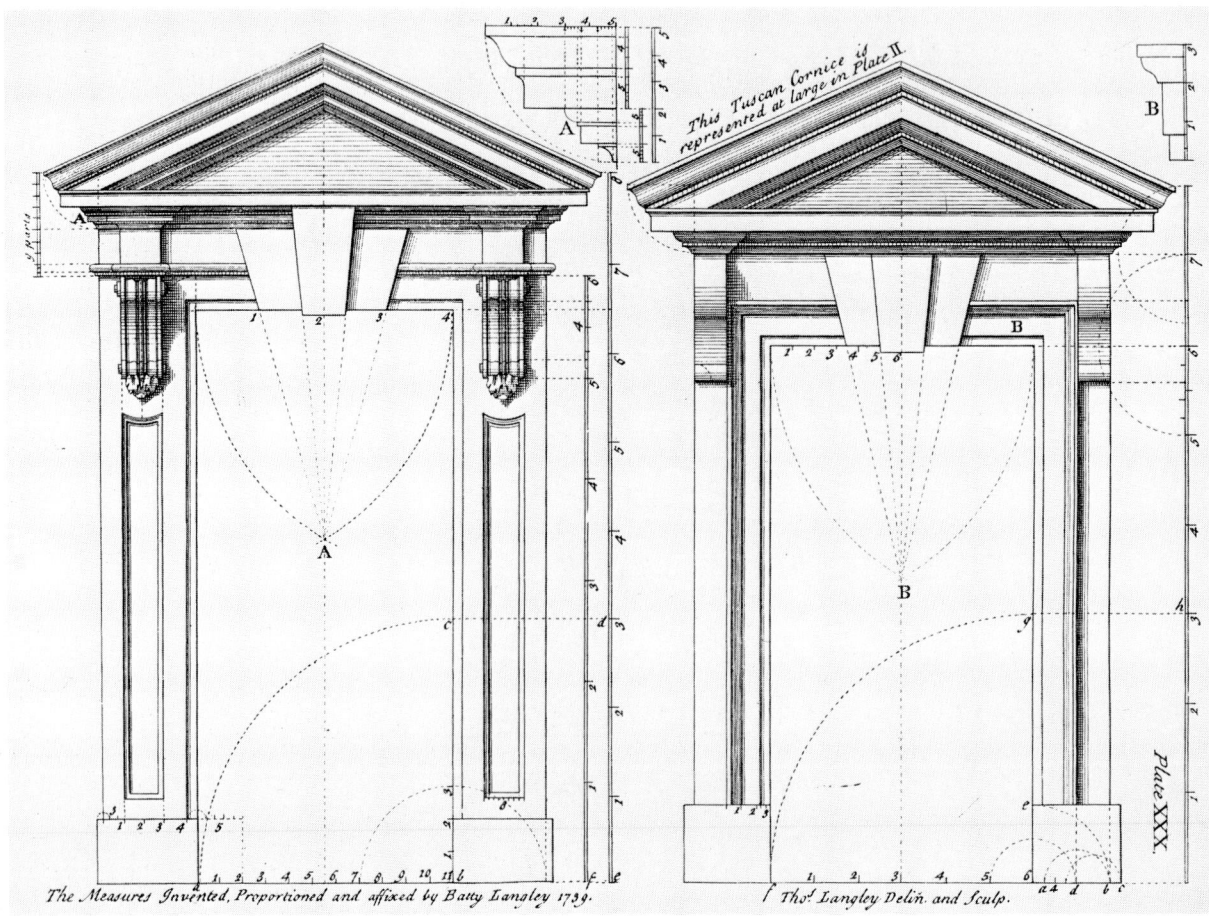

18

19

94

18 This plate from Batty Langley's *The City and Country Builder's and Workman's Treasury of Designs* is interesting for several reasons. It is dated 1739 and is therefore 11 years later than Gibbs' *Book of Architecture*. Yet it is obvious that doorcase A is taken directly from Gibbs (see plate 15) and in publishing an old-fashioned design, Langley not only fails to acknowledge Gibbs, but insinuates that it is his own design. Langley did, however, give more information about the proportioning. He showed how the door void could be elongated while retaining a classical logic. The circles were divided into seven equal parts which then determined certain other dimensions of the doorcase. (The ear of the architrave, C, relates to the circles division). As the plate shows, one-sevenths of the circle could be added to the height of the void until a satisfactory proportion was reached. Batty Langley said of these designs, "And when it happens, for want of a proper height, that a pediment cannot be made; then in all such cases the cornice must break forward and be supported by trusses (consoles) as A, plate . . . xxxi, . . . to carry off the rains. It also very often happens, that even when frontispieces may be finished with pediments; that the projection of the pediment will not be sufficient to protect the entrance from the insults of rains; therefore in such cases, the pediments must advance forward, and be sustained either by trusses, as exhibited in plate . . . xxxi . . . or by pilasters or columns." In the light of this functional statement, it is surprising that the only doorcase design (excluding porchs) to keep rain off successfully was abandoned by about 1730

19 Plate xxx from the same book. The huge dropped keystone is very much in the Gibbs tradition, and the drawing shows neatly how the centre for the keystone was found by dropping an arc equal to the door width until it coincided with the door's vertical centre line, A. Plate B shows a simplified 'Tuscan' version of the same structural type

20 An astonishingly exact example of a doorcase based on the Gibbs-inspired design which Langley published in 1745. This doorcase built in the late 1720s and so pre-dating Langley's book, must come straight from Gibbs. It stands in Stepney Green, London E 1

21 No. 31 Albury Street, Deptford, London SE 8. This street was built between 1700 and 1720. The developer was William Lucas, a master builder who had been employed by Thomas Archer on his nearby St. Paul, Deptford (1712–30). There were many highly-trained craftsmen available in the early 18th century as a result of the demand for their services during the rebuilding of the City of London after the Great Fire. As the rebuilding of the City Church and St. Paul's Cathedral drew to a close in the early 18th century, new employment was found for these craftsmen by the passing of the Act for Fifty New Churches in London of 1712. In fact only 11 churches were built and St. Paul, Deptford was one. Possibly, since he had already worked with them, William Lucas employed a body of experienced wood carvers to decorate the doors of Albury Street. Certainly, Albury Street has an astonishing selection of deeply-carved, pine wood consoles. Practically all are different, and many of the designs are based on nautical as well as classical motifs for Deptford was a naval town. Interesting too is the fact that although the consoles are highly individual, the basic structure of the doorcases are extremely uniform. Each has a pair of consoles supporting a flat cornice, and usually supported by single panelled thin pilaster strips. The deepness of the carving meant these consoles could not support even these small cornices and they were in fact supported by pieces of wood fixed in them and then let into the façade. The fine panelled door is original and, since these were the days before fanlights became fashionable, occupies the whole of the void

22 No. 12 Millman Street, Bloomsbury, London WC 1. These houses were developed during the early 1720s and it is highly probable that the door dates from then although the façade has been rebuilt in the late 19th century. A very neat design, advanced for its date, the consoles were already totally classically correct and totally unoriginal. Unlike Albury Street where the carved work dominated the design and was supported by the joinery, here, only a few years later, the joiner has taken over the design and merely used fragments of fancy carving as foils for his work. The masked keystone was a standard classical motif and the fanlight seems to be an original feature of the composition, which, if it is, makes this a very early example of the use of a curved fanlight

23 No. 8 Millman Street, Bloomsbury, London WC 1. Of the same date as No. 12, this example is simpler and even more the product of the joiner. Particularly interesting is the comparison between the contemporary doors of NO. 8 and NO. 12, and the way the fanlights are related to the overall design. Both these houses have now been demolished and were allowed to stand empty for five years to hasten dereliction. The doorcase of NO. 12 was saved but that of NO. 8 was destroyed

24, 25 Doorcases from Meard Street, Soho, London W 1. These examples were extremely old fashioned, being made about 10 years after those in Millman Street. Meard Street is dated 1732 and here the carver enjoyed one of his last moments of supremacy over the joiner. The feature of the doorcase is very much the huge carved Corinthian consoles with acanthus leaves licking over them and flicking up at the bottom

24

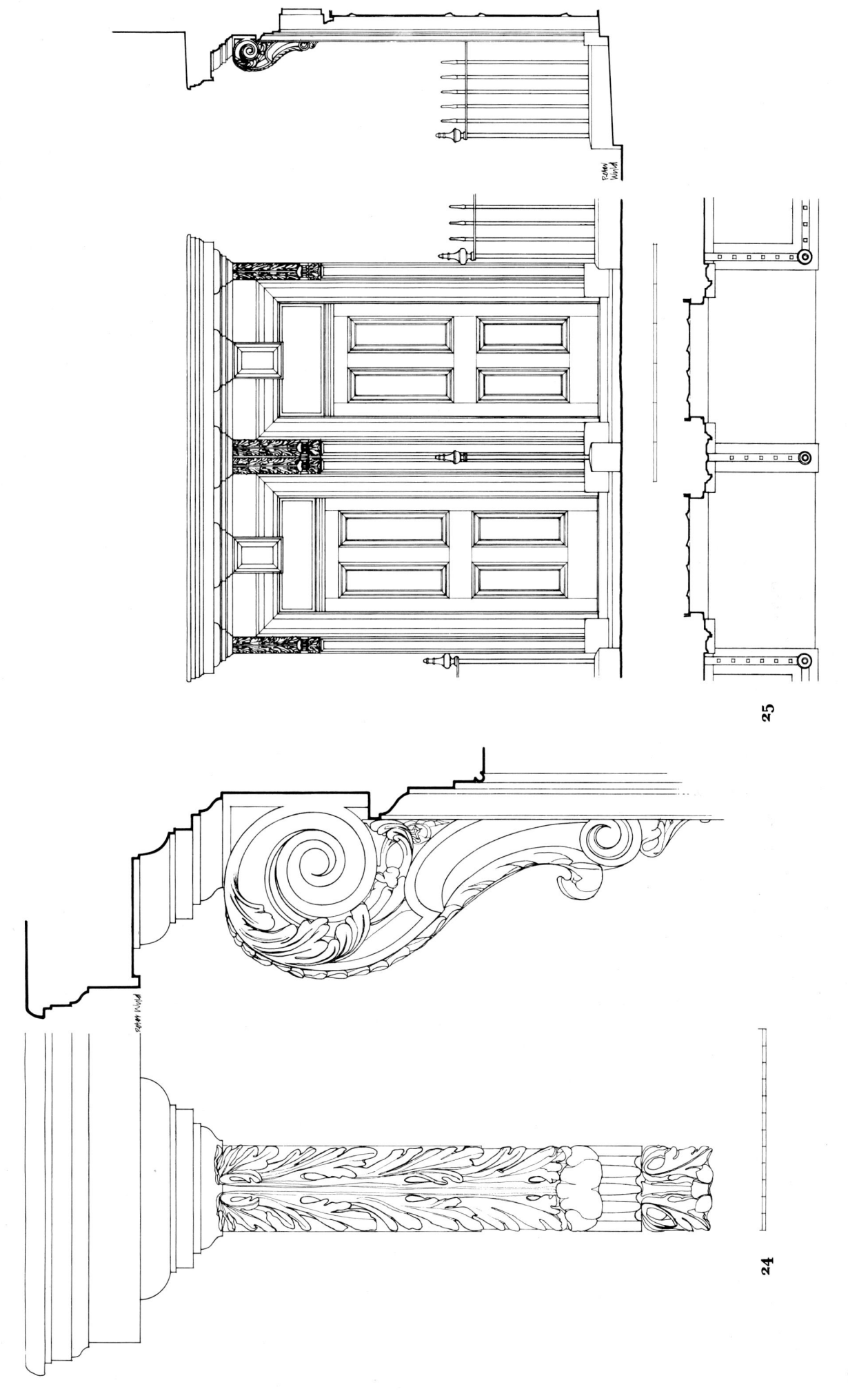

25

26

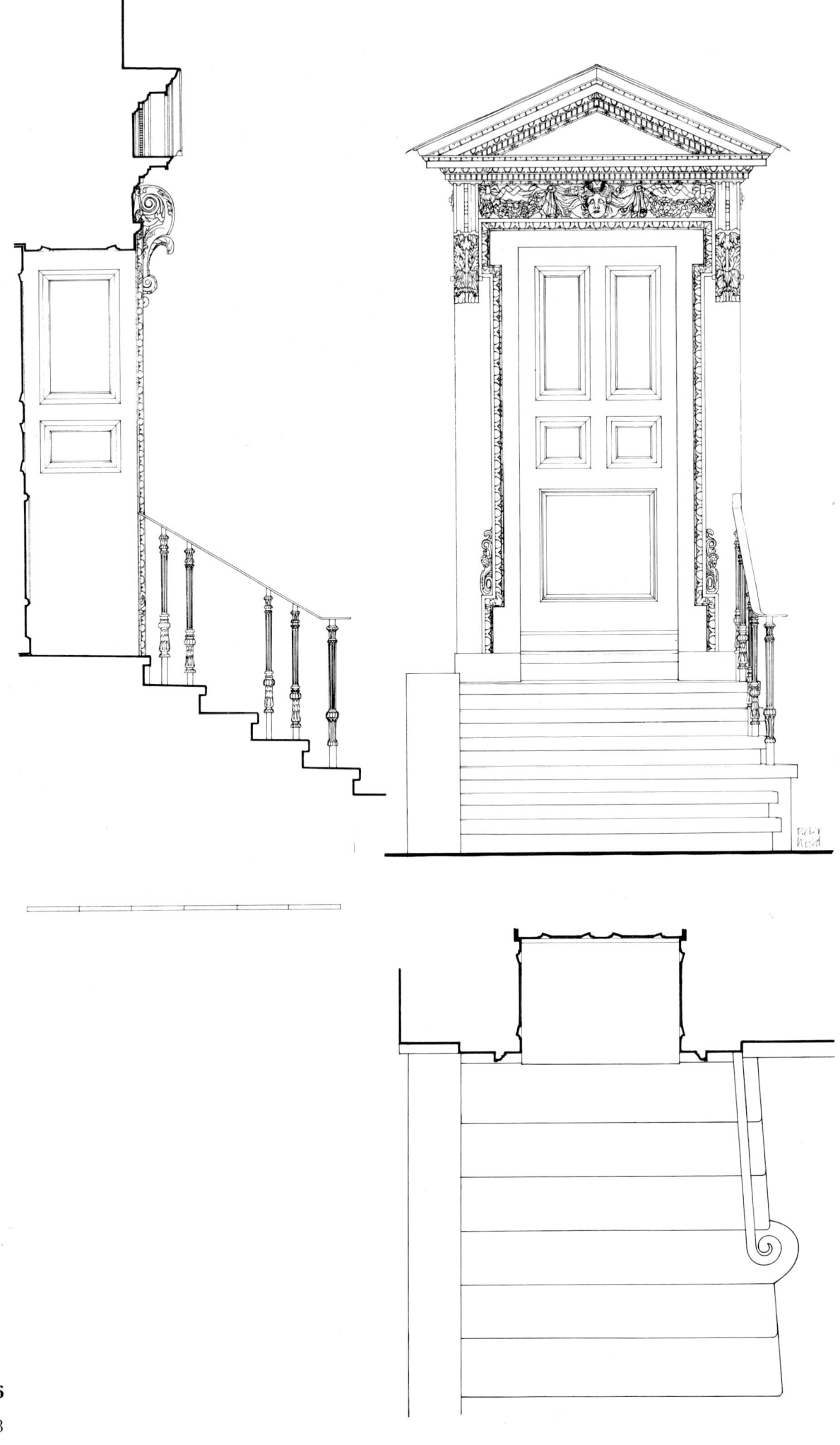

26 Doorway in Stoke Newington Church Street, London N 16. It is difficult to date this door accurately, but it very likely dates from the 1730s. These very rich doors (there are four in a row) contain a plentiful mixture of standard classical motifs but motifs that were more commonly used in 18th-century London for interior door surrounds rather than street doorcases. The richness of this doorcase is therefore not derived from the early 18th-century tradition of individuality and adaption, but is the product of interior classical convention. The consoles are enriched by standard acanthus leaves while the frieze is filled with a perfect mask, swags and cartouche. This all adds up to a rather rich Palladian composition but with a touch of Gibbs-type Baroque. Very Gibbs is the carved architrave with little scrolls at the bottom, and very Palladian the egg-and-dart moulding which forms the surround. The door is original for its panels align with those on the doorcase jambs but there is still no fanlight

27 This example from NO. 1 Greek Street, Soho, London W 1, which was equipped for the rich merchant and MP Richard Beckford, shows what the consoled doorcase had become to the world of high fashion by the mid 1740s. It is of stone and a highly dignified, restrained and impersonal piece. The pulvinated frieze is a typical Palladian feature of Roman ancestry and the rectangular fanlight space appears original. The obelisks flanking the door were a favourite feature for grand houses during the middle of the century

28 Also dating from the 1740s, but a long way from the fashionable West End, Fournier Street, Spitalfields, London E 1. Like the doorcase in Soho, this example also stakes its claim to dignity by its classical correctness and reserve. In fact the relationship of the consoles to the rest of the doorcase is identical with that of Greek Street, for the consoles are attached to a plain band outside the architrave that surrounds the door. The main difference between these doorcases of the 1740s is not that one is pedimented, or that one is of wood and one stone, but that the general effect of cold correctness in the Greek Street example is strangely reversed by the heavy romantic rustication which appears in the Fournier Street door. Unlike Greek Street, this could never have been a door through which one would glide with dignity into a rich interior. The heavy imposts which break back and form a cornice separating the fanlight from the door, indicate that by this date the fanlight was conceived very much as part of the overall doorcase design

29 A pair of doors from Walnut Tree Walk, Kennington, London SE 11, built during the 1750s. Like the Fournier Street example, the fanlights are integral parts of the design, but more importantly, these doorcases contain definite Gothic motifs. While the 1750s was generally, a decade of austerity, correctness and dignity in façades and their details, these little doorcases prove to be the exception. All through the classical period in England Gothic motifs were used, either naturally as vernacular survivals or consciously as revivals. As early as 1742 Batty Langley had published his extraordinary *Gothic Architecture Improved* in which he attempted to cater for the growing interest in Gothic and very insensitively attempted to rationalise and 'improve' it by forcing it to conform to a classical régime. The astringent aesthete Horace Walpole commented on this work and its author in his *Anecdotes of Painting* published in 1762–71, "I must mention a more barbarous architect . . . Batty Langley who endeavoured to adopt gothic architecture to Roman measures . . . All that his book achieved, has been to teach carpenters to massacre that venerable species". In the light of this the surprising thing about these doors is not that Gothic motifs are used, or even that they have possibly been 'improved' by Batty-Langley-type proportioning, but rather that the Gothic motif of the foil and quatrefoil are blended so effortlessly with regular classical motifs. In place of a triglyph or mask in the frieze a quatrefoil is used, and in the pilaster strip, beneath the Doric guttae a trefoil tops the panel

30 This doorcase in Kennington Lane, London SE 11, is situated nearby Walnut Tree Walk. The façade around it has been completely rebuilt this century, but the date of the surrounding buildings is 1780–1800. Kennington Lane is however much older in origin and it is possible that this house may date from before 1780. Certainly the design of the doorcase would suggest this, with its rustic blocks of a type common during the first 30 years of the 18th century

30

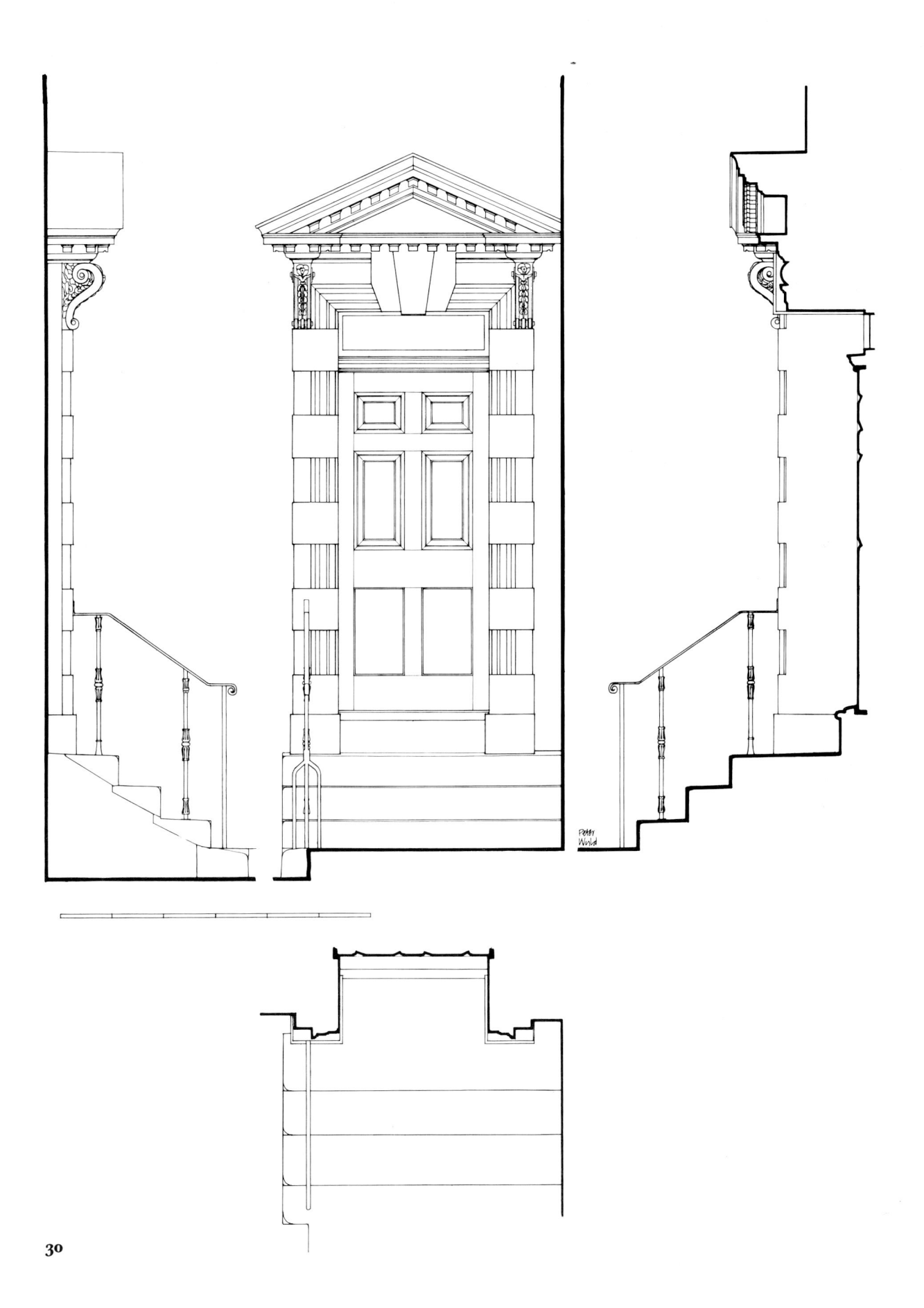

31 No. 9 Dombey Street, Bloomsbury, London WC 1. This street was laid out in 1680s and rebuilt in the 1760s, with this doorcase dating from then. Again, like the examples from Greek Street and Fournier Street, the consoles are fixed outside the architrave on a strip that is a vertical continuation of the frieze. This is a basic structural and design difference that separates these from the examples in Walnut Tree Walk, Meard Street, and Albury Street in which the consoles sit on pilaster strips. The extraordinary feature of this door is its elongated proportion and fanlight. The fanlight is probably later as it does not relate comfortably with the top parts of the doorcase jambs. The ramped-up ironwork is a pleasing 18th-century feature

32 A pair of doors from High Street, Islington, London N 1. These date from 1750–1770, but the boldness of the consoles, which are unusual in being finished without bottom twists, and the imposts made them very reminiscent of patterns published by Gibbs in 1728 and by Langley in the 1740s. The dwarf ironwork is very peculiar since, in every detail but its proportion, it is very dignified. Can it have been cut down?

33 A definite monster, now destroyed, that once enlivened a mid-18th-century house in Greatorex Street, Whitechapel, London E 1. In all but one detail it is of a type that became very common from 1750 onwards. The exception is that, where columns ought to be, there are enervated little consoles propping up the capitals of the missing columns

33

34

35

34 The beginning of the Neo-Classical influence shown in this door from Surrey Street, Strand, London WC 2, which dates from the 1780s. The Adam brothers' influential, if financially disastrous, Adelphi had just been completed west of Surrey Street, by 1772, and their decorative style had spread all over London (see plates **25** and **85**, pages 65, 132).

The doorcase is a pleasing mixture of traditionally profiled and decorative consoles and cornices, and the favourite Neo-Classical motif of a finely fluted frieze

35 This badly mutilated doorcase from Wilkes Street, Spitalfields, London E 1, is one of the last expressions of the wooden doorcase in London. It dates from *circa* 1800 when fashion was moving toward doors decorated with imitation stone keystones, imposts and rustics, or simply with gauged brick archs and fanlights. Predictably, by the end of its era, the doorcase was entirely the work of the joiner. Even required effects which were impossible to produce by joinery or turning, were no longer carved but, true to the principles of mass-production, made of applied and moulded plaster. The mutilation (the top member of the cornice and the bottom of the consoles are missing) weakens this composition, but even when complete it would have been an enervated and rather half-hearted design.

A similar, unmutilated example exists in Cannon Street Road (see plate **10**, page 89)

36 The end of the line—both for the Georgian type in general and this house in particular. The house stood in Dock Street, Stepney, London E 1, from approximately 1830–1973. It was a perfect example of the Greek Revival as applied to domestic architecture and all the details, though in essence standard classical motifs, were modelled on solid Greek precedents. The main consoles of a bold outline, were decorated with austere and simplified anthemion motifs and were echoed in miniature by undecorated consoles which supported the fanlight. The fanlight was typical of the 1830s with its cast-iron lily bud bars, and equally typical of the period was the twin-panelled, studded door. The cornice, of a vigorous simplicity equal to that of the imposts, lies across the railings where it was thrown during demolition

Pedimented and columned doorcases

The pedimented and columned doorcase was, more than any other type, the standard method of door enrichment during the Georgian period. Unlike other varieties which came and went or were greatly modified by fashion, the design of the columned and pedimented doorcase remained relatively constant. Its parts and proportions were derived from solid classical precedents and principles and there was little opportunity for structural invention and novelty without deviating from what was classically 'correct'. In the early part of the 18th century this could, and was done, by Baroque architects such as Nicholas Hawksmoor and Thomas Archer but one of the many results of the Palladian dictatorship that began to rule English architectural taste after 1720 was that this type of Baroque inventiveness died out. If an architect had continued to practice it he would doubtless have had difficulty in finding clients, because the remarkable thing about Palladianism and taste was the almost universal recognition and acclaim it won throughout fashionable England.

As with all thorough revolutions, the Palladians, once in power, began to consolidate their position with an ideological attack on their deposed Baroque predecessors. One of the most astonishing of these attacks, calculated to exterminate Baroque from the fashionable world of potential clients and patrons, was delivered by Robert Morris in his *An Essay in Defence of Ancient Architecture* published in 1728. This book is relevant here, because in attempting to prove how Palladianism followed ancient architectural precedents more 'accurately' and was therefore 'superior' to the Baroque, Morris compared two doorcases, shown here in plates **37** and **38**. The first example (plate **37**) he said was lately erected in London, and the second (plate **38**) was Morris's own Palladian design given for comparison, a design which he claimed was in keeping with the principles of the ancients, and indeed the very principles of Nature. Of the Baroque door he wrote, "There can be no regulated proportions, no universal standards (of absolute necessity), particularly adopted to the execution, because fancy alone has had the superiority over truth and reason, in the extravagant address of the composition, the production of novelty and insensible singleness. What possibility is there of forming a true method of division in the minuter parts, when the whole is the result of an entire independency upon even the general rules and methods of the ancients, and repugnant to its precepts?" The consolidation of the Palladian position in attacks such as this was an architectural symptom of an age which was looking for reason and order in all things and the personalised Baroque was first attacked and then eliminated, simply because its chaotic inventiveness appeared to threaten the new, urbane and readily distinguishable civic order.

It is significant that Morris, for his 'perfect' designs, should have chosen to use Doric columns. In England, from the early 18th century through to the early 19th (when the very idea of decorated door-surrounds fell from fashion), this basic concept of a miniature temple front surrounding an entrance was developed. One of the most important factors in this development both in columned and pilastered doorcases, was the choice of classical Order and this choice was determined by the wider influence of fashion. In the very early 18th century, when English Baroque flourished, there was a definite attraction to the showy and rich Corinthian Order. As Palladianism and relative austerity gathered impetus the Corinthian fell from fashion almost completely by 1720, to be replaced by the more ascetic Doric and Ionic Orders. Since each of the Orders had its own specialised decoration, proportions and possibilities, the following illustrated analysis of pedimented and columned doorcases is divided into the following Order-based sections: Corinthian, Ionic and Doric.

37

38

105

39 Morris' model in Montpelier Road, Twickenham, for plate **37**

Corinthian doorcases
Not many columned Corinthian doorcases were used on the street elevations of 18th-century standard terrace houses. When used on external doorcases, the Corinthian Order was generally simplified by the use of pilasters instead.

40 A doorway designed in 1676 by Christopher Wren in King's Bench Walk, Temple, London EC 4. The whole design is in gauged brick work (which in itself was influential in establishing the popularity of the technique in the early 18th century), except the capitals which are of carved stone. Wren has not attempted to be classically 'correct' and has topped the Corinthian capitals with an entablature of almost Tuscan austerity

This inventiveness on Wren's part was something that could not be tolerated by the later Palladian generation which interpreted it either as ignorance or conceit (who could improve on the Ancients?). Isaac Ware, the strict Palladian theorist and protégé of Lord Burlington, wrote in his *Complete Body of Architecture* in 1756, "... the parts (of the doors) be all proportioned; that no way be given to a vitiated fancy in adding unnatural ornaments; no placing of the entablature of one order over columns of another, as we see too often in London in what are called composed door cases". As taste moved from Baroque freedom, Wren's free approach became inconceivable. This house, and others in King's Bench Walk, is important in that it introduced the idea of using columned door surrounds in domestic terrace architecture rather than the standard canopy and brackets then in general use

39

40

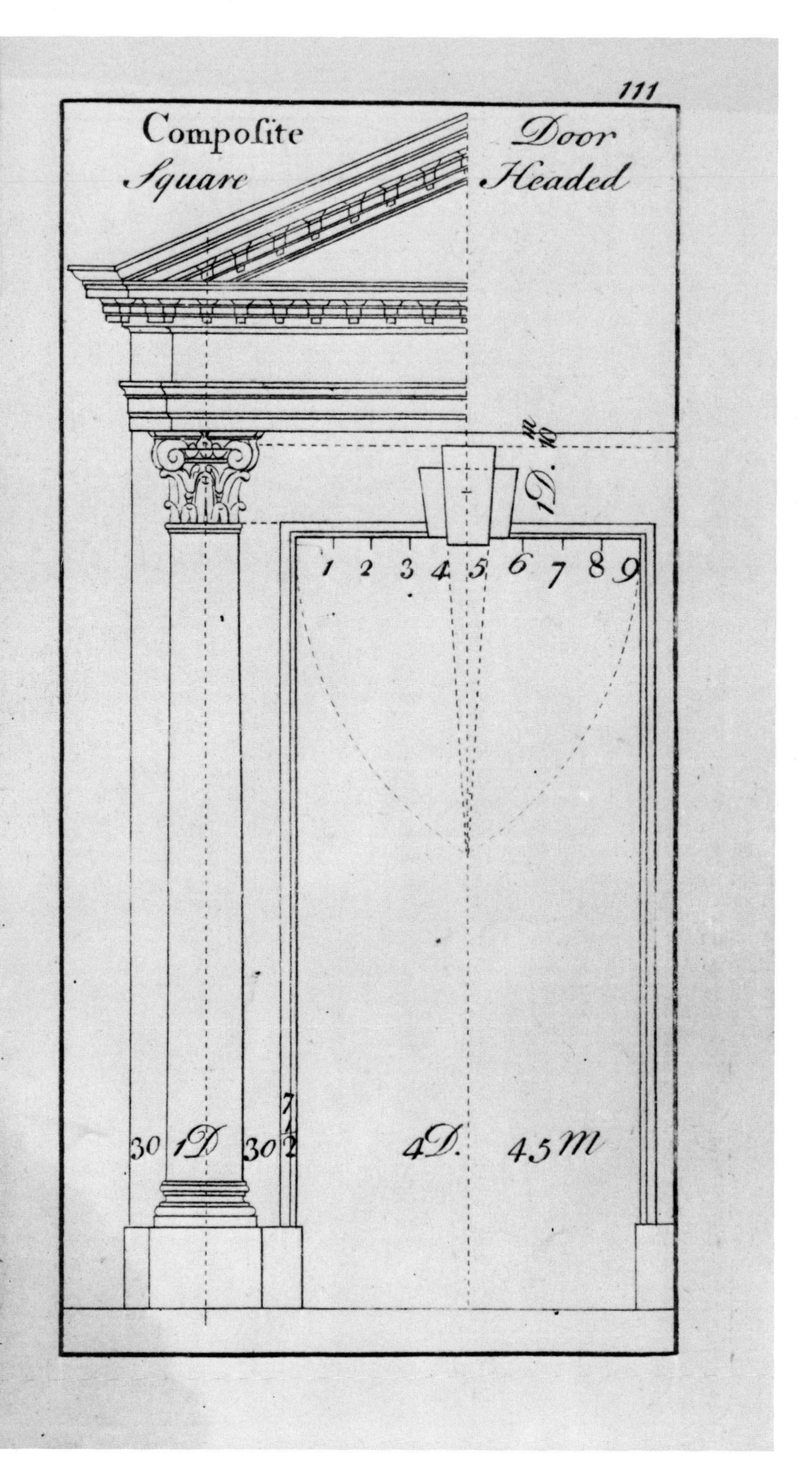

Composite Square Door Headed

111

1 2 3 4 5 6 7 8 9

30 1D 30 7½   4D.   45m

41 Closely related to the Corinthian capital was the Composite capital, a Roman invention intended as a hybrid of the Corinthian and Ionic Orders. This finely proportioned example was published in 1751 by Batty Langley in his *The Builder's Director, or Bench-Mate*. Once the decision had been taken by the designer to use a certain Order then the proportion of the door was to a large degree determined and since the Corinthian column was more elongated than the Doric, the door void would also be more elongated. But this design by Batty Langley illustrates a neat trick. The astragal moulding beneath the capital aligns with the top of the door void and the actual capital stands against a surface. The surface is used to provide a space for the keystone to splay into (since a keystone was wanted space had to be provided since it could not break into the entablature above the door void). The provision of this area for the keystone meant that the door void would lose some possible height, for without the keystone, it could have reached right up to the bottom of the entablature.

What Batty Langley did to compensate was, simply, to increase the size of the void (which is a double-square proportion from the top to the base of the columns), by adding a plinth to the columns of the same depth as the area lost beneath the entablature. Once the principle was accepted that the bases of the columns did not have to form the base of the doorcase, endless tricks could be performed with this little plinth to stretch and control the proportions of the door void without fouling up the proportions of the columns and their relationship with the other classical elements.

The diameter of a column was the module by which all the proportions of its related ornaments were determined and each Order had its own fixed proportions. It was correct, for example, to have more space between Tuscan columns than Corinthian. On this design Langley has marked '1D' on the bottom of the column meaning 1 diameter. Since the column tapered, the diameter varied, but the rule was to take the proportioning diameter from the bottom of the column. The diameter, for subtle proportioning, would then be divided into 60 equal parts called minutes and the 30 minutes on each side of the 1D meant that those dimensions should be half a diameter in width. 4D relates to the width of the door which should be 4 diameters in width. Of course the proportioning of the door void could be worked out in one of two ways. If based on the Isaac Ware doctrine of doors being 6 feet by 3 feet, the door void was fixed and the proportions of the columns of the whole doorcase were determined from that. Contrariwise the exact height and diameter of the columns could be fixed and then the width of the door void worked out

42 An ultimate form of Corinthian doorcase. This type of pediment was specially developed to go with the enriched Corinthian Order and it enjoyed a short period of limited popularity from the late 17th to the early 18th centuries. Somewhat surprisingly, this example was published in 1756 by Isaac Ware in his *Complete Body of Architecture* and despite its fall from fashion into disuse, he appears to have still considered it a standard solution if one wanted to build a Corinthian doorcase with a rich pediment. Isaac Ware did, for he used this design for Chesterfield House which was finished in 1752 and demolished in 1937

Ionic doorcases

The Ionic Order was versatile. Potentially, it was capable of carrying much decoration, and also of being stripped down to almost Doric austerity. This versatile quality made it popular both with the early Baroque designers and the Palladians and it remained popular right through the period, for the new interpretation given to classical motifs by the Neo-Classical architects of the late 18th century, and by the Greek Revivalists of the early 19th century, particularly involved the Ionic Order. Increasingly it became the thing to proportion the Ionic capital to Greek rather than to Romano-Renaissance proportions, and to decorate the Order with Greek motifs. In a sense, the Ionic Order became a common symbol of the change in fashion from the Romano-Palladian interpretation of the classicism to that of the Greek-inspired Neo-Classicists. In comparison the difference between Roman and Greek Doric was more extreme. Its intrinsic austerity together with the exceeding stumpiness of the Greek Doric as marked by Sir William Chambers, made it unpopular in the late 18th century even amongst the Neo-Classicists. When it was used it was usually heavily decorated with Greek motifs not belonging to the Order as at Adam's Adelphi (see plate **85**, page 132). Unlike its plain and heavy-footed brother, the Greek Ionic had the necessary elegance, as well as novelty, to appeal to the 18th-century eye. In 1764 James 'Athenian' Stuart, joint author of the *Antiquities of Athens,* was very proud that the Ionic capital of his NO. 15 St. James Square matched exactly the proportions of those of the Erechtheum in Athens, and in the early 19th century Ionic became almost the trade mark of Sir Robert Smirke.

43 Ionic doorcases, both columned and pilastered, from James Gibbs' *Book of Architecture* published in 1728. One of the most striking things about these three examples is the unexceptional relationship the door void has with its decoration. Presumably the void is proportioned to the diameter of the column or vice versa, but otherwise the designs are merely based on the standard idea of the miniature temple front as given out by Italian Renaissance architects. As the century progressed a synthesis between function and decoration took place and the result of this fusion appeared in both Ionic and Doric doorcases after about 1750.

Although very standard in the light of later developments, the design and details of these three doorcases are also fairly revolutionary for the 1720s when many speculative builders were still running up houses with heavily carved, hooded and bracketed door surrounds. When an ordinary builder did design doors based on these patterns (see plates **48**–**53**) he simplified them and it is very rare, for example, to see in a London Street a doorcase with columns that stand against pilasters.

The design on the left contains features that were widely used amongst designers throughout the century. Keystones with masks were still being placed to smile, grimace or stare blankly down at passers-by in the 1820s, but the idea of combining the keystone with an eaved architrave door-surround had died out by the 1750s. The design on the right contains the much repeated idea of placing a pilaster against a rusticated surround. This was a standard motif even before Gibbs published this book, as was the pulvinated frieze. All three door voids are given extra height by the placing of the columns and pilasters on plinths

43

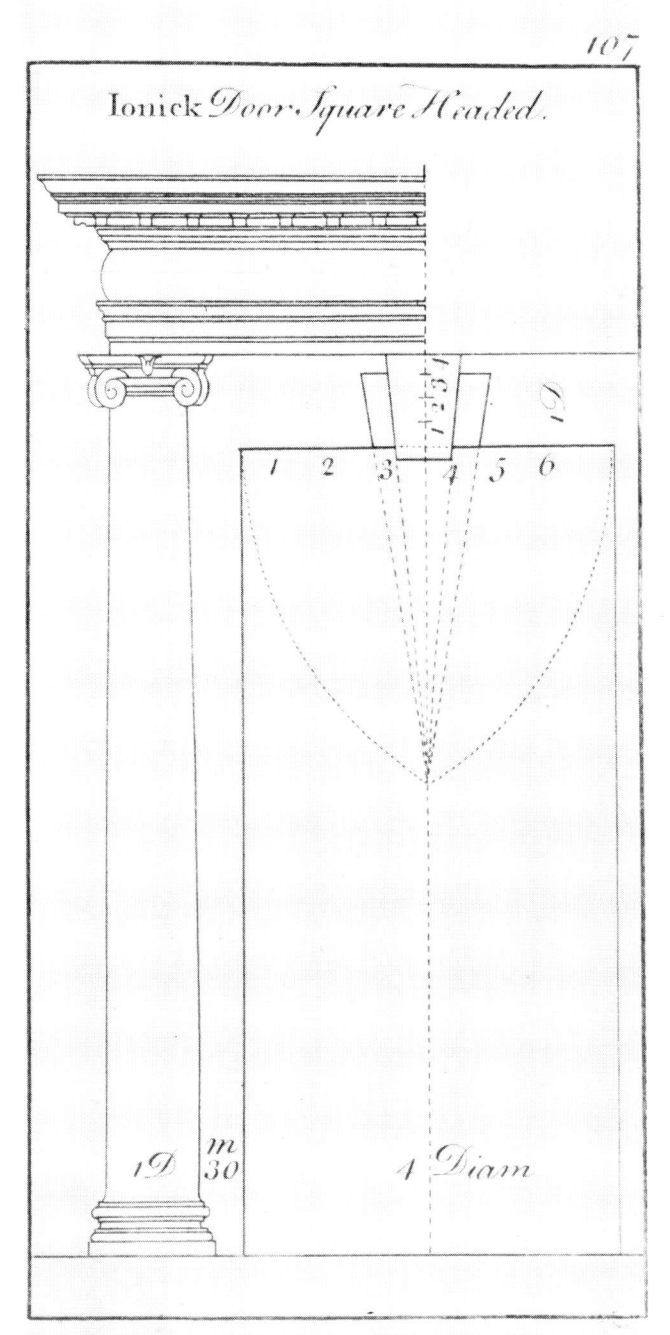

44

45

44 A pattern from Batty Langley's *The Builder's Director, or Bench-Mate* of 1751. The details of this design are fine, with small modillions, almost dentils, and a pulvinated freeze. As with the doorcase in plate **41** from the same book, the D refers to the diameter of the column and since a diameter was divided into 60 minutes, the 30M refers to half a diameter. Other members such as the keystone, which occupies a space 1 diameter deep, are divided into various points to facilitate fine proportioning. The splay of the keystone is found, as before, by dropping an arc equal to the width of the void until it coincides with the vertical centre line of the void. This point then becomes the centre for the splaying of the keystone

45 An early example, *circa* 1717, of the Ionic Order applied to a doorcase from Great Ormond Street, London WC 1, but now in Great James Street, Bloomsbury, London WC 1. It shows how, by using all the available tricks a doorcase could be enriched and yet remain classically correct. Since this doorway was put together when the Baroque was still an acceptable, and even a fashionable influence, no compunction was felt about breaking the entablature—leaving just stumps above the capitals—to allow the insertion of a fanciful piece of decorative carving. The little of the frieze that remains is pulvinated and decorated with scales and bands. The capitals themselves are of standard Roman proportion, while the shafts are fluted and their bottom parts filled with cables. All this was set against a rusticated door surround with a carved keystone and semi-circular top. The segmental pediment was a feature in use from the 1680s to *circa* 1720, although it was more common between 1700–1715

111

46 No. 14 Fournier Street, Spitalfields, London E 1, showing a doorcase of *circa* 1727 which is, and always was, extraordinary. Obviously a showy effect was wanted here and to achieve this the designer fused two types of doorcase into one entirety. His design object was to combine the practical rain-shielding advantages of the canopy, of which there are several in Fournier Street, with the prestigious and fashionable pedimented and columned doorcase.

To begin with, a regular columned door surround supporting a segmental pediment was drawn up and the pediment was then broken forward to become a kind of curved hood. In the process the frieze and cornice were discarded and the pediment ceased to be the jutting forward variety. The architrave was left behind, stuck against the inside of the hood and the pediment was coffered like the ceiling of a dome. To support the unexpected jut of the pediment the standard columned doorcase had to be adjusted and therefore, rather clumsily, an enervated pair of brackets and scrolls were stuck over and through the remnants of the entablature with the effect of supporting the hood by destroying the entablature. Without these brackets the hood would look top-heavy, but it is astonishing how clumsily they were applied, with no attempt to relate them to the capital or entablature. Below this confusion and contradiction the design continued as if nothing had happened. The architrave curves gently over the void to define the height of the actual door and is enriched by a keystone in the form of a carved console. Below this architrave and around the door, a thin band of rustication delicately strengthens the joint between door surround and door void.

In his attempt to achieve dignity, the designer also elongated the door by placing the columns on high pedestals. Since the width of the door void was fixed by the visual necessity of matching it to the width of the window above (which itself could not vary much for reason of convenience and proportion) this was the only method of gaining height while retaining the correct proportions for the columns

47 A pattern for a columned Ionic doorcase, with either segmental or triangular pediment, published in 1746 by Batty Langley in his *The Builder's Jewel, or the Youth's Instructor, and Workman's Remembrancer*. This is essentially the same kind of standard door as published by Gibbs in 1728 (see plate **43**) and was commonly used up to *circa* 1760. In this plate Batty Langley is reflecting and prolonging a taste rather than innovating and this pattern was widely copied on a national scale as well as all over London. To the detriment of individual craftsmanship and 'regional' variety in detailing, designers gradually took the easy way out and increasingly copied from such pattern books as this

48 No. 30 Elder Street, Spitalfields, London E 1, built in 1725 by a master carpenter. The major difference between this built example and Langley's preceding pattern is the rusticated door surround, but the most

interesting feature of this design is the actual door. The door void has the usual semi-circular top and in other surviving examples it is practically invariable for this semi-circle to be occupied by a fanlight, leaving a rectangular shape below for the door. But here, the door itself also has a semi-circular top. In accordance with later fashion, such a curve as this would be sawn off and a fanlight inserted

49 No. 818 Tottenham High Street, London N 17, showing an Ionic doorcase also derived from a pattern book. Again there is a pulvinated frieze, a carved grotesque keystone and a rusticated door surround, but this time there is a fanlight

50 No. 66 Leman Street, Aldgate, London E 1, built *circa* 1760 and again showing the influence of Batty Langley's *The Builder's Jewel* (see plate **47**) which was nearing its eleventh edition in 1768

51 No. 6 Great Ormond Street, Bloomsbury, London WC 1, built in the early 1720s by Edward Chapman, a mason. Although designed to the standard 'correct' pattern for Ionic door surrounds, this example displays some individualism. The shafts of the columns are fluted and the frieze plain, but the cornice is enriched with egg-and-dart mouldings

52 A 1742 example of an Ionic doorcase from Lincoln's Inn Fields, Holborn, London WC 2. This is very close to the Langley pattern, but for the heavy, rusticated door surround

53 No. 13 Devonshire Square, London EC 2. The difference between this doorcase and the preceding example in Lincoln's Inn Fields is only one of scale. There is no fanlight and even as late as the 1750s fanlights were still optional and functional rather than fashionably *de rigueur*. Or was it perhaps that the City was such a conservative place that even the fashion for fanlights came late?

54 No. 22 Cross Street, Islington, London N 1, dating from 1780. The door void, instead of sitting between and below its decoration, is embraced by it and the two elements very subtly blend to make a single design. The whole entablature is broken and exists only as a topping for the columns. Through it, and into the space of the pediment's tympanum moves the arch of the door void. Instead of the Ionic capitals sitting above and beside the door void, they now nestle closely below it and in fact become structurally related to it because the imposts of the door arch align with the volutes of the Ionic capital. (This linking is more obvious in Doric doorcases of this design, for the Doric capital and the impost moulding could be made of the same profile.) Also, since the soffit of the pediment became visible due to the entablature being broken an appropriate moulding could be used to decorate it. Despite the sophistication of this doorcase design, in which a synthesis was achieved between use and decoration to make it an entirely integrated object rather than merely a door void surrounded by an essentially unrelated column and pediment, that of the actual door remained standard, and is of a type that was being executed some 50 years before

55 The preceding doorcase showed the fully-developed synthesis of use and decoration in the Ionic doorcase. This example, from Silver Street, Edmonton, London N 18, although probably later than the Cross Street door, shows an earlier transitory stage. The entablature breaks back from the columns but does not entirely disappear, while the cornice carries on and links the two complete blocks of entablature above the columns. The capitals remain in their old place in relation to the door void and its imposts. It is a very cold embrace, but embrace it is, for the breaking back of the entablature and the rising of the arch into the area between, instead of beneath, the capitals leads to a certain blending between the void and its enrichments

Doric doorcases
The greatest ornament of the Doric doorcase was paradoxically its austerity, and this severity with the addition of various refined motifs belonging to the Doric Order, engendered a distinctive set of solutions to the basic problem of decorating a door void with columns and entablature. Like the Ionic doorcase, the Doric started off in the early 18th century simply as a lofty pediment and entablature supported by columns, having little to do with the door that was slipped in underneath it. But again, as with the Ionic examples, after *circa* 1750, decoration and function were combined.

Because of its essential simplicity the Doric doorcase was always popular with speculative builders. Expensive carving and decorations could be dispensed with and yet the doorcase would still be 'correct' and visually pleasing. The Doric was also the perfect Order to combine with more lavish effects. When carving was wanted, as for example in the bracketed and scrolled cantilevered doorcase common in the early 18th century, Doric pilasters were used as a natural foil for the rich acanthus leaves of the brackets (see plate **7**, page 88). As the century moved on, the Palladian desire for refined simplicity even affected the stripped-down Doric Order. Whereas early examples were enriched with carved metopes, by the mid century these had vanished and were followed even by triglyphs. After 1780 or thereabouts it was therefore common to see doorcases in the Tuscan Doric Order in which the columns were squatter, the freize plain, and the mouldings of the capital and entablature extremely simplified. Such proportioning and decoration would have been unacceptable, in a fashionable sense, even in the mid century and in 1756, Isaac Ware, in his *Complete Body of Architecture*, echoed the general Palladian opinion then prevailing, "The peculiar diminution of the Tuscan being too great to be born, on so near and so distinct a view, should exclude it from use in the ornament of the door."

The fact that within twenty years of this opinion being published Tuscan doorcases were not only being made, but made in great numbers, shows clearly how completely the Palladian autocracy fell from favour as the new concept of Neo-Classicism, greatly influenced by the relative austerity of Greek ruins, flooded into Europe after 1760.

56 The Doric has a good pedigree. This pattern for a Doric window or door surround was published by Sebastiano Serlio in his *Tutte l'Opere d'Architettura* of 1584

57 Doorcase NO. 14 Suffolk Street, Strand, London WC 2. Although the house was built in the 1680s, the doorcase itself quite likely belongs to the 1720s and is a typical example of the way in which the Doric Order was handled in the early part of the century. It is very correct, very dignified, and even if the door void was not below it, the lofty surround would not be in the least affected. The imposts of the door-void arch are enlarged into Doric pilaster capitals, but in no way relate to the enclosing columns. Typically, the metopes are carved rosettes and the soffit of the cornice is also decorated with carved rosettes. The fanlight is presumably a very early and practical object lesson in admitting light to the hall but not a thief

58 The preceding pattern repeated in NO. 796 Tottenham High Street, London N 17 built *circa* 1730. This doorcase has more carving, a dentilled cornice and a fret pattern on the soffit of the architrave

59 A basic Doric door surround at NO. 34 White Hart Lane, Tottenham, London N 17, built between 1720–30. The proportions are perfect and it is a piece of pure joinery with a complete absence of carving. Originally, the columns probably had moulded bases. The brickwork of the façade, particularly the gauged work of the window arches and string course, is also a perfect example of its period

60 Square-headed Doric doorcase from a mansion in Rotherhithe Street, Bermondsey, London SE 16, built during the 1750s. The fact that it is unpedimented makes it unusual, as it was nearly always thought necessary to top columns with a pediment

57

58

59

60

61

61 A page of patterns from Abraham Swan's *A Collection of Designs in Architecture* published in 1757. The Ionic and Corinthian doorcases at the top of the plate are too ornate for exterior use, but the two Doric examples at the bottom are typical examples of doorcases which had been decorating façades for nearly 40 years. The proportioning scale shows that the entablature measures one quarter of the depth of the columns

62 Doorcase in Croom's Hill, Greenwich, London SE 10, built *circa* 1760. It is the same width as the example in Abraham Swan's pattern book (i.e. six triglyphs wide) and also has the same pattern of rustication

63 While traditional Doric door surrounds were being put up, the 'synthesised' variety, more closely combining decoration with function (see plate **54**) had already made its appearance. This example at NO. 43 Parliament Street, Westminster, London SW 1, is a perfect example of the blend between decoration and function, for the decorative mouldings of the Doric capitals continue to form imposts for the arch of the door void and then run across the door void itself as an architrave to separate the fanlight area from the actual door below. The unusual width of the door has caused the fanlight to be elliptical instead of semi-circular

64 Another slightly smaller example of the 'synthesised' Doric doorcase from Harpur Street, Bloomsbury, London WC 1, built *circa* 1760

65 A plate dated 1789 from William Pain's *Practical House Carpenter*. This is another example of the way in which pattern books consolidated and spread ideas already current in architecture, rather than assuming an innovatory role and here, only the fanlight is extraordinary. To accompany this plate, Pain gives a concise description of the way this kind of doorcase was proportioned:

"Doric front drawn half an inch to a foot: the clear passage 3 feet 6 inches, the height 7 feet 2 inches, the height of the column 7 feet 4 inches, to be divided into nine equal parts, one of which parts will be the diameter of the column at bottom; give one of them to the sub-plinth, half a one to the base, half a one to the cap of the column, and two to the entablature, that will be 30 minutes to the architrave, 45 minutes to the frieze, and 45 minutes to the cornice; the distance from centre to centre of the columns is 6 diameters 15 minutes, which will take 5 modillions; to find the pitch of the pediment set the compasses at *a* in the tympan of the pediment, and draw the circle *b c e*, then set the compasses at *c*, and draw the arch *b*, *d*, *e*, which gives the height of the pediment at *d*; this method will give the pitch of any pediment"

66

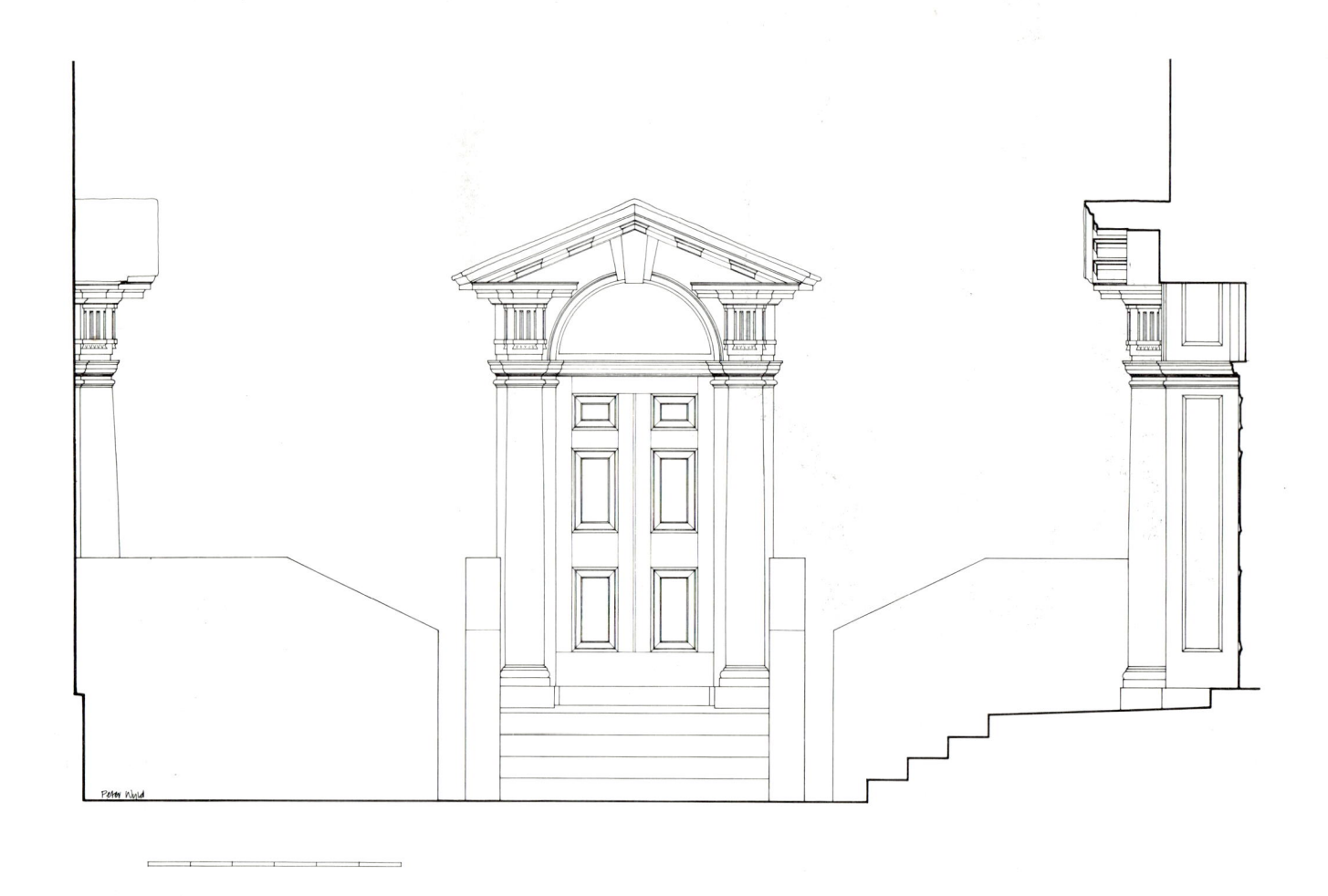

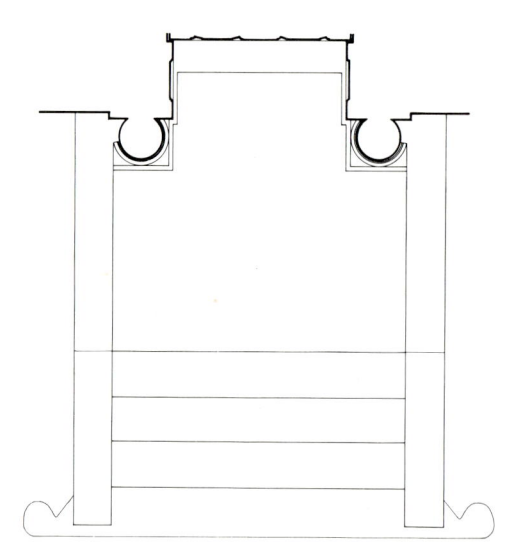

66 House in Mare Street, Hackney, London E 8, dating from 1715, but the doorcase was added between 1760–80

67 This doorcase in Grove Terrace, Hampstead, London NW 5, was built between 1775–85 and although later than previous examples showing the move towards 'synthesised' Doric (see plates **63** and **64**) it is a good instance of the transitory stage in Doric doorcase design

68 The influence of Neo-Classicism has crept into this Doric doorcase at NO. 36 Elder Street, Spitalfields, London E 1. The capitals are in fact not pure Doric but are based on those in the Tower of the Winds, Athens. This design was first introduced to the general public in 1762 when the first volume of James Stuart's and Nicholas Revett's *The Antiquities of Athens* was published (it is said that a gentleman in Greece obligingly demolished his house to give them a better view of the Tower).

It was not until Robert Adam adopted this motif and used it in great quantities in his developments in the late 1760s and 1770s that it entered the repertoire of the average joiner and it is therefore likely that this doorcase dates from the 1780s as does the delicate fanlight. Other Neo-Classical elements may be seen in the fluting that runs along the impost and architrave and around the curve of the door arch

69 This late 18th-century doorcase in Kennington Road, London again displays the influence of Neo-Classicism. The triglyphs are portrayed as flutes and take the place of metopes

70 Definite moves towards the Tuscan are apparent in this late 18th-century doorcase on Dial House, Tottenham High Street, London N 17, which itself dates from 1698. The Doric triglyphs have been replaced by oval panels and the moulding of the capitals and entablature greatly simplified

71 This early 19th-century doorcase at NO. 175 Long Lane, Bermondsey, London SE 1, is a strange mixture and belies the idea that up to *circa* 1820 classical details developed in a continuous and related direction. Here there is a return to the old separate relationship between door decoration and door function, as well as a return to the practice of blending different architectural Orders (the columns are Doric and the entablature Ionic).

As the 18th century ended with a great input of new classical ideas, influences and archaeological discovery, some of the old confusions and freedoms present in the buildings of the early 18th century re-emerged. Suddenly there was no longer, as in Palladian days, a 'right' and a 'wrong' way to do things and a craftsman could be seduced by his fancy once again

Pilastered doorcases
The development of the pilastered doorcase is closely related to the columned examples if one considers its development only in terms of the fluctuating fashions for different architectural Orders. But construction itself dictated certain independent developments in pilastered doorcases quite apart from such fashionable considerations, and for subtle reasons of finance combinations and expressions of classical motifs were possible in pilastered doorcases which were not possible in the columned variety. It was for example cheaper to build a two-dimensional pilaster out of brick than a three-dimensional column and similarly it was easier to break a pilaster with rustic blocks than to break a column (see plate **82**, page 131). Again, if time and money could be saved by not shaping and glueing a column, more of both could be expended on the capital and entablature and for this reason, there are many more examples of Corinthian pilastered doorcases than Corinthian columned examples. The following examples of pilastered doorcases are laid out in chronological sequence since certain treatments of them transcend the disciplines of the architectural Orders.

72 Although scarcely a pilastered doorcase this reconstructed example at Bradmore House, Broadway, Hammersmith, London W 6, is an important specimen of the Baroque interpretation of classical motifs to make an original and imaginative composition. This house was built in the 1700s and its architect may have been Thomas Archer

72

73

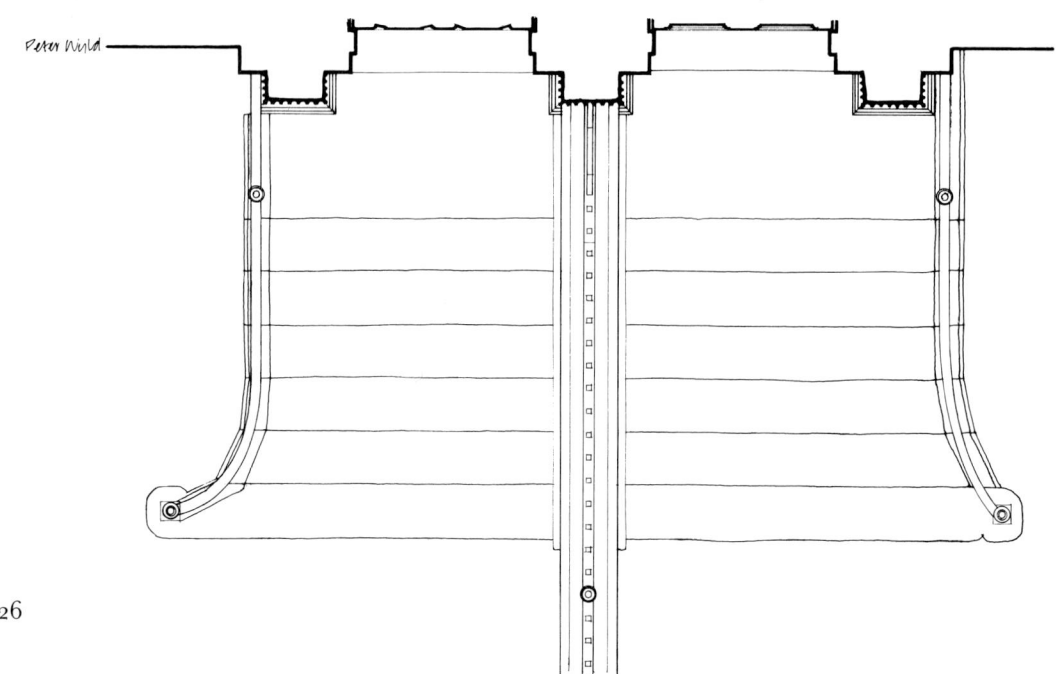

73 Paired Doric doorway *circa* 1705 in Clapham Old Town, London SW 4. Even though the paring causes a few irregularities, this is an extraordinarily correct example for its date when one considers that the standard doorcase solution during that period was the heavily carved and imaginative cantilevered type (see pages 84–89). The use of entasis on the pilasters is particularly good. This very slight convex curve to correct the optical illusion of concavity on totally straight verticals was of course essential in the construction of columns, but joiners frequently felt they could dispense with this effect when putting together pilasters

74 An early, correct and finely proportioned Doric doorcase in Brabant Court, City of London, dating from the early 1720s. A sophisticated, rather Baroque refinement is apparent in the way the entire entablature and pediment break forward over the pilasters

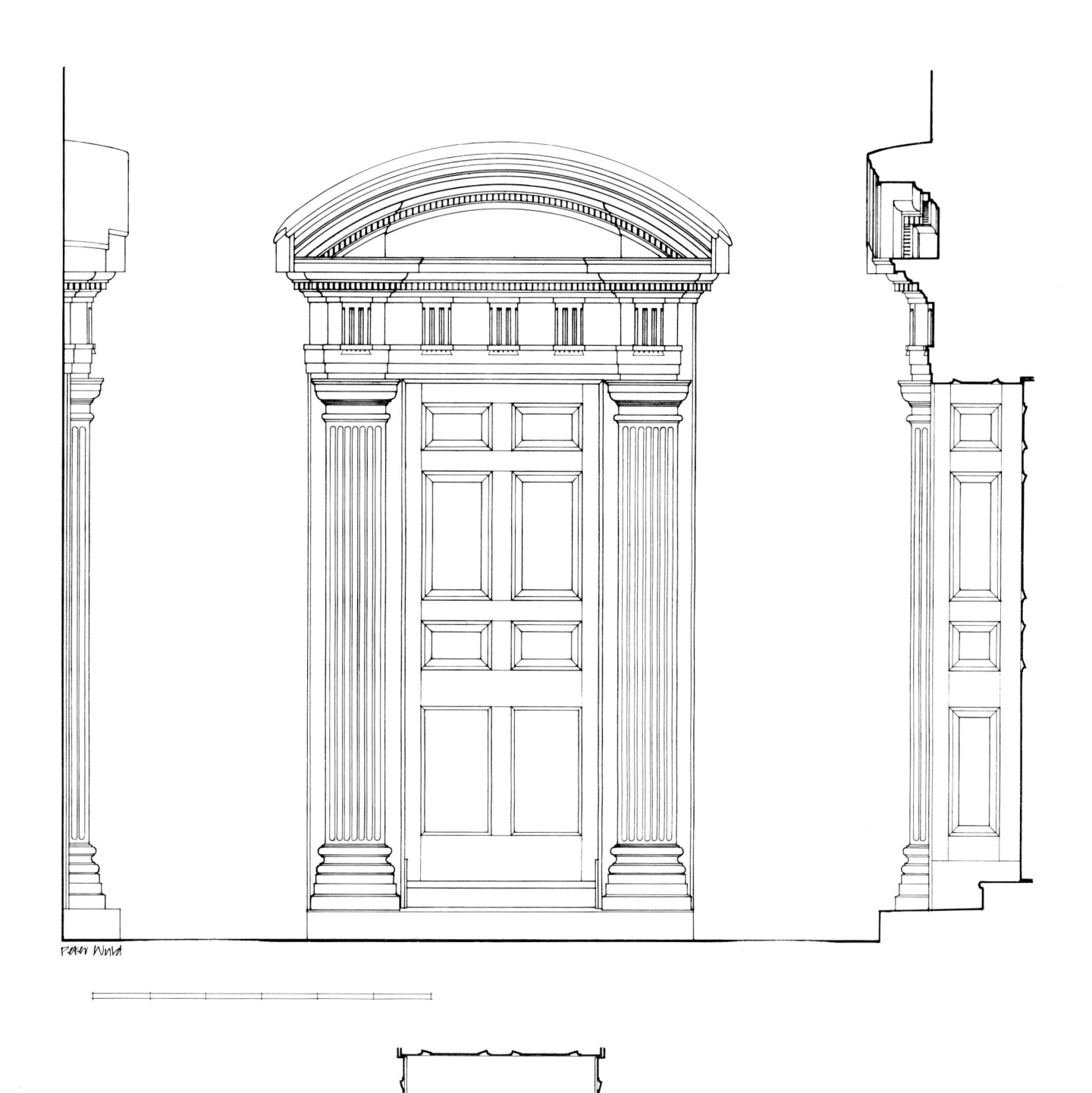

75 Another perfectly proportioned Doric doorcase in Elder Street, Spitalfields, London E 1. The house was built in 1726 and its developer was Thomas Brown, a pavior. As plates **73** to **75** indicate, the use of the Doric Order on pilastered doorcases was popular during the early 18th century and in contrast to the liberties taken with contemporary Corinthian columned doorcases, they were impeccably correct. Despite such correctness, this doorcase in Elder Street, does contain a certain 'regional' quality in its use of rustication. Although rustication of pilasters has a good Classical pedigree it was a device not often used except in Spitalfields during the developments which took place there during the 1720s. Spital Square contained many examples and although all these have been demolished, others still survive in Elder, Folgate and Wilkes Street. The fanlight probably belongs to the early 19th century, as does the strangely decorated architrave that separates it from the door below

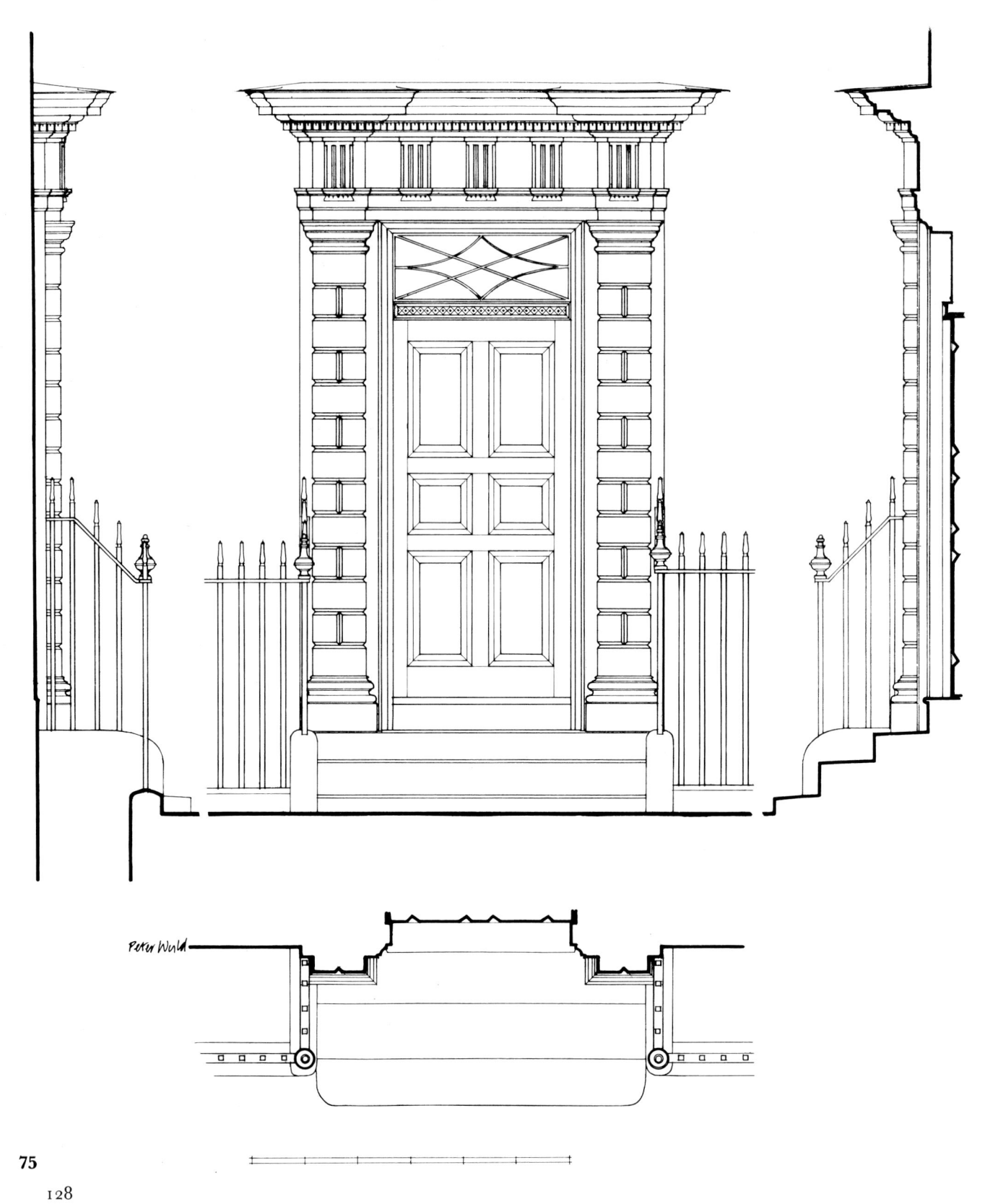

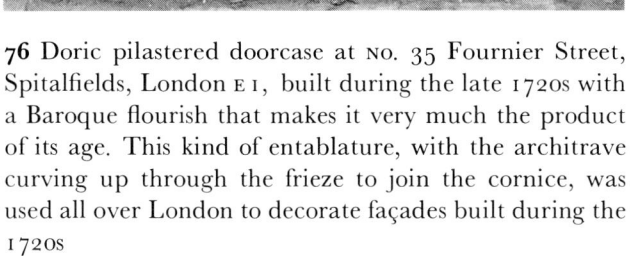

76 Doric pilastered doorcase at NO. 35 Fournier Street, Spitalfields, London E 1, built during the late 1720s with a Baroque flourish that makes it very much the product of its age. This kind of entablature, with the architrave curving up through the frieze to join the cornice, was used all over London to decorate façades built during the 1720s

77 Corinthian pilastered doorcase dating from the mid 1720s at NO. 142–152 Long Lane, Bermondsey, London SE 1. Although heavily restored, the design appears to be original and it is thought to be the only example of a Corinthian swan-necked pediment on a modest house in London

78 Pattern for a swan-necked doorcase from *Palladio Londinensis, or the London Art of Building* published by the Colchester-born carpenter William Salmon in 1734. Here he strangely combines Composite columns with an Ionic entablature. As Composite and Corinthian proportions are virtually the same, the doorcase here and in plate **77** have unusually elongated door voids without the use of plinths

129

79 This doorcase at no. 5 Wandsworth Plain, London sw 18, built in 1723, is basically identical to the example in Long Lane, Bermondsey (see plate **77**) but lacks its swan-necked pediment. Like Salmon's preceding example, the door void is three times as high as it is wide

80 Another pattern for a doorcase from William Salmon's *Palladio Londinensis* showing the ideal Doric doorcase in the form it circulated throughout the country. The curious feature of this pattern is not that this design had been perfected nearly 30 years earlier, but the fact that it is too wide. Most examples of this type of doorcase are five triglyphs wide and this is six, but apart from width the other proportions in the pattern are very fine and standard. The entablature is one quarter the depth of the columns and the depth of the door void relates to this proportion, since the proportioning circle is divided into quarters and like the entablature, an extra quarter is added to make the full depth

81 Strangely, the Ionic Order was infrequently used in the decoration of pilastered doorcases during the first half of the 18th century and this sadly derelict example from Helmet Row, Finsbury, London EC 1, dated 1737 is unusual. The dearth of Ionic pilastered doorcases is quite inexplicable, particularly since James Gibbs published designs for them in his influential *Book of Architecture* in 1728. This doorcase is also unusual in being built of stone rather than wood, a material rarely used in London during this period. Overall, this doorcase is a very straightforward Roman Ionic design. The frieze is pulvinated and decorated with scales and extra height is achieved by the placing of the pilasters on plinths

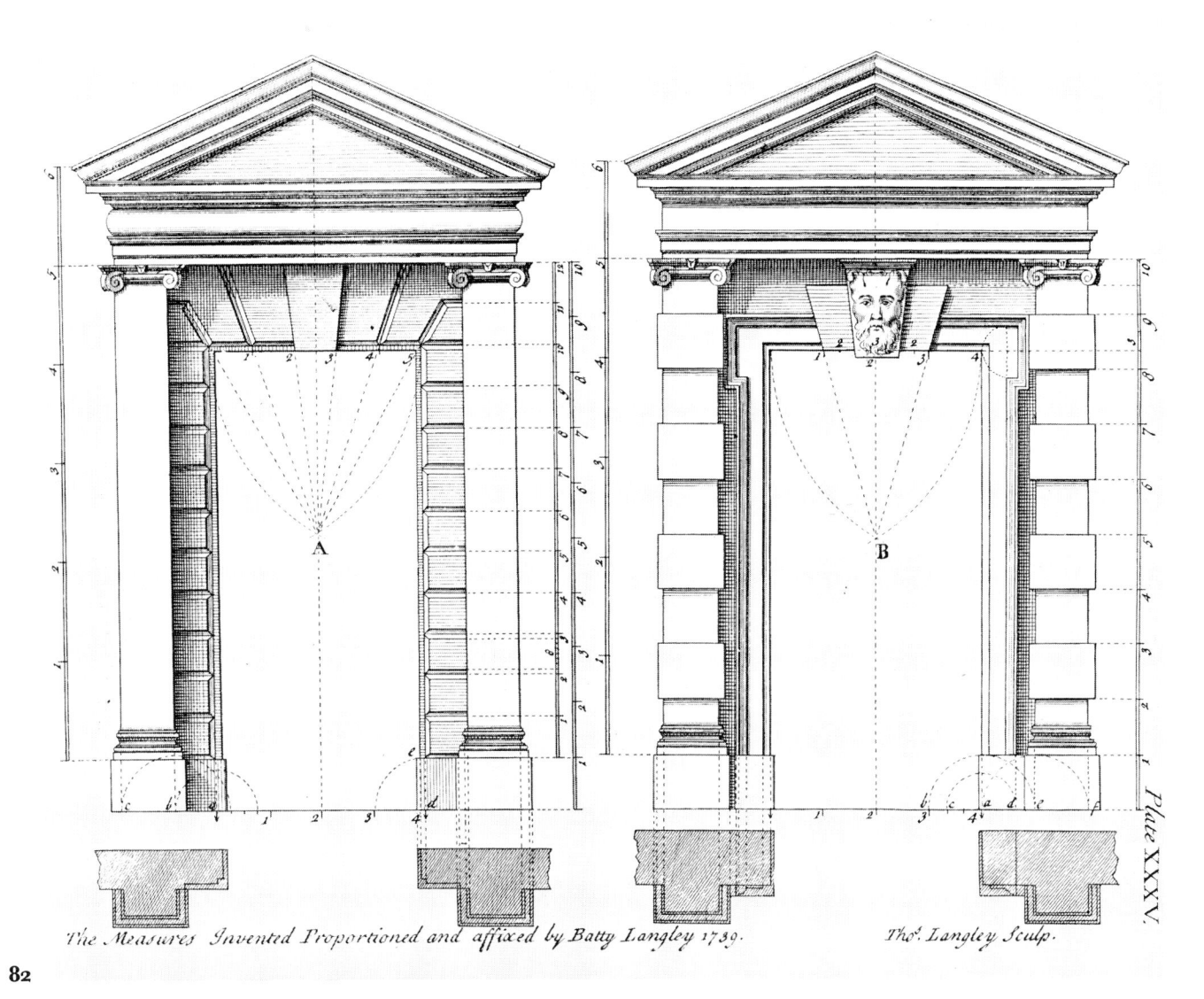

82 Plate from the 1745 edition of Batty Langley's *The City and Country Builder's and Workman's Treasury of Designs*, showing patterns based on a Gibbs' original. Door 'A' in many ways resembles the preceding example from Helmet Row, Finsbury. These patterns are particularly interesting because of the detailed instructions they give on proportioning: the Ionic entablature, like the Corinthian, is shown as being one-fifth the depth of the pilaster shaft

83 Corinthian pilastered doorcase at NO. 61 Stepney Green, London E 1, an example which must originally have been part of a paired design. The façades of the surrounding group of houses appear to date from the 1740s and presumably so does this doorcase. If this dating is correct, the doorcase shown here is one of the last expressions of Roman Corinthian in doorcase design before it disappeared from the repertoire of the fashion-conscious joiner

84 Ionic door surrounds built between 1789–95 at NOS. 152 and 154 Lambeth Road, Lambeth, London SE 1, showing how the new, slightly deformed, Neo-Classically-proportioned Ionic volute had found its way into the work of the average joiner. Such Neo-Classical detailing to a large degree stemmed from the work of the Adam brothers at the Adelphi begun, between 1768–72, and to keep abreast of demands from fashionable patrons, the jobbing joiner had to quickly familiarise himself with a complete new vocabulary of decorative motifs

85 Very little now survives of the Adelphi, a large group of palatial houses built on the banks of the Thames by Robert and James Adam, but this doorcase in Adam Street, Strand, London WC 2, displays a very good selection of the new decorative elements displayed and popularised in that development (see also plate **86**). Structurally it is still a pilastered door surround supporting an entablature, but there is no attempt to conform to long-accepted ideas of 'correct' proportioning. The pilasters are merely slim, elongated vertical panels and contain a somewhat traditional wave motif with the additional enrichment of anthemion leaves. The capitals of the pilasters are based on an example from the Tower of the Winds, Athens (see page 12) and structurally, the entablature is simplified. The architrave is plain and shallow and the cornice contains only very delicate mouldings. All the decoration is loaded into the frieze which contains roundels above the capitals and then breaks back to continue as a fluted surface. The fluting halts abruptly in the centre of the frieze to admit a decorative panel containing two sphinxes facing each other across a vase

86 The immediate influence of Neo-Classical doorcases in the Adelphi is apparent in this door, one of a pair, at NO. 33 Cross Street, Islington, London N 1. The house itself was built *circa* 1760 and the original doorcase was replaced by this, the latest fashion, during the 1770s. A comparison with plate **85** will show that while every element of the Adam Street doorcase is also apparent here, each detail has been slightly and individually modified

87 More Neo-Classical influence in the doorcase of NO. 2 Millman Street, Bloomsbury, London WC 1, demolished in 1971. The house was built in the early 1720s but the doorcase is post-1775 and probably belongs to the early 1780s. This doorcase contained an excellent ensemble of Neo-Classical motifs including Tower-of-the-Winds capitals and a fluted frieze with anthemion leaf motifs above the capitals. The cornice was dentilled and the architrave wrapped itself around the sides of the door void in the traditional manner. The door, with its heavily fielded panels, presents a strange contrast to its immediate Neo-Classical environment and may have been retained from the original doorcase of the 1720s

Door surrounds

This form of door decoration, which consisted simply of surrounding the door void with a two-dimensional motif, had a sound classical precedent since both Sebastiano Serlio and Jacopo Barozzi Vignola designed differing varieties of door surrounds made up of rustic blocks. Rustication was incorporated in the vast majority of door surrounds during the Georgian period and it swept into fashion on the Baroque wave that was repelled in the 1720s by the rise of Palladianism. Some of the purest examples of rusticated door surrounds in London are to be found on the extraordinary houses built in Hanover Square in 1715 by Whig politicians and generals who favoured a German Baroque manner as a compliment to the Hanoverian Dynasty.

88 Rusticated door surround at NO. 17 St. George Street, London W 1. The doors are vertically linked to the rest of the façade by rusticated aprons which are beneath each window

89 Plate showing three rusticated door surrounds from James Gibbs' *Book of Architecture* published in 1728. Gibbs published many designs for this kind of door surround and used them himself to such an extent that rustic blocks lining door or window voids became known as 'Gibbs surrounds'. In these three examples Gibbs has aligned the rustic surrounds with classical Orders by giving them moulded cornices. The boldness of the rustic blocks demand an almost Tuscan profile to the cornice but, if desired, the cornice could be discarded and the top of the composition finished off as at the sides, with a keystone breaking above the alternating long and short blocks. The pattern on the left is very closely based on a Renaissance model and the pedimented centre pattern is similar to those actually executed by Gibbs at St. Martin-in-the-Fields between 1721–26. The pattern on the right, with a mask on a console to serve as a keystone and rustic blocks laid as quoins, was once a fairly common entrance design for such plain and functional buildings as warehouses, factories, stables, arsenals and prisons (see plate **90**)

90 Entrance of the Whitechapel Bell Foundry at NO. 34 Whitechapel Road, London E 1, showing a rusticated door surround based on a plate in James Gibbs' *Book of Architecture* published in 1728 (see plate **89**). Practically all London door cases were wooden structures imitating designs originally intended for stone but here, with the building-brick quality of the bold, quoined rustic blocks and the heavy key-stone, it seems rather absurd that they are merely a soft-wood façade only a few inches deep and totally non-structural. The door itself is unusual in so far as all its panels are flush and its general proportions and materials suggest it was built during the late 1720s or 1730s

91 Rusticated door surround from a house in Twickenham, Middlesex, which is very similar to the pattern used by James Gibbs for St. Martin-in-the-Fields. This example dates from the 1720s, possibly before the publication of Gibbs' *Book of Architecture* in 1728, for Gibbs, although he disseminated and popularised this type of design did not himself invent it

92 Rusticated door surround at NO. 4 Parkshot, Richmond, Surrey, a design similar to that in Hanover Square (see plate **88**) and as published by Gibbs in his *Book of Architecture*. This example dates from the 1720s but although the adjoining house was also built during that decade, the concave door surround of NO. 3 is very probably a later alteration (see also examples in Fournier Street, Spitalfields and Ormond Road, Richmond in plate **108**, page 146)

93 Rusticated door surround at NO. 10 Syon Road, Twickenham, Middlesex. Although not based directly on any Gibbs' pattern, this example is very much Gibbs in spirit with intermittent blocks breaking the architrave of the door. The flavour of early 18th-century English Baroque is also apparent in the huge, slightly dropped keystone which splays into the very deep frieze and in the flat dentilled cornice

94 Plate showing two rusticated doors from Batty Langley's *The City and County Builder's and Workman's Treasury of Designs* published in 1745. The Palladians abandoned the rusticated door design so favoured by Gibbs and after the mid 1720s permitted rustication to be used on principal façades only as a background for other correct classical elements such as columns and pilasters. It was not until Palladian rule faltered in the 1760s that pure rusticated doorways enjoyed a new vogue, but Batty Langley, ever pursuing an almost standard policy of curious plagiarism, printed an entire series of Gibbs rusticated designs in the 1745 edition of this book, without regard to the requirements of contemporary fashion.

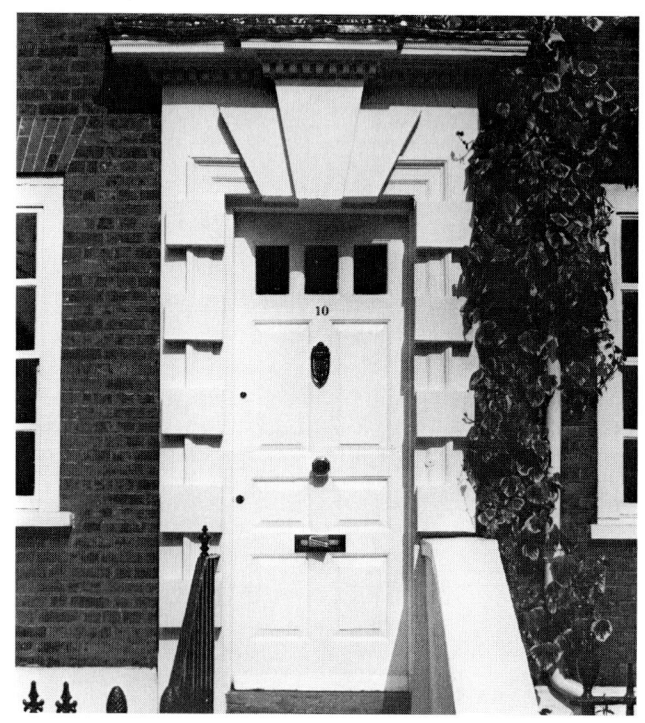

This plate forms an interesting companion to the Gibbs' original (see plate **89**) because here Langley gives detailed instructions on proportioning. The design on the left, with its applied consoles and cornice, would have been more acceptable to contemporary Palladian taste, because the rustication has been subordinated to the classical Order. Apart from the presence of a pediment, the design on the right is a direct copy from Gibbs and would have been too boldly forthright for the refined taste of the 1740s

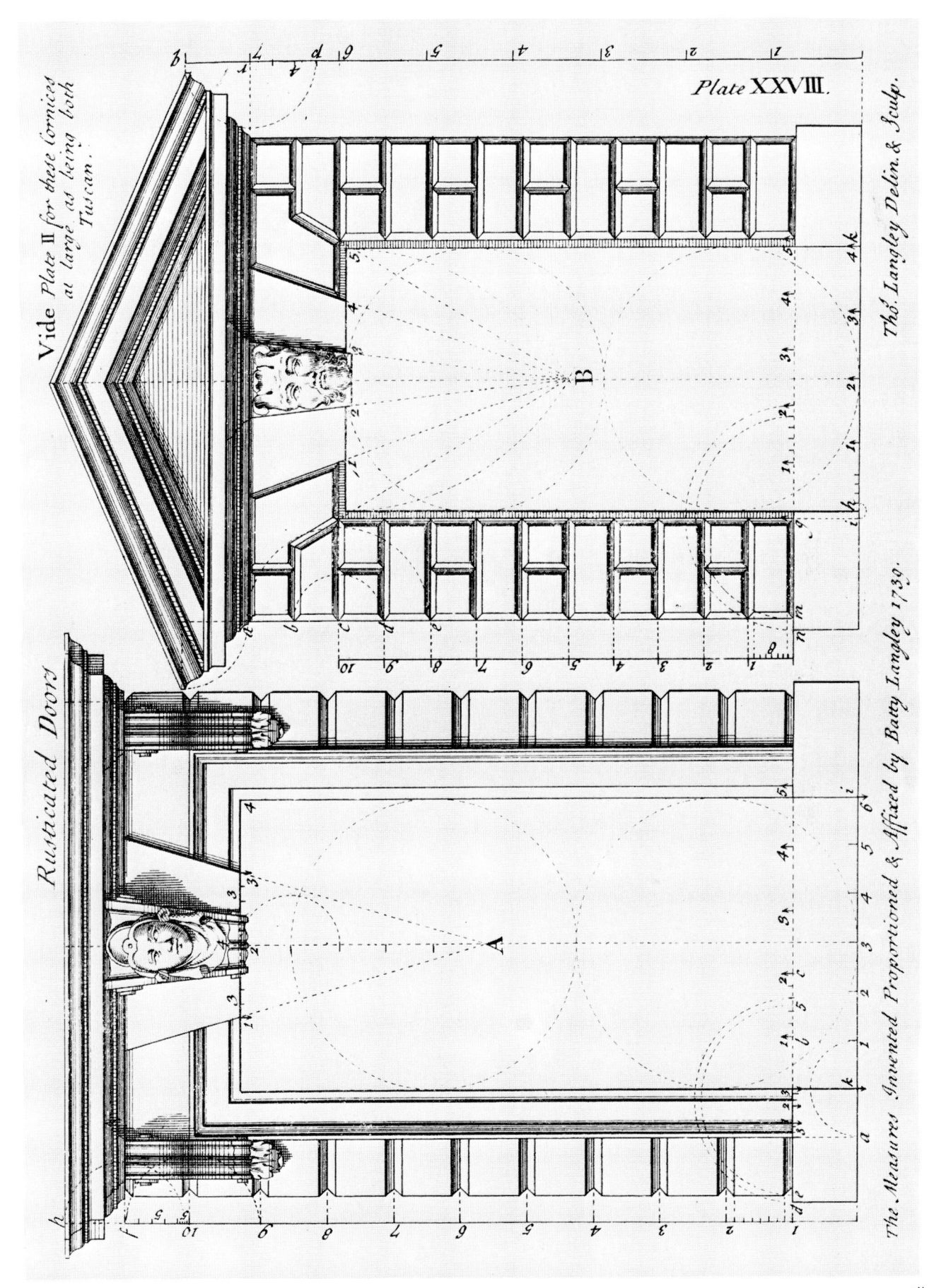

Rusticated Doors

Vide Plate II for these cornices at large as being both Tuscan.

Plate **XXVIII**.

Thō. Langley Delin. & Sculp.

The Measures Invented Proportioned & Affixed by Batty Langley 1730.

95 Plate showing a rusticated door surround incorporating Coade stone from Mrs Eleanor Coade's *Etchings of Coade's Artificial Stone* published in 1799. This material was an artificial cast stone successfully marketed in the 1770s by Mrs Eleanor Coade and later by Coade & Sealy of London. Appearing at precisely the moment when taste would accept, and even required, refined simplicity and classical repetition of motifs, the success of this versatile building material was due in no small part to its timing. Recognising that the fulfilment of these aesthetic requirements related exactly to the capabilities of artificial stone, Eleanor Coade immediately aligned its manufacture with the demands of fashion and so successful was this alignment that Coade stone not only supplied architectural fashions but became a vogue in itself.

Etchings of Coade's Artificial Stone was not only an advertising booklet but a form of retrospective exhibition catalogue, as the particular design used in this plate had been used in the Bedford Square development in Bloomsbury approximately twenty years before. In this design the Coade company revived a design for bold, vermiculated blocks, a form of decoration admirably suited to artificial stone, but although the blocks themselves are as vigorous as anything produced in the early 18th century, other details such as imposts and joinery are designed in the new and delicate Neo-Classical manner

96 This rusticated door surround in Bedford Square, Bloomsbury, London WC 1, dating from 1775–80 is a built example of the Coade pattern shown in plate **95**: even the joinery details tally with it

97 Coade stone, rusticated door surround in Batty Street, Commercial Road, Stepney, London E 1, built between 1800–10. Although this example has been abused it is interesting to note that it is a slightly scaled-down version of the preceding design built in Bedford Square (see plate **96**). Not only are the blocks slightly smaller but the keystone lacks vermiculated side pieces

98 Coade stone door surround at NO. 27 New Road, Whitechapel, London E 1, built between 1800–10. This Coade stone design is scaled down to an even greater degree than that in plate **97** and is part of a terrace in which all the doorways are dressed in the same way although the masks on the keystones vary. This kind of small-scale Coade stone door surround decorated doors all over London as the age of mass production arrived and any remaining 'regional' variations in decoration were totally abandoned as builders ordered all their details from pattern books

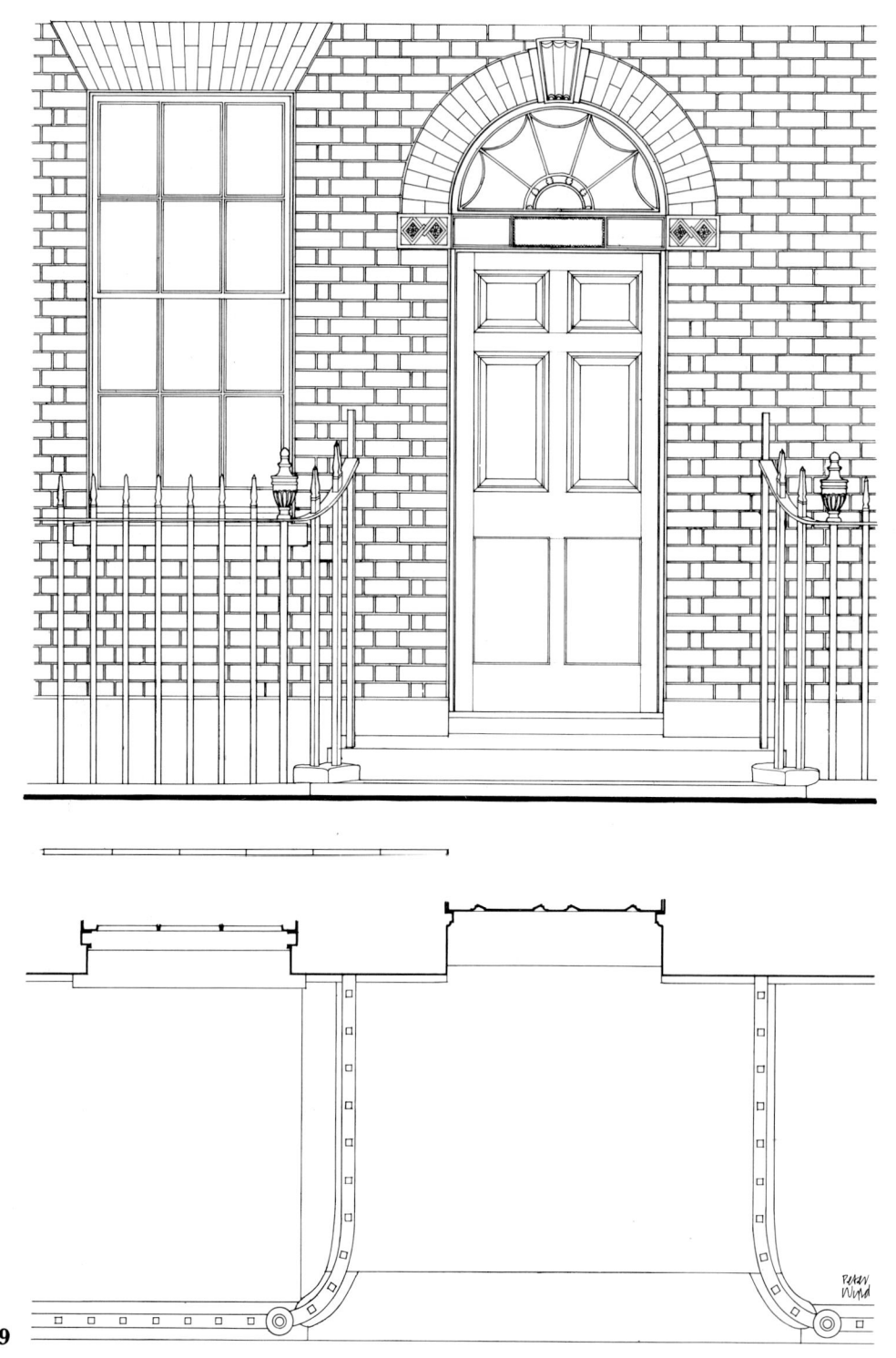

99 Example of keystone and impost design in Coade stone dated 1790 from Huntley Street, Holborn, London WC 1

100 Rusticated door surround in Coade stone at NO. 41 Grafton Street, Tottenham Court Road, London W 1. Here the rustic blocks are plain and emphasis is transferred to the impost by the use of blocks with rounded mouldings. The deeply fielded door is a type which remained in constant use throughout the 18th century

101 A pair of early 19th-century Coade stone door surrounds at NO. 143 Kennington Lane, showing vermiculated rustic blocks and keystones

102 Pair of unusual door surrounds at NOS. 40 and 42 Stepney Way, Whitechapel, London E 1, forming part of a development built during the 1820s. By the 1820s designers were beginning to permit their individual fancies to rise above the limits of the motifs laid down by classical precedent for door decoration. Sir John Soane for example, an architect of the same idiosyncratic originality as Vanbrugh, was already using basic classical elements as abstract decoration and expressions of this same free and innovatory spirit could be found in even the smallest terrace house. Here the designer has constructed trunks of mouldings out of cement and wrapped them around the door void. It is likely this motif is derived from the reeded architrave so popular at the time for such internal features as fireplaces

100

102

101

103 A delicate and more classically 'correct' door surround at NO. 57 Ashfield Street, Whitechapel, London E 1, belonging to the same 1820s development as the preceding example (see plate **102**). This kind of door surround with impost and keystone became very common during the 1790s and the panelled door itself is a very good specimen of Regency design

104 Pair of doors from The Paragon, Hackney, London E 9, built *circa* 1830. From the 1830s onwards the use of Greek motifs became increasingly curious and reflected the way standards of aesthetic judgement in architecture were breaking down, presaging the eclectic confusion of the later 19th century. There were no longer any generally accepted criteria to govern the taste of workmen and the products of their self indulgence were often as grotesque as those of early 18th-century workmen has been fresh and original. Especially extraordinary in this example are the fanlights with their ogee profiles

104

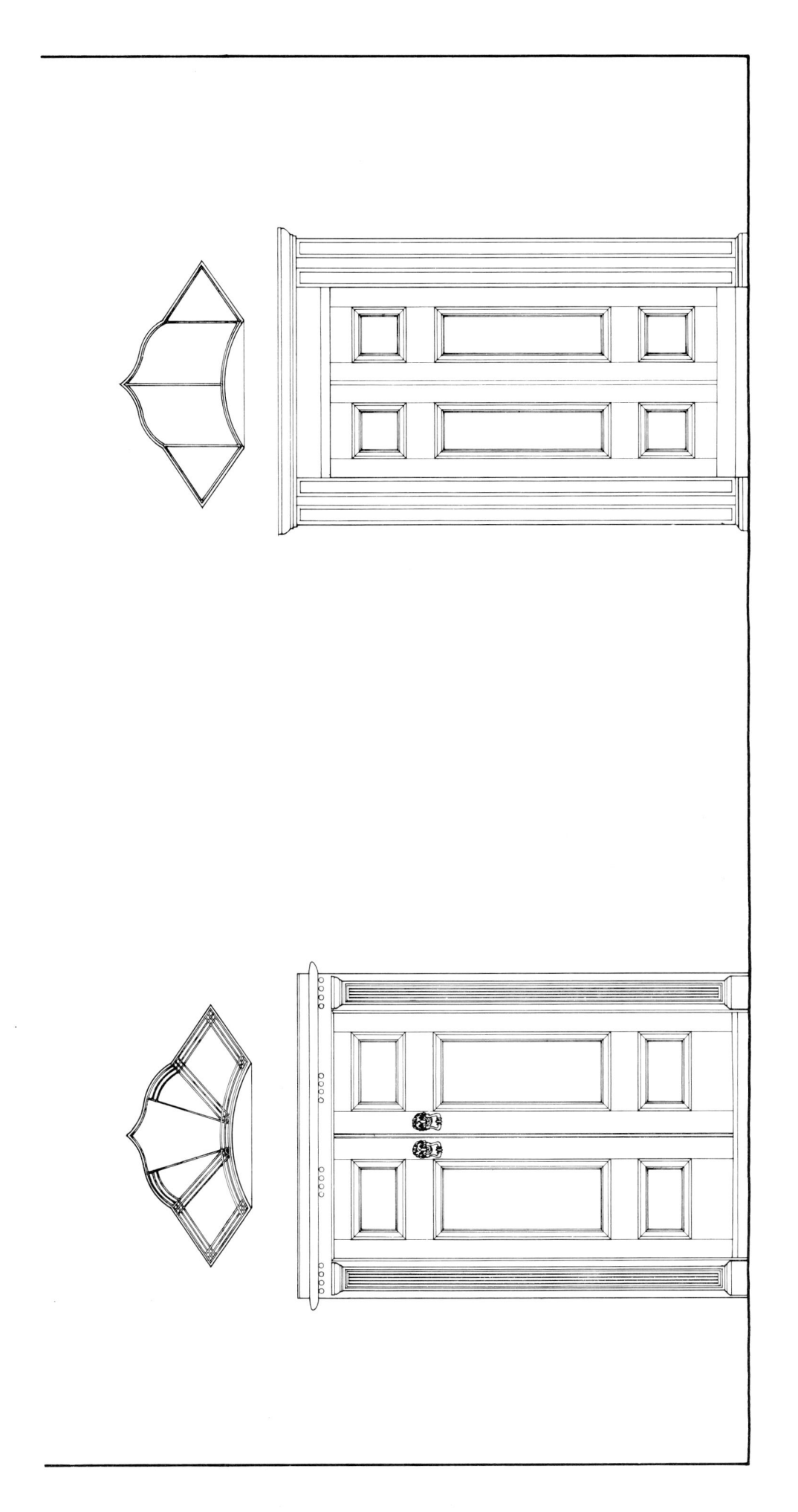

105

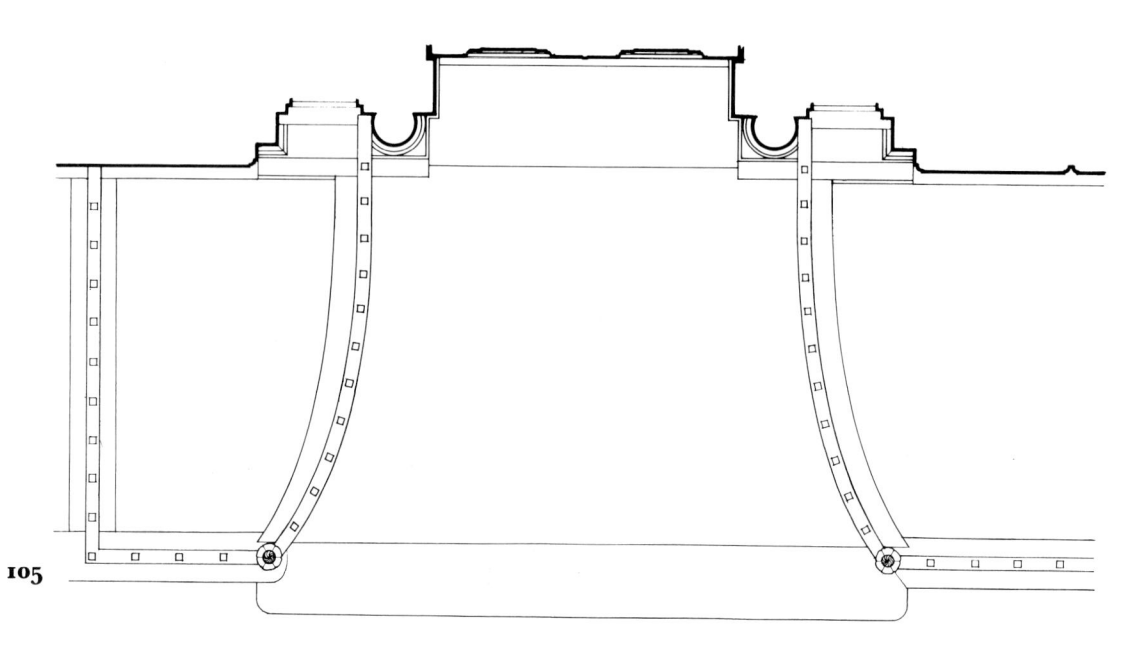

Door voids

Significantly, it was not until the late 18th century that this most basic of door types, the door void, was developed and used in quantity as an architectural ornament. This type of doorcase is simply explained by saying that the outline of its sides and arch strictly defined the extent of the doorway and that all decorations, such as fanlights, columns and pilasters, were placed *within* the actual door void. In practice, the borderline between this type and the preceding door-surround type (see pages 134–143) was very flexible and a door containing columns and fanlight within the door void could also, as at Kennington Common (see plate **106**) have impost and keystone.

The idea of the doorway being just another void in a façade and the same width as window voids, was much used by mid 18th-century Palladians in such developments as The Circus and Royal Crescent, Bath, but this rigid discipline did not find widespread favour in London much before the early 19th century. The origin of the type in London can however be traced back directly to the 1760s when Robert Adam popularised the fanlight as a principal decorative element of a door. Since the fanlight had to be placed necessarily within the door void, the placing of *all* decorative elements within the void was a natural progression, particularly so if, as at Mansfield Street (see plate **105**), the fanlight determined the form and position of related decorative elements.

105 No. 7 Mansfield Street, London W 1, showing all the fundamental elements of the door-void type. The doorway is divided into three vertical units by a pair of Greek Ionic columns and from their capitals springs a semi-circle giving a Venetian-window-type motif. The space above the semi-circle is occupied by another concentric band which turns downwards to range with the two smaller windows on each side of the panelled door and the entire semi-circular area of the wide doorcase is occupied by a huge fanlight. The detailing of the joinery and ironwork is Neo-Classical with a fine display of anthemion leaves in the fanlight. Lacking an architrave, the entablature is fluted, with roundels appearing above the capitals.

This example is the basic door-void type and as so frequently happens, its first expression was the most ambitious and complete. As it was echoed in the work of speculative builders throughout London, this form of doorway became diluted by economy and gradually lost both its size and showiness, but the basic principle of severely containing decorative elements within the brick or stucco boundary of the door void was firmly established

106 This doorway at Kennington Common, London SE 11, was built in the 1790s and is a good example of the door-void type as it found expression in London's expanding suburbs. The keystone and imposts are extraneous elements properly belonging to the door-surround type, but the principal decorative effects are firmly contained within the door void. The columns, which have Tower-of-the-Winds capitals probably constructed out of applied plaster mouldings, have been drastically reduced to slender reeds to facilitate them in a door void of standard width, but the fanlight still retains a definite division into two decorative concentric semi-circles

107 A basic treatment of the door-void type at NO. 40 Maple Street, Fitzroy Square, London W 1, built *circa* 1800 and demolished in February 1974. Decoration here is reduced to the panelled door, thin fluted pilaster strips and a meagre, spidery fanlight, by 1800 decorative elements on the door voids of such speculative houses were generally reduced to a cut-brick arch above the door

108

109

110

111

146

108 This door void at NO. 12 Fournier Street, Spitalfields, London E 1, is more ambitious and thoughtful than that shown in plate **107** and although it was built *circa* 1800, it has been inserted in the façade of an earlier house. Again, its main decoration is the brick arch, but there are formal elements of decoration within the void. Instead of pilaster strips there is a striking concave recess and the door is divided from the simple fanlight by a boldly moulded band

109 A more formal example of the door-void type, also dating from the 1800s, at NO. 60 Grafton Street, Tottenham Court Road, London W 1. The fanlight is still divided into two concentric parts and the shallow mouldings are of plaster stuck into wood and then painted

110 This house, built in the early 1800s, stood on the corner of Bedford Way and Russell Square, Bloomsbury, London WC 1, and is now demolished. Most of the doorways shown so far had to occupy voids wider than the window apertures above to accommodate their decorative elements within the void, but a re-alignment could be achieved if desired by making the actual door the same width as the window. This visual re-alignment of door and window has been attempted here, giving an actual door width greater than those on most speculative terrace houses of the 1800s, and because of the extra width it has been possible to accommodate almost perfect Greek Ionic columns rather than the usual weedy varieties

111 A surviving house at NO. 32 Bedford Way, Bloomsbury, London WC 1, designed by the speculative builder James Burton between 1805–10. Although very much in character with other terrace houses then being built throughout London, Burton's buildings have a certain individualism in so far as certain decorative elements were constantly used. Particularly common in Bloomsbury is his use of the reeded architrave which appears in this example and the placing of lion masks in the corners of the architrave which, although missing here, may be seen in plate **3**, page 86. The fanlight, composed of circles and segments of circles, is very typical of its period

112, 113 Two doors in Camberwell New Road, Lambeth, London SE 5, dating from the 1820s. The fanlights are still basically similar to that at NO. 32 Bedford Way, Bloomsbury (see plate **111**)

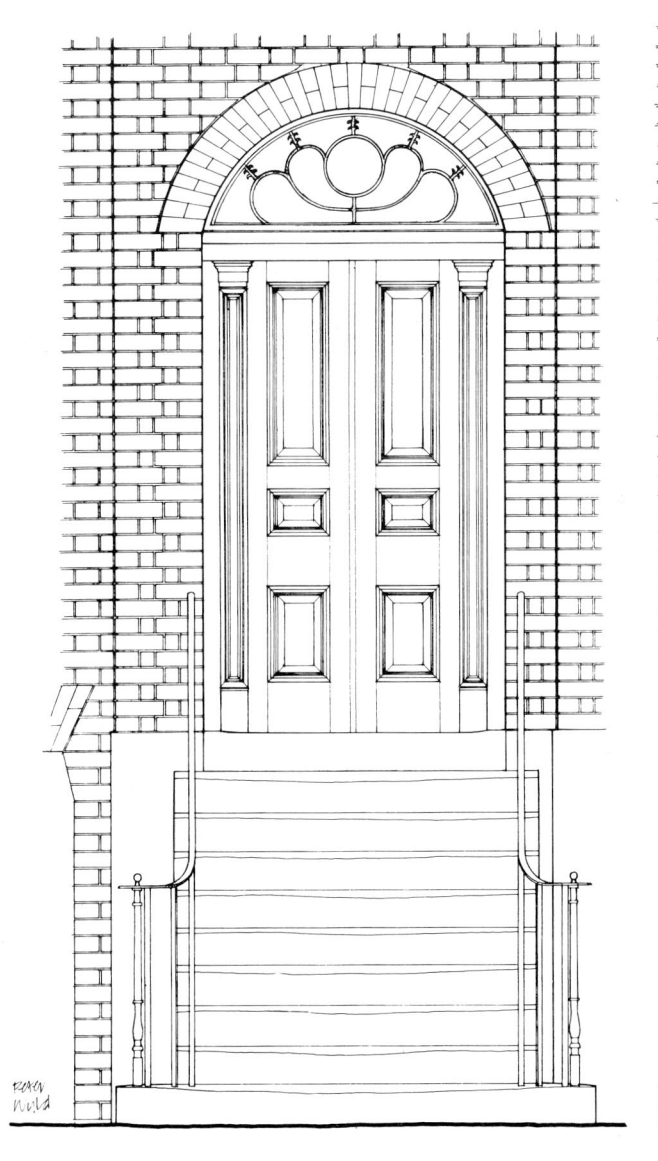

147

114 A very interesting design of the 1820s at NO. 226 Mare Street, Hackney, London E8, showing a tripartite door and window composition contained within a huge arch. The fluted entablature aligns with the impost of the arch and then, sitting centrally above the door, is a Doric attic with small piers

115 This fine doorway at NO. 49 Northdown Street, London N 1, is part of a uniform and pedimented terrace near King's Cross. The handsome Greek Doric columns support a reduced entablature and with the exception of the piers, the attic is cut away to permit the insertion of a traditional fanlight. The rectangular grid fanlight is typical of the 1830s

116 A bold, decisive and very Greek doorway at NO. 18 Woburn Square, Bloomsbury, London WC 1. Built in 1828 this example is one of the last expressions of Georgian architecture in London for within a few years the Greek Revival became heavy and imitative and the handsome synthesis of foreign influences and English building traditions which so readily characterise Georgian domestic architecture, was irrevocably lost. This terrace too will be lost, as it is due for demolition by the University of London

116

Porches
There was never much demand or opportunity for building free-standing doorcases in London as the vast majority of houses, even mansions, stood on or very near the Public Way and as far as the speculative builder was concerned, there was no need to construct an expensive porch when a columned or pilastered door surround would be equally acceptable. Porches properly belonged to free-standing country houses and doorcases to urban terrace houses, but as London gradually expanded into the surrounding countryside in the early 19th century the distinction between town and country blurred and the infant suburbs provided a new opportunity for architectural display. These new houses or villas, often built in strips along older roads, were generally provided with front gardens and besides lending the house an air of landed rural seclusion such a garden also provided sufficient space for the erection of a socially prestigious porch of good classical pedigree.

117 Early 18th-century Corinthian porch at The Water House, Forest Road, Walthamstow, London E 17, a country house when built

118 Ionic porch at NO. 12 Percy Street, Tottenham Court Road, London W 1, built *circa* 1760. This is a rare example of a porch in a totally urban terrace and although it is very shallow, the columns are in fact free-standing

119 Stone porch of Chandos House, Queen Anne Street, Marylebone, London W 1, designed by Robert Adam in

1771. Although austere, this example contains many decorative motifs typical of Adam's Neo-Classicism. The Roman Doric columns are topped with elongated capitals decorated with fine anthemion leaves and the frieze, containing swag-linked ram skulls instead of triglyphs, appropriates the space of the architrave. The simplicity of the stone façade is set off by a display of astonishingly rich ironwork incorporating such Neo-Classical motifs as rosettes, anthemions and darts

120 Coade stone porch of Brunswick House, Albert Embankment, London SE 11, dating from the 1780s on which the decoration is very similar to that designed by Robert Adam at Chandos House (see plate **119**). Roman Doric columns are again used here but, unlike the preceding example, the capitals are decorated with vertical acanthus, rather than anthemion, leaves. The deep frieze contains goat skulls and swags rather than triglyphs and metopes

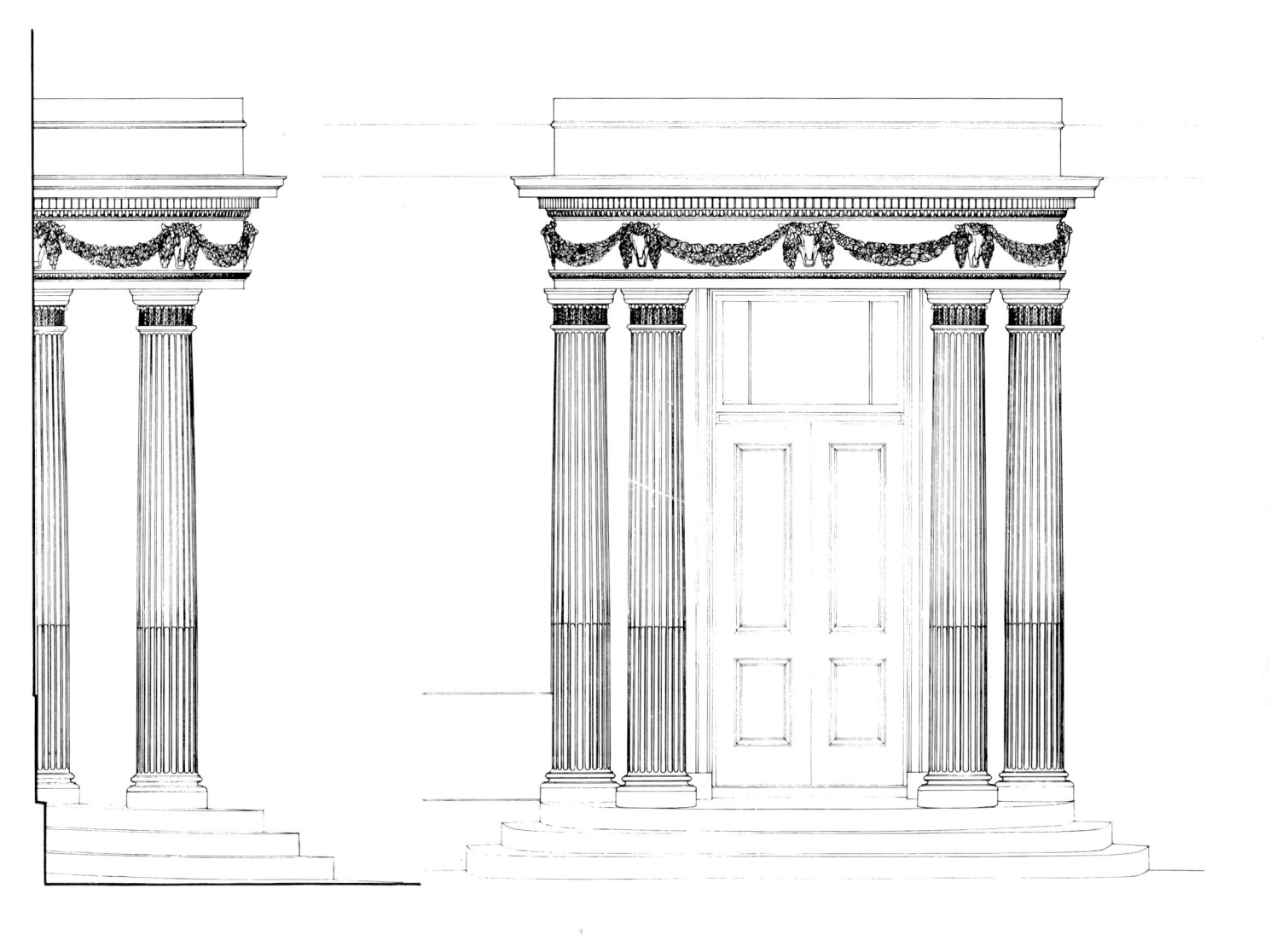

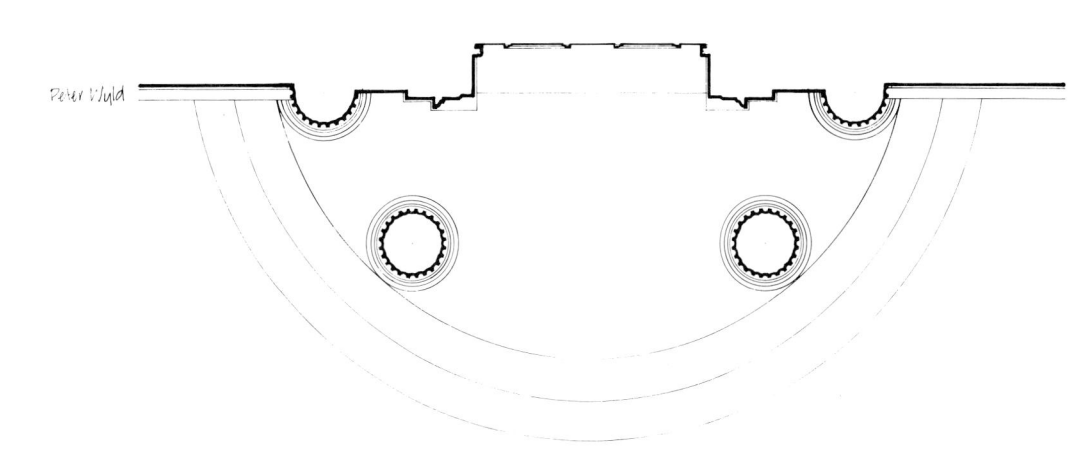

121 Now in a state of dereliction, this Greek Doric porch on a villa in Camberwell New Road, London SE 5, is a typical product of the early 19th century. Unlike its earlier 18th-century manifestations, mass production was acquiring its current shoddy associations and these fashionable Greek Revivalist columns were produced in the cheap, speculative spirit that was beginning to undermine workmanship in the 1820s. The columns are very likely made of brick (tree trunks were also sometimes used) built up into a shaft and then fluted moulds were built around them and cement poured in. Nor has any attempt been made to give the entablature its proper mouldings: instead bricks have been roughly laid with a couple of projecting courses and the whole structure covered with a layer of cement

122 A Greek Ionic porch in Deptford High Street, London SE 8, also dating from the 1820s. Although also built of cement it is a little more imaginative in conception than the preceding example in plate **122**

123 Cast-iron veranda at NO. 363 Hackney Road, London E 2, again dating from the 1820s. This airy device once graced many a suburban villa in London and since cast iron lent itself to a huge variety of decorative motifs, porches of endless invention and variety were virtually guaranteed

123

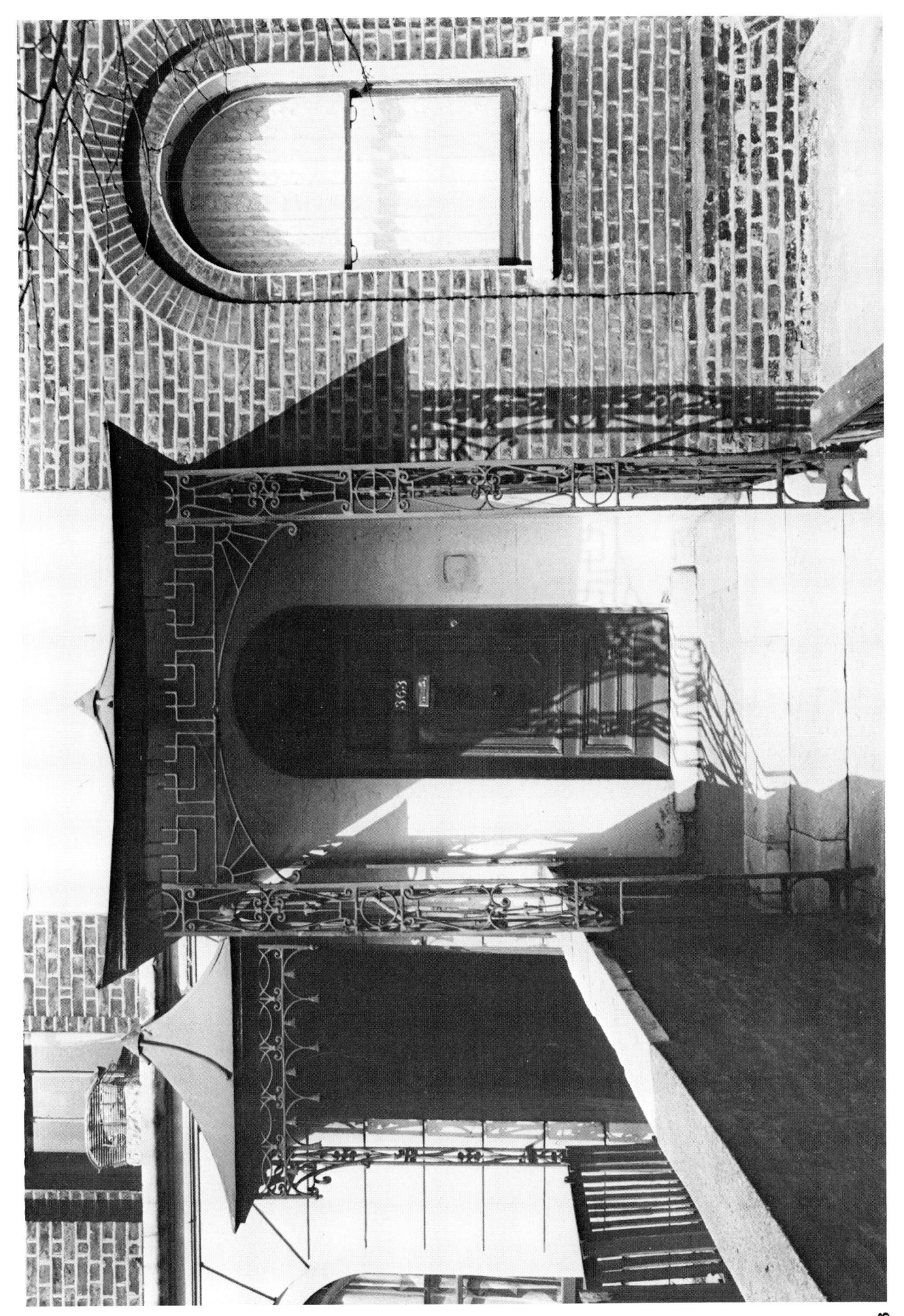

Windows

To talk about windows is to talk about the proportioning of Georgian houses for it was the windows that gave Georgian façades, whether in brick, stucco or stone, their distinctive character and emphasised the all-important relationship between interior and exterior. (The varying heights of the windows on different storeys reflected the *piano nobile* proportioning of the rooms while also dividing the façade into basement, column and attic sections.) If the windows of a house were wrongly proportioned or disposed no amount of carving or other expense could correct the fault and although mere holes, properly cut and placed in the façade could achieve a handsome ornamental effect, attempts were made to enhance their basic impact by the addition of ornamentation. This application of window ornament was often done to the extent that it offended such architectural purists as Isaac Ware. Writing in his *Complete Body of Architecture* in 1756 he wryly remarked, "If any one would know how the publick will receive them, let him take his answer from the bow window. This, from its being uncommon, pleased extremely: those who built it where there was a prospect, were followed by people whose houses were situated where there could be none, and at present we see Venetian windows that look into stable yards, nay that block up one another in the streets. Nor need we go out of the circuit of the new buildings of London, for a house where the Architect has made two Venetians that block up one another."

Scoffing here at the inappropriate use of décor, Isaac Ware railed particularly at bow and Venetian windows, two varieties common by the mid 18th century. The bow, merely an adaptation of the Elizabethan oriel, came into its own in the later 18th century, whilst the Venetian enjoyed a heyday during the Palladian period in the first 60 years of the century.

Basically the bow window could be built as part of a façade in the manner of a bay, or take the form of a bulge stuck on to a regular façade as an addition. It came in many types and was not necessarily semi-circular or segmental, since half-hexagonal and elliptical varieties were quite common in the later Georgian period. Like the elliptical type, another variety with straight sides called the canted bay, did not bulge as much as the semi-circular bow and their popularity late in the century may be explained in the light of the 1774 Building Act which stated that bow windows were "not to be built to extend beyond the lines of the street, nor are any projections allowed beyond them . . ."

The Venetian window, a popular plaything of the Palladians, first appeared in grand houses and then, as Ware records, found its way into any side street or stable yard. Its proportions were subtle and it was capable of a variety of enrichment. Generally occupying a position on the first floor, the Venetian window consisted of a central void, usually twice as high as wide, with a semi-circular space above it. This main void was flanked by two smaller voids, the tops of which aligned with the spring of the central window's arch. As the width of the side windows was not automatically determined by the geometry of the central window, this could lead to problems in design for, if they were made simply half as wide as the main window, the arrangement of glazing bars would be confused. Of this problem Isaac Ware remarked:

"It is common practice, and a common error, to make the side openings one half at the middle; and this is attended with a great inconvenience in dividing the sash squares; the principal light should be divided into three parts for the square, and the side lights should be either one or two of those parts" (see plate 1). The proportions of a Venetian window having been determined, it was then generally dressed in the uniform of one or other of the architectural Orders and indeed the proportions of a window would ideally vary according to the Order with which it was associated: more square for the Tuscan and Doric Orders and more elongated for the Corinthian and Composite Orders.

Plate 2 from Batty Langley's *The City and Country Builder's and Workman's Treasury of Designs* published in 1745, is a good example of an Ionic Venetian window, although Langley in his proportioning has made exactly the error Isaac Ware complains of. Ware's own version of a Doric Venetian window, together with other modes in which such windows could be decorated, is given in plate 1. These are all Palladian designs, but as the 18th century progressed, Neo-Classical architects whilst retaining Palladian proportions, applied their new vocabulary of decoration to windows as much as to interiors and doors. This combination of Palladian proportioning and Neo-Classical ornament drew fire from Sir William Chambers who had already attacked what he considered to be an excessive use of window ornament in his *Treatise on Civil Architecture* in 1759:

"The common sort of builders in this country are extremely fond of variety in the ornaments of windows and indeed in every other part of a building, imagining, probably, that it betrays a barrenness of invention to repeat the same object frequently."

As a foremost late-Palladian denouncer of progressive developments in late 18th-century English architecture and a natural enemy of the Adam brothers, Chambers' judgement of ornament must be taken as extremely subjective, but allowing for this his criticism of proportions is generally very valuable because ideal Palladian window proportioning whether treated with Baroque, Palladian or Neo-Classical decoration, remained standard throughout the Georgian period. Chambers' *Treatise on Civil Architecture*, in its own day a classic text, deals authoritatively with both aesthetic attitudes and physical details and gives for example the following piece of highly informative advice: "If an Order comprehends two stories,

1 Plate from Isaac Ware's *Complete Body of Architecture* published in 1756, showing various Palladian designs for enriching windows. The Doric Venetian window (bottom centre) is proportioned in accordance with Ware's theory that the side windows should equal one-third the width of the centre window

155

Venetian Windows *of the Ionick Order whose Members are described at large in Plates* V. VI.   Plate LIII

4 Diam.   7 Diam.   4 Diam.

2 *Batty Langley Invent and Delin. 1739.*   *Thos Langley Sculp.*

the apertures of the windows should not exceed three modules in width" (a module was the diameter of the column or pilaster of the chosen architectural Order). Although this typically Palladian dictatorial approach was well suited to this particular instance it produced a near absurd result when applied to more subtle questions of architectural design: "In all the storeys of the same aspect, the window must be placed exactly one above the other and those to the left symmetrize with those to the right, both in size, situation, number and figure. The reason for all these things are obvious enough, and therefore it is needless to mention them."

In the manner of an architectural Emily Post, Chambers was simply repeating what had become accepted etiquette in 18th-century building practice, but his rigidity of expression clearly suggests that by 1760, with the dawning of the Picturesque movement and the Gothic Revival, this indefatigable Palladian was already the most established member of a dying race. Isaac Ware set forth the principle of the Palladian *piano nobile* more simply, "The height of windows for this principal storey are to be proportioned to their breadths . . . the most general proportion in plain windows twice the measure of the aperture in breadth for its height." The taking of window breadth as the proportioning module was standard practice in the 18th century. Although the

2 Plate from Batty Langley's *The City and Country Builder's and Workman's Treasury of Designs* published in 1745, showing a Venetian window decorated with the Ionic Order. In this example the side windows are half as wide as the central window

3 A plain Venetian window in Brick Lane, Spitalfields, London E 1, dated *circa* 1740

4 Venetian window on a chapel in Alie Street, Whitechapel, dated 1760. It is decorated with Tuscan pilasters and forms a fine composition framed between two boldly designed doors

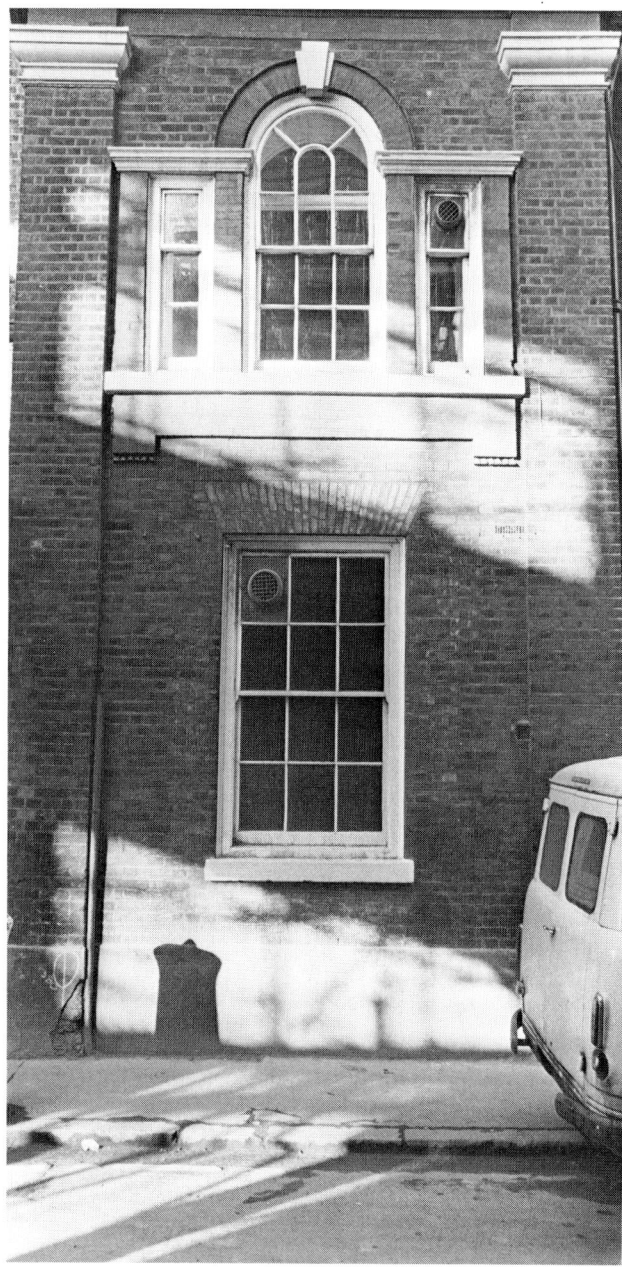

5

5 Frontispiece of a house in Rotherhithe Street, Southwark, London SE 16, built in 1750

6 These three Greek Revival detailed Venetian windows adorn Philip Hardwick's City Club in the City of London.

It is to be demolished so that the National Westminster Bank can build a 600 ft office block

7 Canted bay window on a late 18th-century house in Kennington Lane, London SE 11

breadth of a window varied between 3 feet for small houses and 4 feet for large, the most common dimension was 3 feet 6 inches and this module not only determined the proportions of windows but the entire façade, from the height of the parapet to the width of the façade over the party wall (see page 39). Ware continued:

"As rooms are lower in the chamber floor (the floor above the *piano nobile*) the windows should also be lower; therefore instead of twice the breadth for height, the best measure for these is diagonal, which is one and a half the breadth; this is what the builders express by the name of a diagonal window . . . the attic storey should have the windows square . . . for the mezzanine floors give the windows three quarters of their breadth in height."

Attic windows were always square and thus, being distinctive elements, were used to define the position of the attic if the house was proportioned and faced with a full set of columns, entablature and basement.

Having determined the breadth of the proportioning module, the geometry used in the construction of varying types of windows was a much simpler operation (see plates **8–12**). However, if the window arch was not straight but segmental, elliptical or semi-circular, the procedure became slightly more complicated (see plates **13–16**).

Throughout the 18th century attitudes towards the spacing of windows and to the treatment of window arches developed so consistently that an examination of

8–12 Methods for proportioning windows

8 A square window, often known as an attic window. It would be the top window in a façade, often above a cornice

9 A window one-and-a-quarter times deep as wide. In a five-storey building it would appear on the fourth floor

10 A window one-and-a-half times deep as wide

11 A window one-and-three-quarters times deep as wide. This was a proportion commonly used for second and ground floors

12 The double-cube window, i.e. a window twice as deep as wide, a proportion greatly favoured by the Palladians. It generally appeared on the main floor or *piano nobile*, which was usually the first

13–15 Diagrams to show geometrical techniques for the construction of three types of window arch

13 Segmental

14 Semi-circular

15 Elliptical

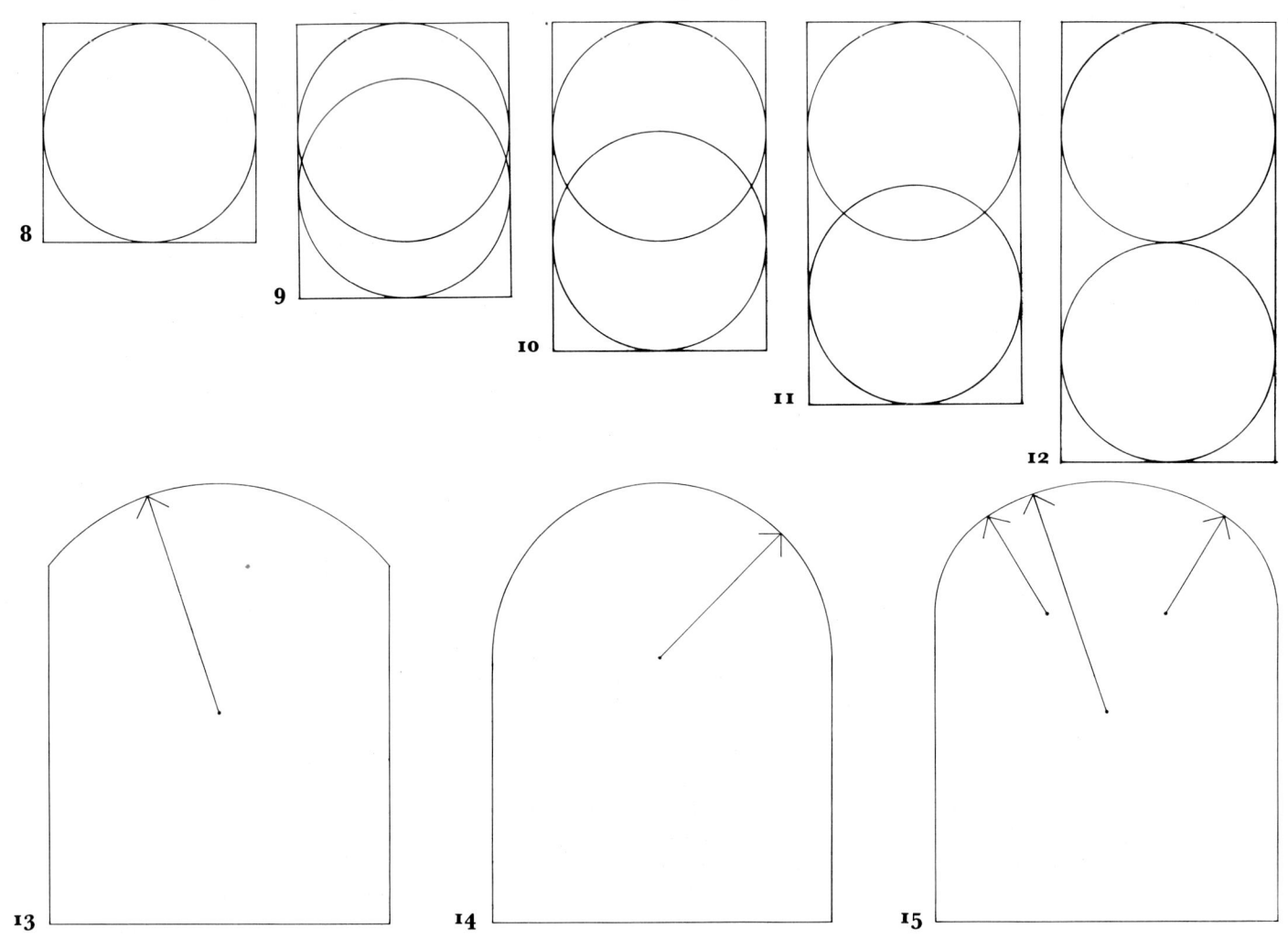

these details alone makes it possible to date an individual house accurately. In the early part of the century the tendency in terrace design was towards achieving horizontality and a house in such a terrace would appear low because of the width of the piers between windows. As often as not, the windows themselves would not display much influence of the *piano nobile* and retain the same proportions in each storey. As the century progressed the space between windows gradually tightened up and a greater feeling of verticality ensued as the *piano nobile* became pronounced. This move towards verticality continued until, by the early 19th century, the first-floor windows of terrace houses were at least twice as high as wide and reducing in height floor by floor, finally terminated in square attic windows just below the parapet.

Although window spacing was a consistent development the changes in the use of the window arch were more subject to arbitrary fluctuations of fashion. During the 1700s straight window arches were common but were almost totally superseded between 1710–30 by a segmental variety. In the 1730s the straight arch reappeared once again in force and although it held the field throughout the rest of the Georgian period it was occasionally challenged at the end of the 18th century and the beginning of the 19th by the semi-circular arch and less often by elliptical and ogee specimens.

Just as important as the proportioning and spacing of the window void is the proportioning and design of its contents and here a true revolution took place during the Georgian period. During the greater part of the 17th century the English, like most other householders in Europe, kept wind and rain out of their houses by hinged casements divided by stone mullions and transoms into which glass was fixed with lead. But during the 1670s this essentially medieval solution was replaced by the sash window, thought to have been imported from Holland, and after being first used in quantity at Chatsworth in 1676, this novel mechanism proceeded to revolutionise English window design. The sash consisted of two sliding glazed frames running in vertical grooves and its impact on façade design was astonishingly dramatic. The casement window was obviously clumsy and unsympathetic to the carefully considered proportions of a classical façade and the difference in its appearance when closed and open (particularly when the open casement swung back, obscuring immediate brickwork) was excessive and disturbing to the classically orientated mind of the late 17th century. By contrast the cool grid of the sash window not only formed a pleasing design and blended well with a classical façade, whether open or closed, but if neatly constructed, constituted a positive ornament to a building. The speed with which the sash was adopted by builders and casements removed and replaced by sashes shows how much dissatisfaction was felt with the traditional window form.

Being recognised as one of the ornaments of a façade, the sash immediately fell under the sway of fashion, and of its constituent parts, the glazing bar itself, was subject to considerable toying—being fat, flat and plain at the beginning of the period and thin and fancy at its con-

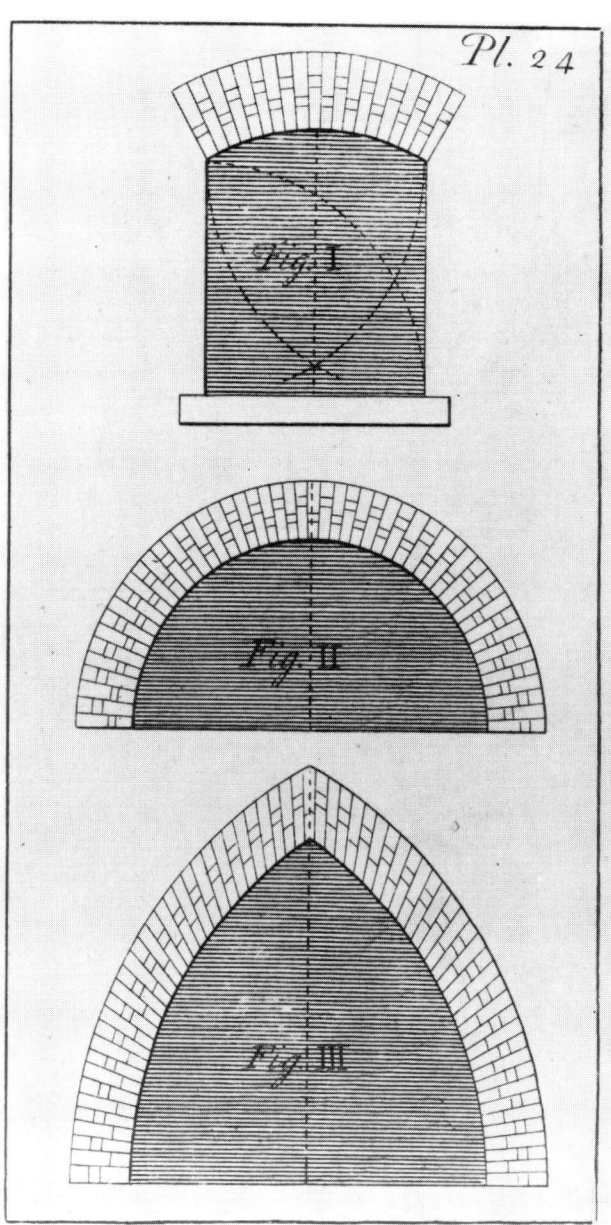

16 Plate from Batty Langley's *London Prices of Bricklayers' Materials and Work* first published in 1747, showing three kinds of window arch. *Fig. I* shows a square window with a segmental arch. The bond making up the cut brick arch is that commonly used for fashionable façades during the 18th-century; *Fig. II* shows a semi-circular arch; *Fig. III* shows a Gothic pointed arch

clusion. In his *Treatise on Civil Architecture* Chambers wrote of sashes, "Sashes of windows are generally made of wainscot, or mahogany, and sometimes of copper, or other metal . . . the squares of glass are proportioned to the size of the window, these being commonly 3 in width and 4 in height, whatever the dimensions of the window; each sash is composed of two equal panes, placed one above the other."

When Chambers wrote this in 1759 sashes were still in a transitory form and further changes, particularly involving glazing bars, were yet to come. As the 18th century progressed the glazing bar, in common with many other elements in architecture became more refined,

161

17 W   M   X   Y

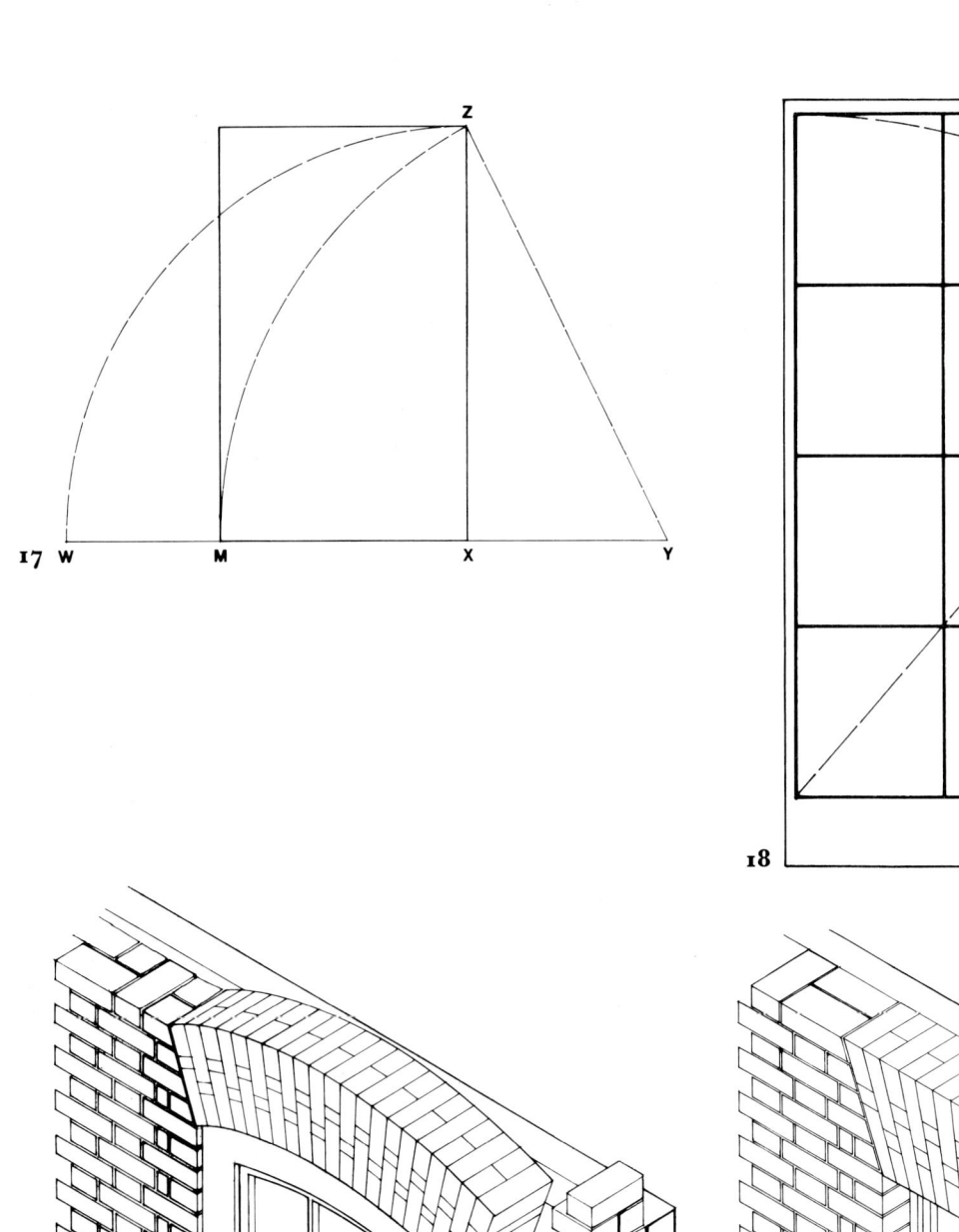

18

19

20

162

thinner and more elegant. Indeed they could be astonishingly thin (generally ½ inch wide by the early 19th century) for as Chambers pointed out, it was becoming the thing to construct glazing bars out of metal which was then painted to suggest wood.

The basic structure of the sash itself was however determined more or less from the beginning. The size of the panes of glass were condensed or elongated according to the proportioning of the window but for an average example, the formula was soon fixed that the width of the window should be divided by two vertical bars and the height divided by three horizontal bars. Although this was the standard design, a more elongated window might be divided by four or five vertical bars and an attic window only by one. Very wide windows would generally be constructed as a number of separate sashes, perhaps two of normal size with a mullion between them, or one normal-sized sash between two small ones.

This basic division was arrived at by a variation on the golden section principle. The proportioning of one pane of glass was not a scaled-down version of the overall window proportion, but more generally a scaled-down version of three-quarters of the window height by its breadth (see plates **17** and **18**). To divide a window void into panes was a very straight-forward operation once it had become standard to divide its width by two bars. Having made this vertical division, a rule would be placed from a bottom corner to a point three-quarters up the height of the window and the points worked off on the vertical bars to ascertain where the horizontals should cross them. By this method the window voids would be divided into twelve equal panes: three wide and four high. To divide the very elongated windows which were not common until the later 18th century, the principle remained the same although for appearances sake, the window would be divided into more panes.

The height of a window of average proportions was divided into quarters for aesthetic reasons but as windows became taller this was no longer acceptable as panes would look deformed and lose their strength if the void continued to be divided by only three horizontal bars. Obviously, the higher a window, the more horizontal divisions were necessary and this was simply done: for a window that looked as if it would require five horizontal elements the individual panes would be proportioned to three-fifths of the window height multiplied by its breadth and on an even taller window requiring six horizontal divisions, the pane would be proportioned to

17, 18 The Golden Section and its application to the proportions of glazing bars

17 To find the golden mean of line wx produce wx to y so that: xy = ½wx. At point x erect a perpendicular so that xz = wx. With y as centre and yz as radius draw an arc cutting wx at M. wx will then be divided at the golden mean by M

18 The Golden Section ideal applied to glazing bars in a window void one-and-a-half times deep as wide

19 Isometric of pre-1709 Building Act window. The box of the sash is exposed and set flush with the face of the external brickwork. The arch is segmental, the cut bricks are laid in a closer, header, stretcher bond sequence. The bond of the façade brickwork, as it meets the window void, is neatly finished off by introducing closers (or quarter bricks). As an extra decoration, the bricks actually forming the window jamb were red stocks, while the rest of the façade might be faced with yellow or grey stocks

20 Isometric of a post-1774 window. The box of the sash is recessed 4 inches from the façade (one brick depth) while also being tucked behind the brickwork of the jambs. The arch, as was common after 1730, is straight and the glazing bars thin. In both examples the bond between the fashionable and well-laid facing bricks and the cheaper place bricks is random

21 Detail from a house in Russell Street, Covent Garden. Although built in 1721, the window is typical of those legal before 1709. The sash box is exposed and flush with the façade

half the window height multiplied by its breadth.

Like cornices, windows were an element particularly subject to building legislation and apart from sheer aesthetic considerations, various Building Acts affected their design throughout the 18th century. When sashes had first been introduced in the late 17th century, glazing bars had been about 2 inches wide, and the box mechanism in which the frames were hung was exposed, painted and fitted flush with the façade. Being so exposed, the wood of the box presented a great fire hazard and a Building Act of 1709 ordered that the box be recessed into the façade to the depth of one brick (i.e. approximately 4 inches) although the actual box still remained visible (see plate **19**). This Act was repealed and super-

22 Window from a house of 1717 in Hanover Square showing the results of the 1709 Building Act. The sash is still exposed, but set back four inches

23 Post 1774 Building Act window. The box of the sash is now not only set back from the façade, but also recessed behind the window jambs

seded by the massive and detailed Building Act of 1774 which put another constraint on sash windows. Now, as well as being recessed 4 inches, the box was required by the Act to be fixed out of sight in the brickwork of the window jamb. This meant that from the street only a piece of wood the size of glazing bar was visible, whereas before the Act anything up to 6 inches of sash box could be seen (see plates **20–23**).

The other official legislation to affect the form of windows during the Georgian period was the window tax although, unlike the Buildings Acts, this tax did not so much influence the design of windows as their disposition and number on the façade. This tax was introduced in 1696 as an attempt by the Government to recoup revenue that had been lost as a result of the population persistently clipping the coinage. The number of windows presumably being considered a fair guide to the size and prosperity of a household, householders were taxed according to how many windows their house possessed, business premises being exempt. In 1710, when the duty was increased, the notorious practise of stopping up windows to avoid taxation began and in 1766 when the tax acts extended to houses with seven windows or more, the number of houses in England and Wales with exactly seven windows was reduced by two-thirds. In 1798 the tax extended to houses with six windows and again by 1800, the number of taxable houses was less than it had been in 1750. Known in the 18th century as the "tax on light and air," the window tax was not reduced until 1825, nor repealed until 1851.

Roofs

One of the oddest things about the roofs of Georgian London is the way they sit like rustic English caps upon more or less correct and classical Italian faces. Possibly the precedent for this combination was set by Inigo Jones in the 1630s when he topped his pilastered palace front in Covent Garden with a vernacular high-pitched roof and dormers. Peter Nicholson in his *The New and Improved Practical Builder and Workman's Companion* of 1823 explains that Inigo Jones determined the angle of his roofs by making the rafters three-quarters the breadth of the building. "This proportion", he writes, "called the true pitch, still prevails in some parts of the country where plain tiles are used". Throughout the Georgian period, the pitched roof, in various and modified forms, continued. Tiles, which needed to be hung with a steep pitch to keep the weather out and which were not superseded by slates until the 1760s, forced builders to use steep pitches over relatively narrow spans. This meant that even the smallest terrace house had to be topped with a lowering cliff of tiles on a great gable end and to avoid this, early 18th-century builders devised a method of covering the span with two or more scaled-down pitched roofs, called after its shape, the M roof. The ridge of the M roof generally ran at right angles to the façade for if it ran parallel, it simply became a double-pitched roof. Occasionally, if a terrace was developed by one builder, the M roof could run across the entire terrace with very little relationship to the individual house units. Especially common in early 19th-century terraces was the practice of giving each house two half roofs rather than one whole one, with the gutter being positioned down the middle of the house, at right angles to the façade, and the top of the pitch positioned at each party wall. Even in the early 18th century, houses built as pairs with mirror plans, would generally share one roof.

The M roof, with its pitch at right angles to the façade, emerged in the late 17th century, lost favour, and then reappeared again later in the 18th century. Its one big disadvantage was that it was only a roof, a basic coverage,

1 Rooftop view of Camberwell New Road, London SE 5, showing examples of the mansard, M-shaped and shallow-hipped roofs in one early 19th-century group

2 The basic pitched roof which was not only the most simple design to construct, but provided a most functional slope to keep out the weather. Before the 18th century, when its pitch ran at right angles to the façade, this type formed the gable end which characterises Medieval and Tudor buildings. In the early 18th century particularly, pitched roofs running in this traditional direction were still used, but the great gable profile was softened by hipping the end of the roof. It should be remembered that Greek pediments are of course the gable ends of shallow-pitched roofs

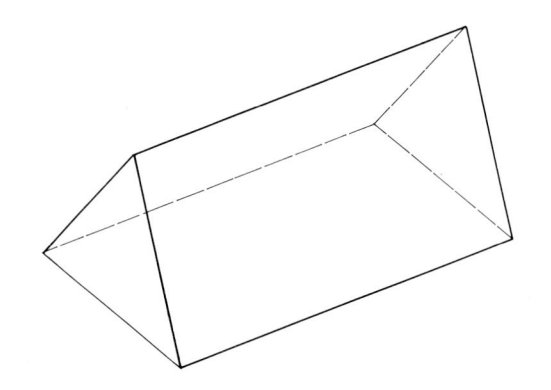

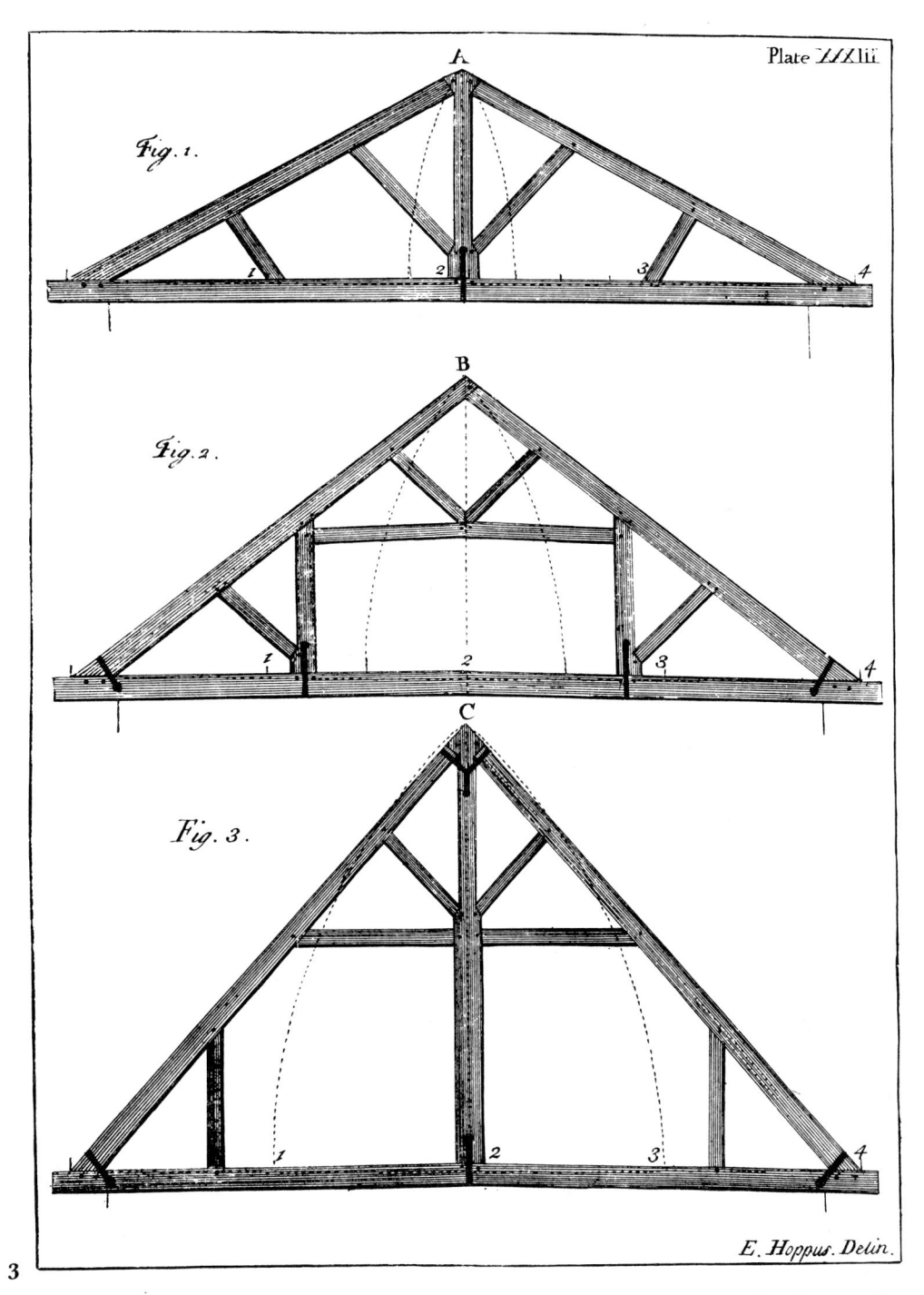

3 Plate from William Salmon's *Palladio Londinensis: or, The London Art of Building* published in 1734, showing three types of pitched roof. In explanation of this plate Salmon wrote:

"The first thing to be considered in Roofs, is the covering wherewith the Building is to be inclosed, as Lead, Pantiles, Slates or Plain-Tiles; they each requiring more Pitch, or Slope, than the other, for which observe the following Rules.

Fig. 1 is a proper Pitch for covering with Lead. To find the perpendicular Height, divide the breadth of the Building into 4 equal Parts, and subdivide the Part between 1 and 2, or 2 and 3, also into 4 equal Parts.
Then take half the Building, and one of those Parts for the length of the Rafter, which said length being used as a Radius, describe the Arches intersecting in A, which gives the perpendicular Height.

Fig. 2 is a proper Pitch for covering with Pan-Tiles and Slate. To find the perpendicular Height divide the breadth of the Building also into 4 Parts: Again, divide one of the middle Parts into 2, and take half the Building and one of those Parts for the length of the Rafter, which will intersect in B the perpendicular Height.

Fig. 3 is a proper Pitch for covering with Plain-Tiles. To find the perpendicular Height, divide the breadth of the Building also into 4 Parts, and take 3 of these Parts for the length of the Rafter, which will intersect in C the perpendicular Height.
This is called true (or common) Pitch, it being most in Use"

whereas others such as the pitched roof and especially the mansard (named after the French architectural classicist François Mansart) could take rooms and be lighted with dormers. The introduction of slates to London in the 1760s meant that builders could attempt to conceal a roof behind the parapet so that it did not disturb the proportioning of the façade. They could do this with more hope of success than the earlier builders with the M roofs because slate could be hung successfully at a much shallower pitch than tiles.

In the early 19th century, despite the English weather, it became fashionable to construct roofs with pitches of a very Mediterranean shallowness, the edges supported by the long-exiled eaves cornice, on villas in the expanding suburbs. As in Camberwell New Road (see plate 1) these villas stand side by side with houses topped with the more traditional mansard, hipped and M-shaped pitched roofs. Nicholson wrote in 1823, "with regard to the present practice, the proportion of the roof depends on the style of the architecture of the edifice; the usual height varying from one-third to one-quarter of the span", and one imagines that not only the pitch but the overall style of roof was dependent upon the type of house and amount of money the builder had at his command.

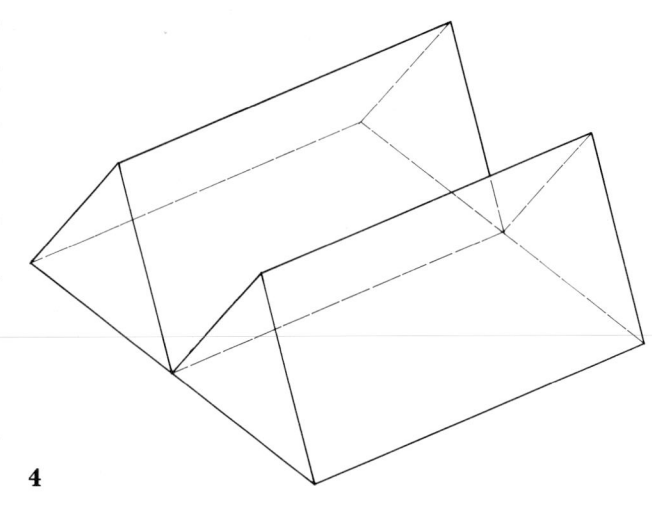

4

4 The double-pitched roof, a design developed to span a building which was too deep for an ordinary pitched roof

5 End-on view of a double-pitch roof in Mount Pleasant, London WC 1

6 Interior view of structural timbering in derelict pitched roof in Great Ormond Street, London WC 1 dating from 1721–25

5

168

6

7 The M roof was the early 18th-century answer to the problem of bridging a span whilst lowering the pitch and this type of roof generally ran with its pitch at right angles to the façade. M roofs were frequently hipped at one end or both, to prevent the archaic phenomenon of gables poking over the parapet

8 Plate from Peter Nicholson's *The Carpenter's New Guide* published in 1792, the first in a long series of publications by this most prolific expert. *Fig. B* shows a very typical M roof with king-post and struts connecting the angled principal rafters to the horizontal tie beam. *Fig. A* has a collar beam

9 Plate showing a plan for an M roof from Batty Langley's *The City and Country Builder's and Workman's Treasury of Designs* published in 1745. In this example one end of the roof is hipped and the other is joined by a linking roof and the rafters are marked but not the purlins. By tracing this drawing and then scaling it up, a workman using Batty Langley's book would be able to produce an M roof quite easily

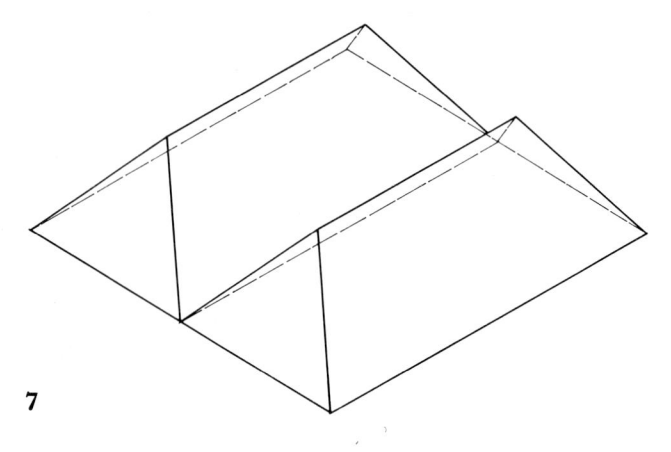

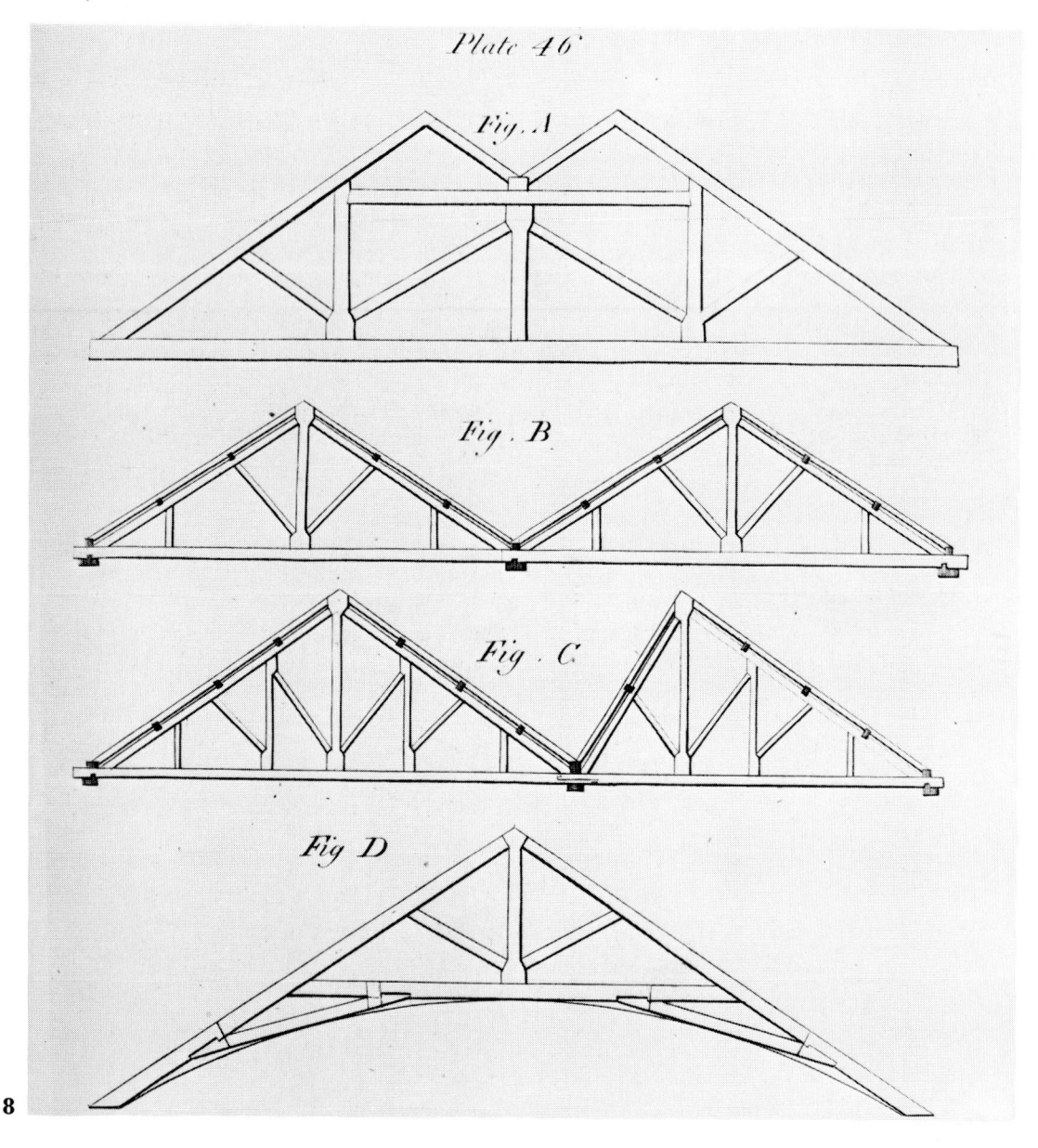

170

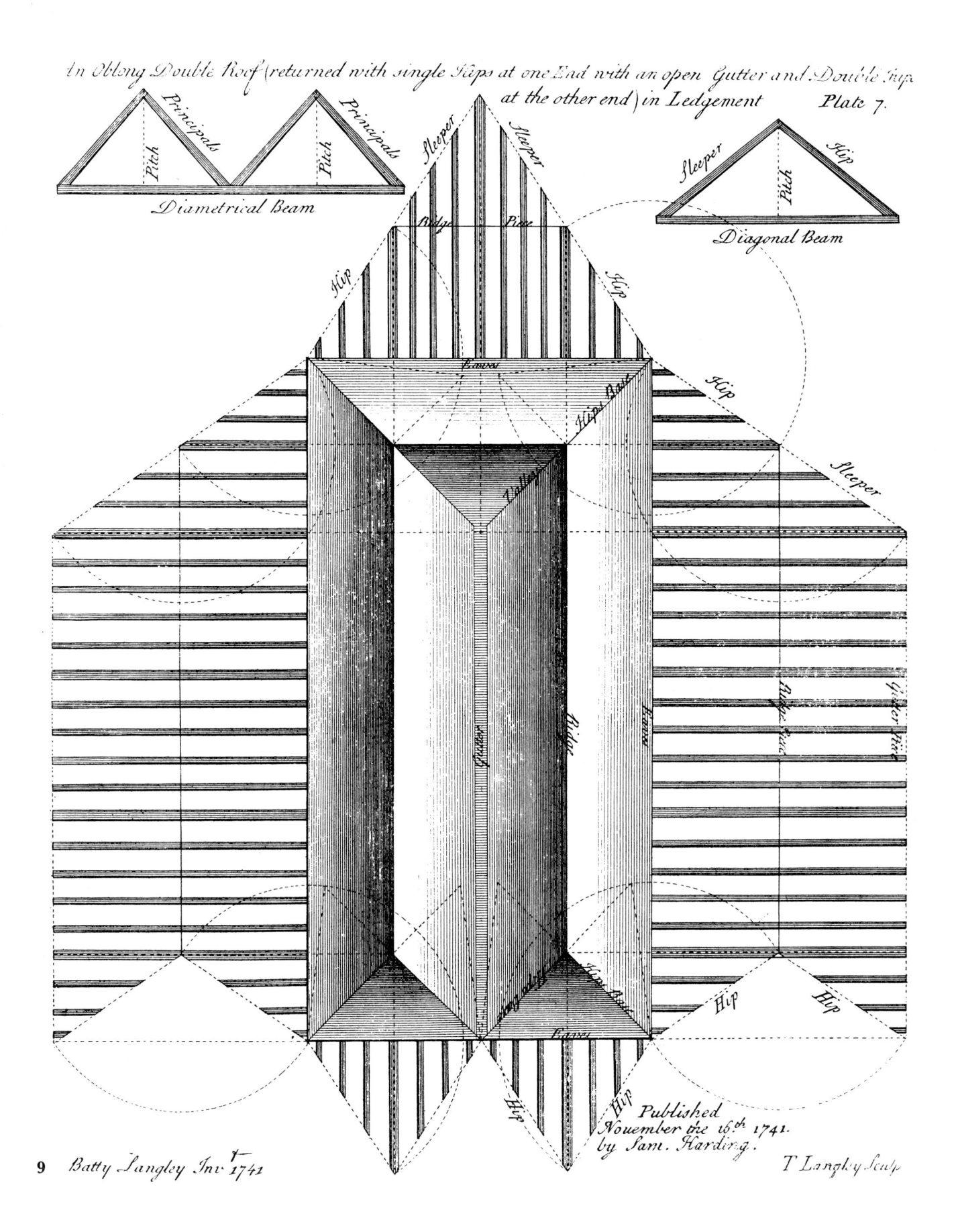

An Oblong Double Roof (returned with single Hips at one End with an open Gutter and Double Hip at the other end) in Ledgement. Plate 7.

9 Batty Langley Inv.ᵗ 1741

Published November the 16.ᵗʰ 1741. by Sam. Harding.

T. Langley Sculp.

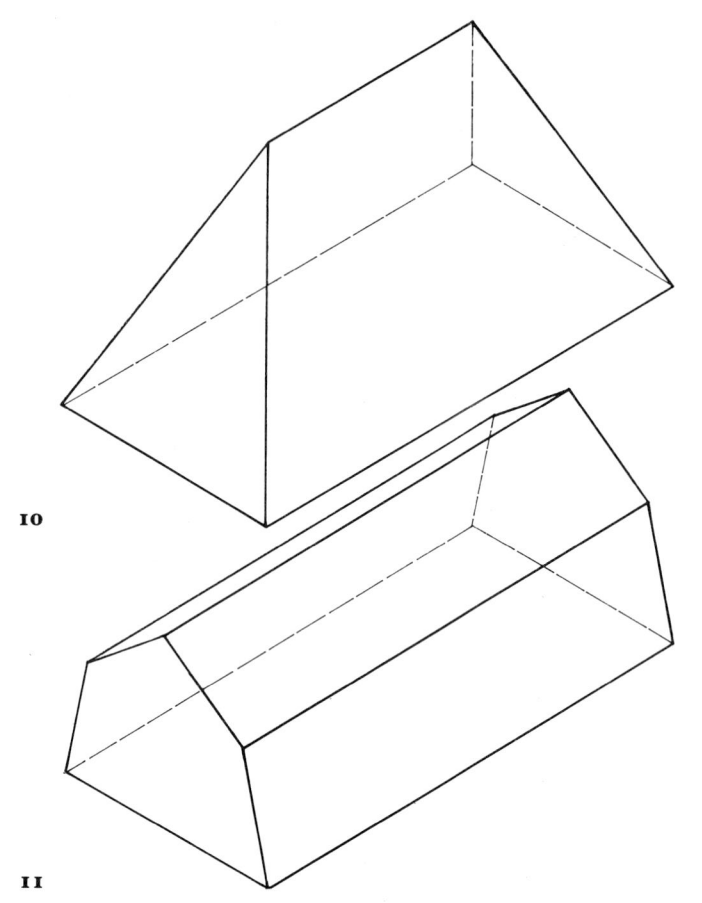

10 The hipped roof, shown here, is another ancient form of roof and is basically a pitched roof with four slopes instead of two, the shorter sides being roofed with small pitched triangles called the hipped ends. Plain hipped roofs are not common in London because, since the majority of houses were built in terrace form, the pitched roof when used simply disappeared into the party wall and no hip was necessary. Although pitches were occasionally hipped on the roofs of ostentatious houses or those built in pairs with no neighbouring party walls, in such instances as these the builder more usually resorted to the half-pitched roof in which party walls would rise approximately half way up the pitch of the roof and then stop. The party wall would then be ramped down to join the parapet while the protruding tip of the table would be hipped back to join the ridge of the roof

11 Example of a gambrel roof, most simply described as a two-angled pitched roof. Although this type of roof may at first glance seem an uncommon sight in London streets, most mansard roofs when used in terraces in fact end up this shape when the roof goes into the party walls and chimney stack rather than being hipped (see plate **12**)

12 Roofs in Southampton Place, Bloomsbury, London WC 1, showing the metamorphosis of the mansard roof into gambrel roof as a result of terracing (see plate **11**)

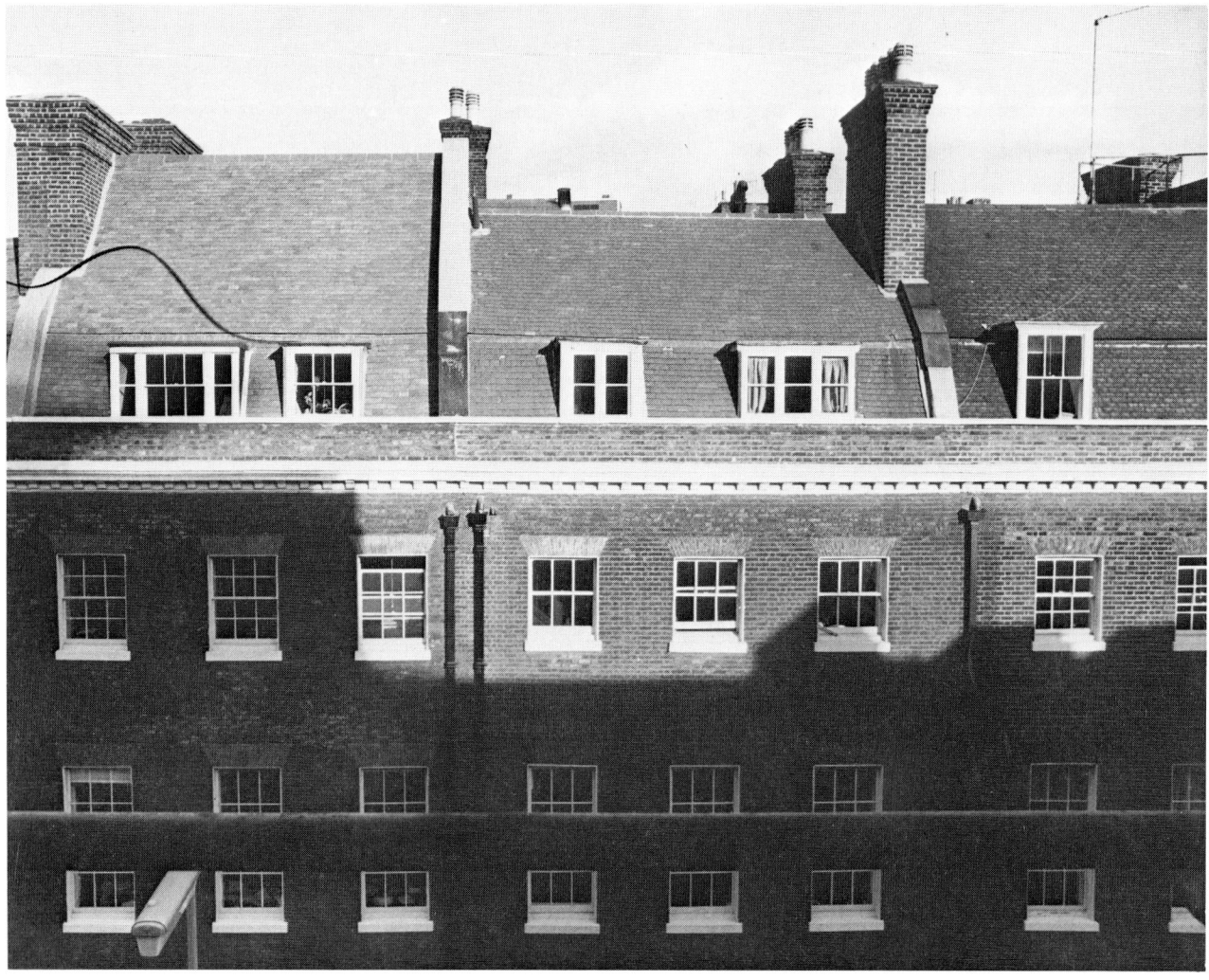

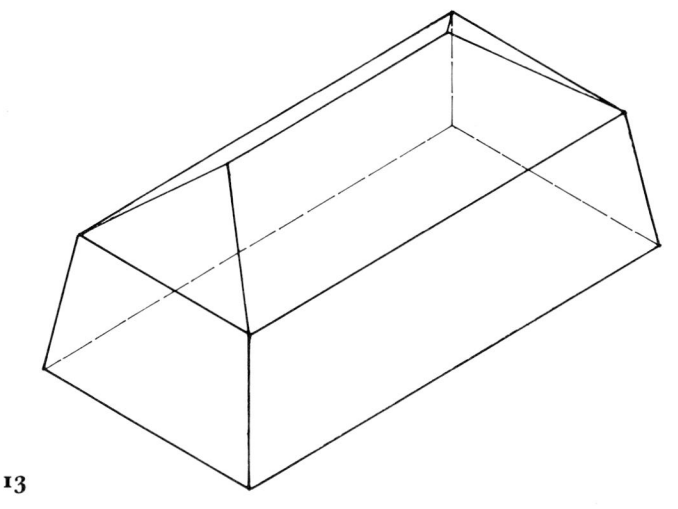

13 The mansard roof has a double slope, the lower being longer and steeper than the upper and was a design very much approved of by Isaac Ware in his *Complete Body of Architecture*. Also known in the 18th century as the kirb roof, it was the ideal solution for the builder who wished to incorporate a large amount of attic space. So great was the roof space that in the 18th century the mansard occasionally had the appearance of an independent little house sitting on top of a large one and in the early part of the century, the cladding of the different pitches was generally in differing materials. The top pitch being rather shallow, was covered with pantiles, while the bottom pitch was boarded in or hung with tiles. Later in the century, after 1765, both pitches could be hung with slate.

14, 15 Two diagrams taken from the *Encyclopaedia Britannica* of 1797 which were intended to show the "unlettered artisan" the structural principles of a mansard or kirb roof:

"Suppose it were required to make a mansard or kirb roof whose width is AB (see plate **14**) and consisting of the four equal AC, CD, DE, EB. There can be no doubt but that its best form is that which will put all the parts in equilibrio, so that no ties or stays may be necessary for opposing the unbalanced thrust of any part of it. Make a chain *acdeb*, (see plate **15**) of four equal pieces, loosely connected by pin-joints, round which the parts are perfectly moveable. Suspend this from two pins *a b*, fixed in a horizontal line. This chain or festoon will arrange itself in such a form that its parts are in equilibrio. Then we know that if the figure be inverted, it will compose the frame or truss of a kirb-roof *a y j c b*, which is also in equilibrio, the thrusts of the pieces balancing each other in the same manner that the mutual pulls of the hanging festoon *a c d e b* did. If the proportion of the height *D j* to the width *a b* is not such as pleases, let the pins *a b* be placed nearer or more distant, till a proportion between the width and height is obtained which pleases and then make the figures *A C D E B* (see plate **14**) similar to it"

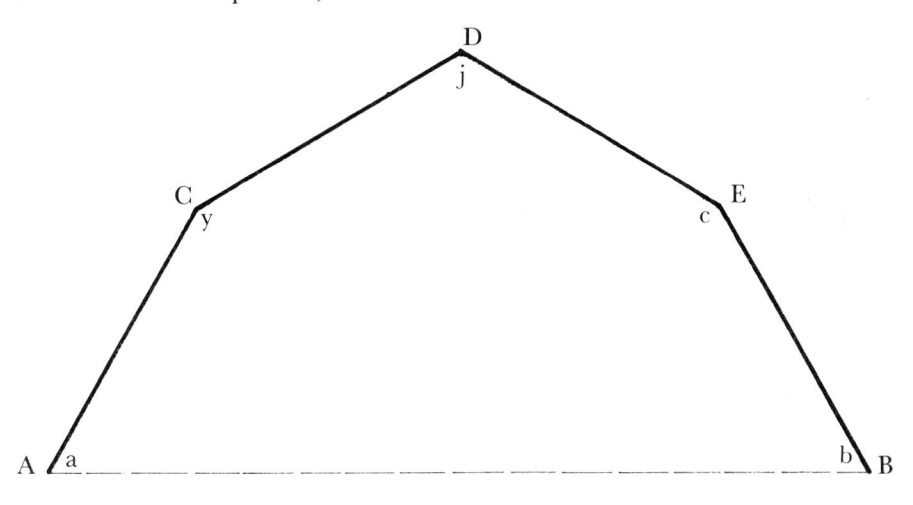

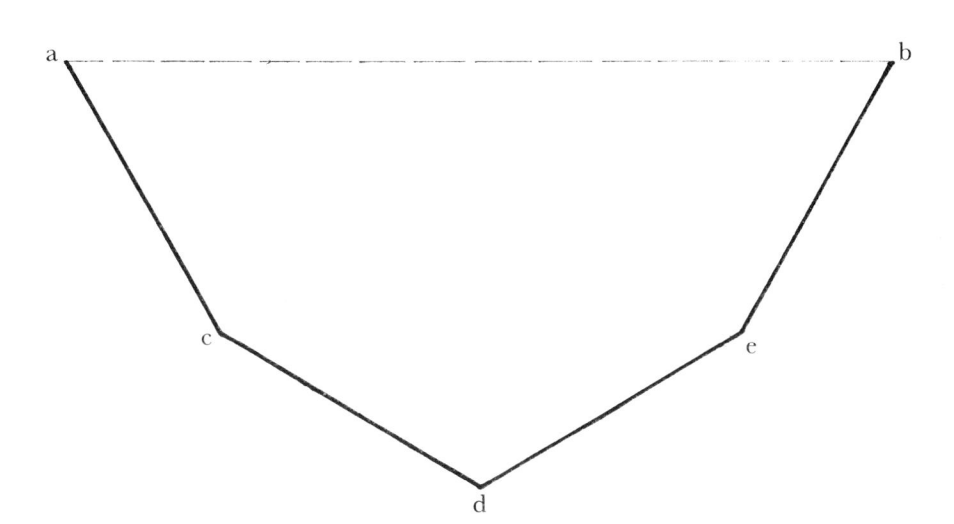

16 Plate from Peter Nicholson's *The Carpenter's New Guide* published in 1792, showing that in terms of construction the mansard roof is simply a king-post truss, the tie beam of which is supported by a queen-post truss. The other various struts were to be accommodated in the event of a door or room etc. being required

17 Plate from Batty Langley's *The City and Country Builder's and Workman's Treasury of Designs* showing the infinite variety of interior spaces which could be achieved with trussed roofs

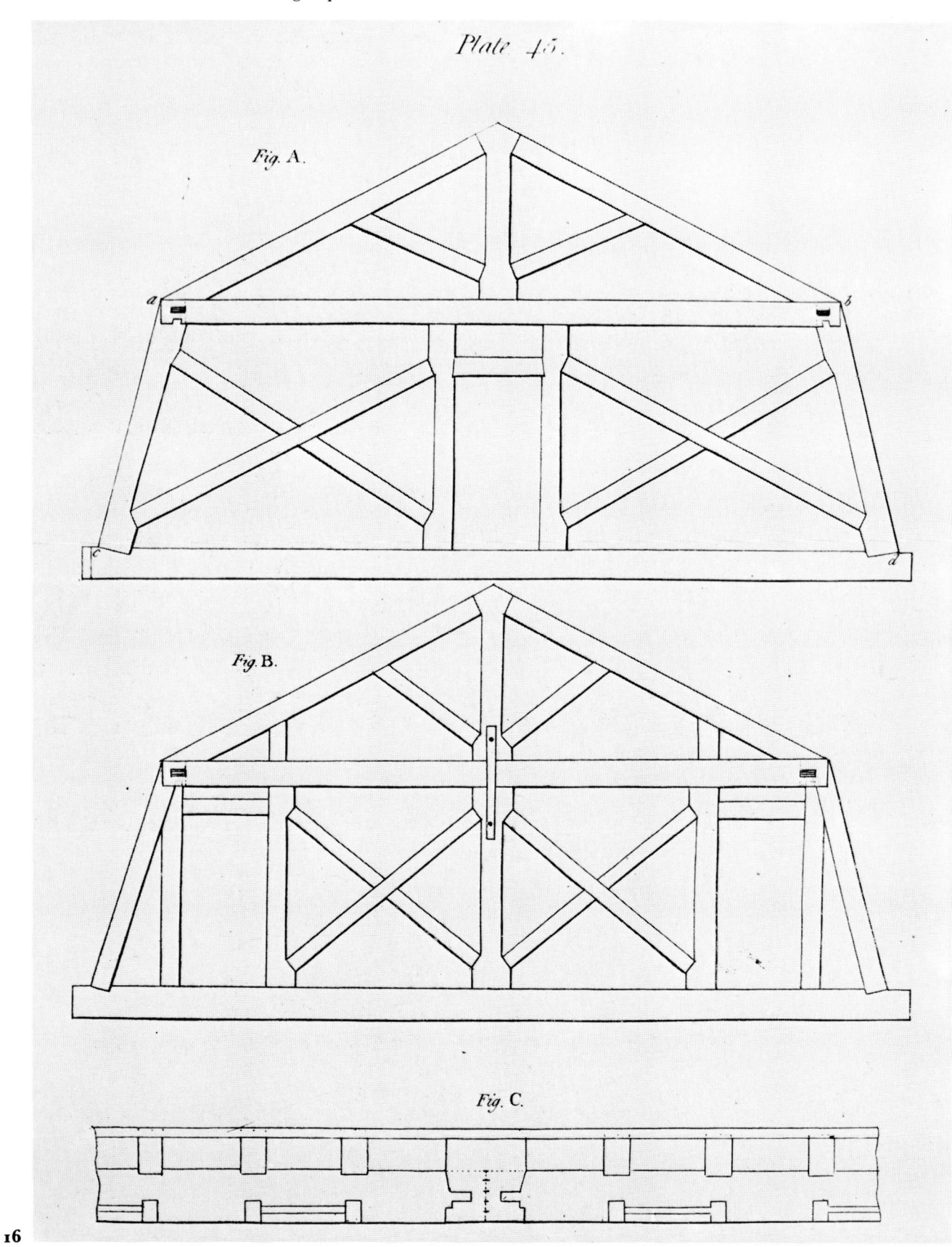

Ten Examples for Truss'd Roofs — Plate 23

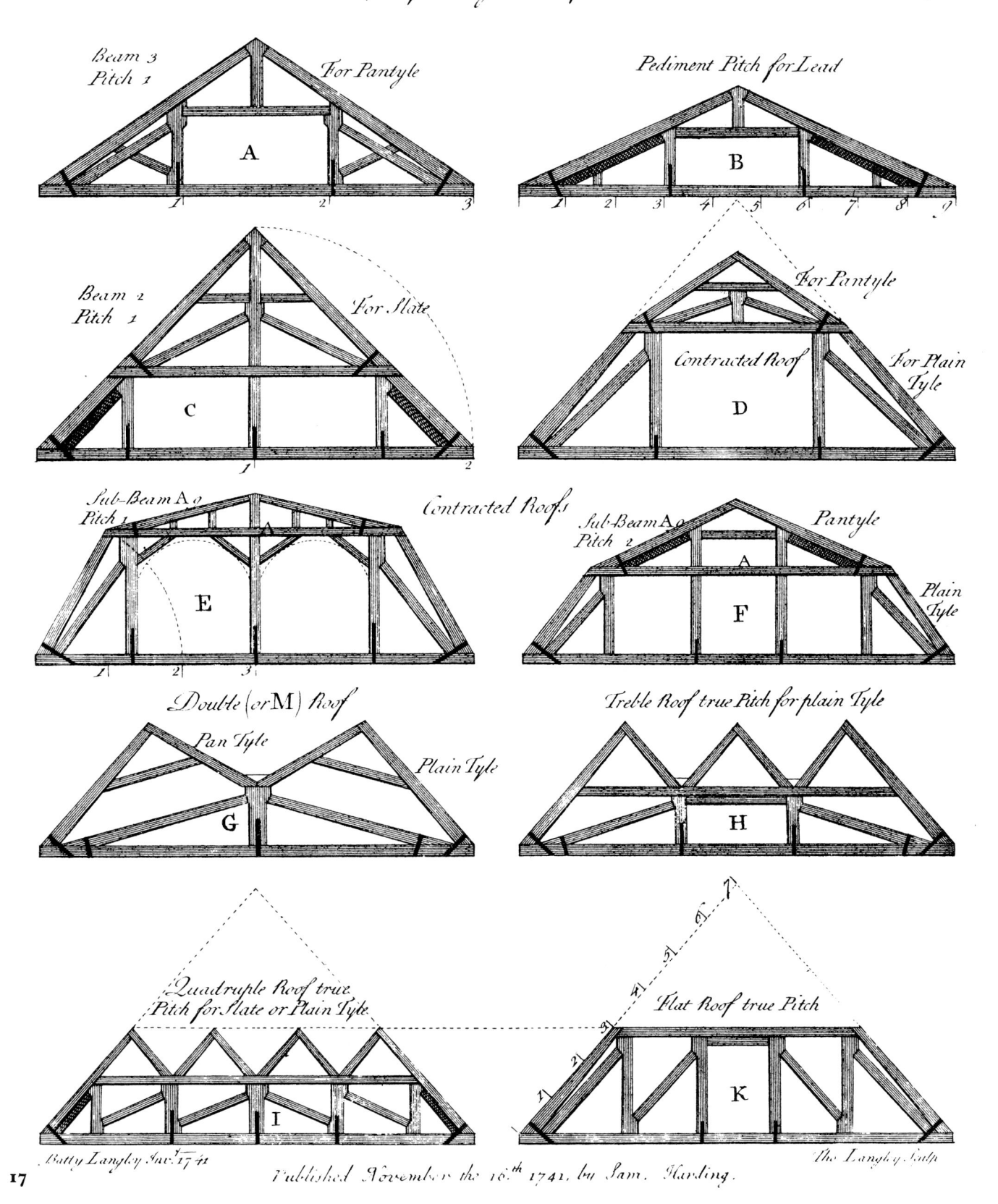

Roof Cladding
In his *Complete Body of Architecture* published in 1756 Isaac Ware describes the types of tiles then available:
"1. The plain tile, which is flat and thin.
  2. The pantile, hollow and crooked, or bent somewhat in the manner of an S.
  3. English glazed pantile.
  4. Dutch.
  5. Gutter tile, made with kind of wings".
He then goes on to say,
" . . . the plain common tile is greatly preferable to any other: but this in its best condition is not comparable to slate."

The tile, pantile and slate were London's main roofing materials during the 18th century, and Isaac Ware reflects the taste of his time. He says, "The neatness and pale look of the common slate gives that covering a vast preference. Having nothing coarse or fiery in the appearance, it agrees perfectly well with the stone or woodwork, and with the grey brick of the chimnies... This preference is so very great that it entirely banishes the use of tiles from elegant edifices or other buildings of expense".

However, when Isaac Ware was writing, slate had not appeared in London in any quantity and it was still a red tiled city. It was only after 1765, when Lord Penrhyn began to develop his slate quarries in Wales, that slate began to be really accessible and cheaper than tiles and the Adam brothers were amongst the first to utilise its advantages. Not only was slate cheaper, but pitches could be shallow and the roof hidden to avoid disturbing the classical repose of the façade. Towards the late 18th century, the transportation of slate on the new canal systems made it even cheaper in relation to tile and many buildings were re-surfaced in the 'new' material. Today many an old terrace carries on its roof, steeply, pitched for tiles, a scaly skin of later 18th-century slates.

18 Domes, cupolas and pendentive roofs were expensive to construct both in materials and time and were therefore not generally used by the speculators who were responsible for building the major extent of Georgian London. But as a result of the special uses to which some roof spaces were put, variations on the preceding basic roof forms did occur and most of these variations were to facilitate the entry of more light into garrets. One of the most obvious examps of this exists here in Fournier Street, Spitalfields, London E 1 where the Huguenot weavers needed good light to work at their garret looms. Built between 1725–30, this peculiar type is a hybrid consisting of a shallow pitched roof sitting on a mansard-like box. As the pitch is too shallow for ordinary tiles, pantiles have been used here, with weather boarding on the box

19 The desire to light this early 18th-century house at NO. 55 Monmouth Street, Covent Garden, has led to huge dormers, with their own little hipped roofs, being let into the angle of the roof pitch. This way of roofing dormers was common in the early 18th century when only tiles were available and which needed a steep pitch on which to hang

18

19

PART III ELEMENTS: MATERIALS

Brick

Long before the Georgian period began and long after it had drawn to a close, bricks were the standard building material in London. As it was not available locally, stone was an expensive luxury and in the Cities of London and Westminster wood had been banned as a major structural or facing material after the Great Fire. The size of bricks during the period varied little and from 1571–1776, despite all the Acts and charters specifically governing brick size, dimensions only varied between $8\frac{1}{2} \times 4 \times 2$ inches and $9 \times 4\frac{3}{8} \times 2\frac{1}{4}$ inches. (The only exception to this was the brick tax of 1784 which, for several years, caused some bricks to expand in size to $10 \times 5 \times 3$ inches. See page 191.) Consistency in brick size was matched by a similar consistency in choice of bonding for although brickwork techniques offered a wide range of possibilities, Flemish bond held the field almost without rival. Introduced in the early 17th century, Flemish bond did not fall from favour until the early 19th century when the Gothic Revival and a return to 'true' English architecture led to the revival of the English bond.

Colour, the most superficial quality of a brick wall, was subject to change however. Red, purple or grey bricks with red dressings were fashionable from the late 17th century to *circa* 1730 when taste gradually moved away from such 'hot' colours to more discreet brownish-greys and pinkish-greys. By the mid 18th century grey stocks were supreme, although in fact more often brown than grey in appearance, and by 1800 yellow marl or malm bricks were used throughout the expanding capital to such an extent that they became known as London stocks.

These London stocks were made from a nearby chalky clay, but whether yellow bricks became fashionable because London's own red clay reserves had become exhausted or because fashion demanded lighter colours and therefore yellow clay had to be found, will always be debatable.

In his *Complete Body of Architecture* of 1756 Isaac Ware neatly sums up the mid-century change of taste from 'hot' to 'cool' brick colour. "Of the manner of using bricks. We see many beautiful pieces of workmanship in red brick; and to name one the front of the greenhouse in Kensington Gardens will be sure to attract every eye that has the least curiosity; but this should not tempt the judicious architect to admit them in the front walls of buildings. In the first place, the colour is itself fiery and disagreeable to the eye—it is troublesome to look upon it; and in summer it has an appearance of heat that is very disagreeable; for this reason it is most improper in the country, though the oftenest used there from the difficulty of getting grey. But a further consideration is that in the fronts of most buildings of any expense there is more or less stone work; now one would wish that there should be as much conformity as could be between the general naked surface of the wall and the several ornaments which project from it, the nearer they are of a colour the better they always range together... There is something harsh in the transition from red brick to stone and it seems altogether un-natural; in the other the grey stocks come so near the colour of stone that the change is less violent, and they sort better together. For this reason also the grey stocks are to be judged best coloured when they have least of the yellow cast; for the nearer they came to the colour of stone, when they are to be used together with it, always the better. Where there is no stone work there generally is wood, and this being painted white as is commonly the practice has yet a worse effect with red brick than stone work; the transition is more sudden in this than in the other; but, on the other hand in the mixture of grey brick, and white paint, the colour of the brick being soft there is no change."

Although firing affects the colour of bricks if they are over-burned and glazed, the colour of bricks depends almost entirely on the colour of clay from which they are made. The colour of clay varies from area to area and until the opening of the canal system during the 1770s, which made the transportation of building materials cheaper and easier, bricks had a very strong regional character and colouring. In London however, such regional distinctions were frequently overlooked for if architectural fashion demanded certain colours fashion was supplied, and even before the Industrial Revolution and indeed, even before the days of Wren, special bricks were 'imported' for certain building works: particularly fine Sussex rubbers for use in gauged brick arches. The use of red cutting bricks for gauged brick window arches and continued throughout the 18th century but more surprisingly, the cheap place bricks which were used for unseen work such as party walls and piers were practically always red and in fact Peter Nicholson notes in his *The*

1 Plate from Peter Nicholson's *Mechanic's Companion* of 1825 showing a selection of bricklaying tools used during the Georgian period: *Fig 1* brick trowel; *Fig. 2* brick axe; *Fig. 3* square; *Fig. 4* bevel; *Fig. 5* jointing rule; *Fig. 6* jointing; *Fig. 7* hammer; *Fig. 8* raker; *Fig. 9* wire pins; *Fig 10* rammer; *Fig. 11* pick axe; *Fig. 12* camber slip; *Fig. 13* banker and rubbing stone.

There appears to be an error in this early 19th-century plate and the bottom item should in fact be *Fig. 13* instead of *12*. Although in the accompanying text to this plate Peter Nicholson's list of tools is longer than that given, for example, in the 1703 edition of Joseph Moxon's *Mechanik Exercises, or, the Doctrine of Handy-works*, it is clear that the same basic tools remained in use throughout the Georgian period

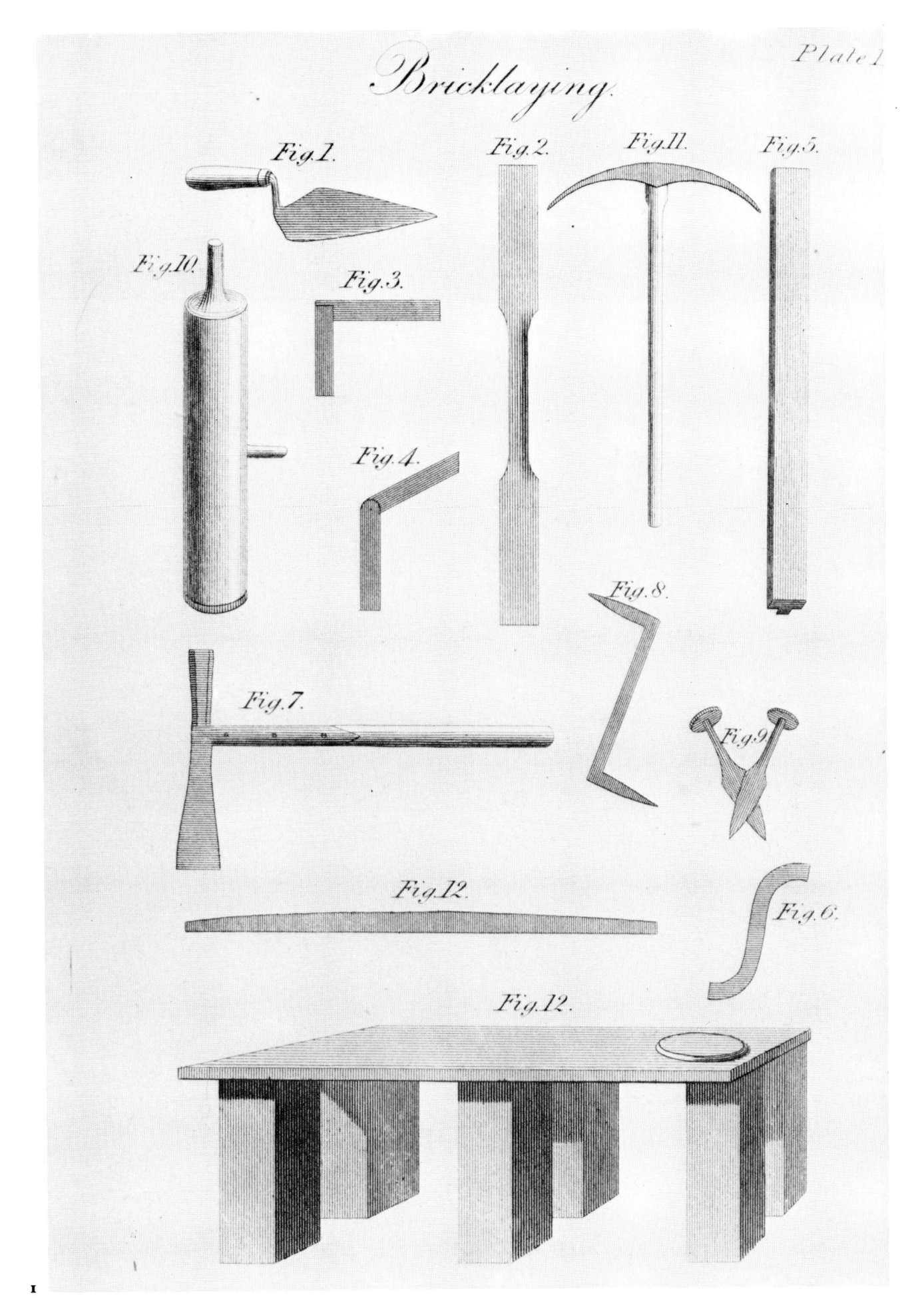

Bricklaying.

Plate 1.

Fig. 1. Fig. 2. Fig. 11. Fig. 5.
Fig. 10. Fig. 3.
Fig. 4.
Fig. 8.
Fig. 7. Fig. 9.
Fig. 12. Fig. 6.
Fig. 12.

New and Improved Practical Buider and Workman's Companion of 1823 that place bricks are redder than stocks. Some place bricks were simply under or over-done or otherwise were faulty stock bricks, but some were especially made of inferior clay and it would seem that colour and quality go together.

Writing in 1703 Richard Neve in his *The City and Country Purchaser* explained the basic types and qualities of bricks in contemporary use:

". . . those which derive their names from accidents are clinkers, Samel or Sandal. Those from their dimensions are the great and small (or statute) and Didoron, Tetradoron and Pentadoron. Those from method of making are place, and stock bricks."

It is surprising that Neve mentions Tetradoron and Pentadoron bricks since these names were not generally used in the 18th century although they were explained by Vitruvius in his *De Architectura*. Vitruvius stated that the Romans used Greek Lydian bricks 1½ feet long by 1 foot wide and that since 'doron' meant palm, other varieties of bricks such as the teradoron were five palms wide. Neve then proceeds to explain the two basic types of brick in use throughout the Georgian period: place and stock: "Place bricks and stock bricks are of two kinds that

2 Detail of a gauged brick pilaster and arch from the Blue Coat School, Caxton Street, London SW 1, built in 1709

3 Three types of facing brickwork from the Blue Coat School: on the left is shown fine rubbed red bricks, in the centre ordinary greyish-brown stocks and on the right red decorative bricks

receive their names from the method of their make-up. Place bricks (generally made in eastern parts of Sussex) are so called because there is a place just where they strike (or mould) their bricks which is a level smooth piece of ground, prepared . . . to lay them singly down in rows as soon as they are moulded and there they are left until a little dried". Samel bricks, Neve described as "Those which be out most in a kiln . . . they are very soft, and will soon moulder to dirt". Of stock bricks he wrote, "These differ not from place bricks in form; their difference lying conceal'd in the quality of the earth; they are made upon a stock" Statute, small or common brick, Neve wrote, "ought to be $9'' \times 4\frac{1}{2}'' \times 2\frac{1}{2}''$.

As regards the disposition of stock and place bricks in Georgian building, Isaac Ware's recommendations are a rather structurally dangerous example of the 18th-century obsession with good appearances or 'façadism': "Grey stocks are made of purer earth and better wrought, and they are used in fronts of buildings being the strongest and handsomest of this kind; the place bricks are made of the same clay, with a mixture of dirt and other loam material and are more carelessly put in hand, they are therefore weaker and more brittle, and are used out of sight and where less stress is laid upon them: the red bricks of both kinds are made of a particular earth, well wrought and little injured by mixture and they are used in fine works, in ornament over windows and in paving."

In terms of 18th-century building economy, Ware's remark that place bricks are bad and should be "used out of sight and where less strain is laid upon them" is a violent contradiction. Expensive, handsome and strong stock bricks were used where they could be most admired —in the elegant façade—but the façade was not structural, since the floor joists were supported by the piers between the windows and by the party walls. Inevitably, being unseen, these structural elements were constructed with cheap, unsightly and weak place bricks: a truly dangerous, though almost universally practised, economy in speculative domestic building.

Bonding

The essential characteristic of an 18th-century brick façade was its unique combination of structural and decorative elements. If a wall is to have strength, the bricks must be properly laid and bonded, but the Georgian bricklayer, acutely conscious of the beauty of fine brickwork, made such a point of the regularity of bond and joint that the proper structure of a wall became its major ornament. The brick details from the Blue Coat School, Caxton Street, London SW 1 shown in plates 2 and 3 illustrate the subtle relationship between structure and decoration in an early 18th-century façade. On the left of plate 3 is a pilaster of expensive red cutting bricks. They are smaller than the stocks, about five courses of them were equal to four of stocks, and being finer and softer, their corners could be rubbed square to make very tight jointing possible. Although red cutting bricks could be used to build structural walls if a builder could afford

4 Skin-deep beauty: the fashionable façade of this house in Elder Street, Spitalfields London E 1, built during the 1720s, is only $4\frac{1}{2}$ inches thick

Bricklaying.

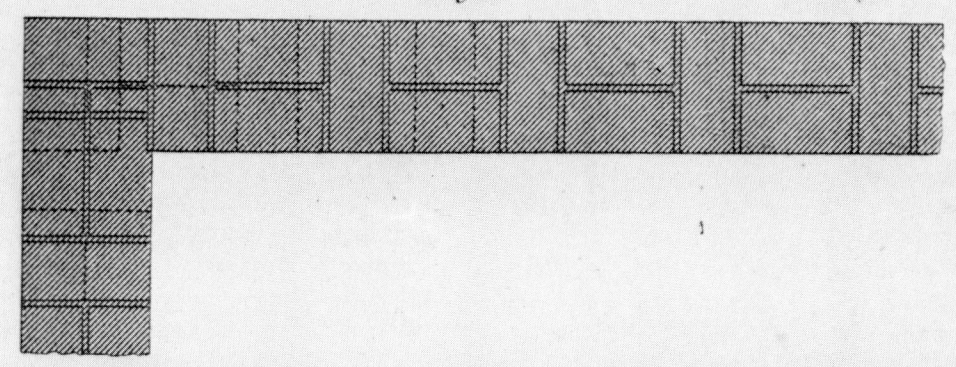

Plate 3.

Fig. 1.

Fig. 2.

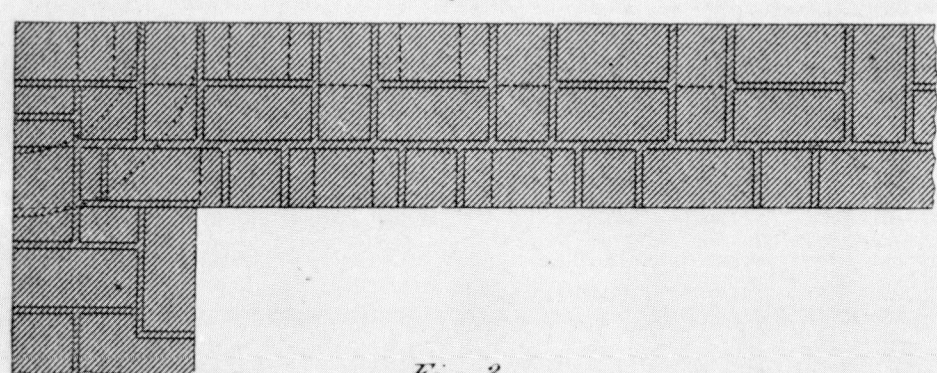

Fig. 3.

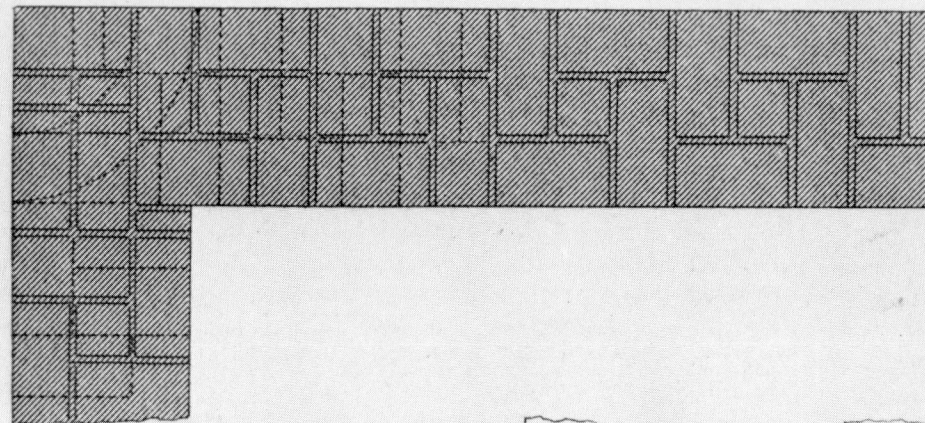

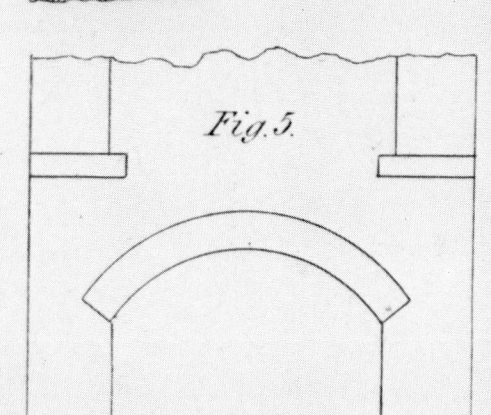

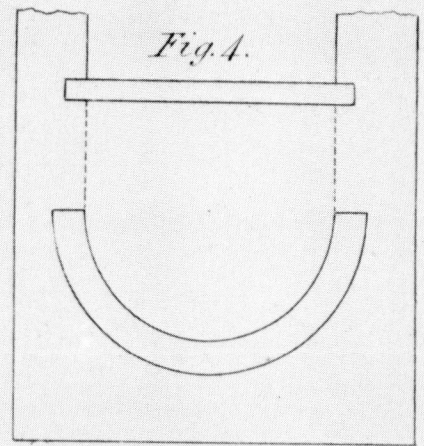

Fig. 5.

Fig. 4.

them, cutting bricks were, as here, mainly used as decorative elements. Brick window arches were commonly constructed with cutting bricks because, being fine, such bricks could be keyed to an arch more accurately. The two types of brick on the right of plate 3 form an even more subtle blend of the practical and the decorative. The bond is a perfect example of Flemish with headers, stretchers and quarter bricks called closers. The bricks near the corners (right) are red whereas the others (centre) are ordinary greyish-brown. This dressing with red bricks was the common way to treat window jambs, corners, in fact any change of plane, in a façade during the first quarter of the 18th century.

Flemish bond had first appeared in England *circa* 1630 (Kew Palace built in 1631 is thought to be the earliest existing example of it) and by the early 18th century it was *de rigueur* to use Flemish in any façade with a pretension to fashion. Peter Nicholson argued in his *The New and Improved Practical Builder and Workman's Companion* of 1823 that the Flemish bond was difficult to execute well because a workman as he laid it had to remember the course below which was difficult to see being hidden by a layer of mortar. This increased the chance of perpends failing to coincide and if this happened the wall would not only look unsightly, but would also be liable to split.

Nicholson wrote, "The outer appearance is all that can be argued in favour of Flemish Bond, and many are of opinion that, were the English mode executed with the same attention and neatness that is bestowed on the Flemish, it would be considered as equally handsome... To obtain it [Flemish bond] strength is sacrificed, and bricks of two qualities are fabricated for the purpose. A firm brick, often rubbed and laid in what the workmen term a putty joint for the exterior [Nicholson then describes the method in which a whole façade of fine rubbed bricks would be built. This would be extremely expensive and although it had happened, occasionally, in the time of Wren it very rarely occurred during the 1820s for façades were, in Nicholson's time, generally made of yellow marls], and an inferior brick for the interior substance of the wall [place bricks]; but as these did not correspond in thickness, the exterior and interior surface of the wall would not be otherwise connected together—than by an outside heading brick, here and there continued of its whole length; but as the work does not admit of this

5 Plate from Peter Nicholson's *Mechanic's Companion* of 1823 showing "... Various specimens of Flemish bond according to the different thicknesses of walls. The dotted lines show the disposition of the bricks in the courses above. *Fig. 1* a nine-inch wall where two stretchers lie between two headers, the length of the headers and the breadth of the stretchers extending the whole thickness of the wall. *Fig. 2* a brick-and-a-half wall, one side being laid as in *Fig. 1*, and the opposite side, with a half header opposite to the middle of the stretcher opposite the middle of the end of the header. *Fig. 3* another disposition of Flemish bond where the bricks are similarly disposed on both sides of the wall for half-bricks." *Figs. 4* and *5* show relieving arches

at all times, from the want of agreement in the exterior and interior courses, these headers can be introduced only where such a correspondence takes place, which, sometimes, may not occur for a considerable space".

This had been the practice all through the 18th century, and explains how easily a house could have its face lifted and be re-fronted in the latest fashion without interfering with the rooms behind. Simply, not only was the façade built independently of the structural piers behind, but it was not even bonded to them, or was only bonded where back and front courses happened to coincide. In this way the façade could be designed and built without any great consideration being given to the structural requirements of the house and gave the architect a delicious freedom to indulge in fashionable conceits.

The example from Elder Street, Spitalfields in plate 4 shows an extreme result of this façadism. Built during the 1720s this house looks fashionable and substantial but, from within, with its panelling removed, one sees that the fashionable façade is only $4\frac{1}{2}$ inches deep. It appears to be Flemish bond from outside, but actually the headers are snapped and similarly, the piers between the windows are separated from the fashionable skin by a 3-inch gap: an early example of a cavity wall!

Nicholson, in his *The New and Improved Practical Builder and Workman's Companion* of 1823, explains the construction of varying thicknesses of Flemish-bond walling and his description is illustrated in plate 5, but as well as the type of bond remaining constant, there were certain techniques of bonding, not peculiar to Flemish bond, which were used throughout the Georgian period. While discussing the use of brick ornaments in the façade, Batty Langley in his *London Prices of Bricklayers' Materials and Work* of 1748 describes red brick dressings to windows, "Those which are rubbed only are chiefly the sides of jambs of windows, and the external angles or quoins of buildings, which workmen call returns, which generally consist of alternate courses the one of a stretcher, the other a header and closer, or the one a stretcher and header, and the other a header, closer and stretcher."

The first and simpler form of dressing was by far the most common. Only on very ambitious houses did the bricklayer extend the red dressing to $1\frac{3}{4}$ bricks wide. The use of a quarter brick or to be more exact, a brick cut in half lengthwise so as to present an area in the façade half as wide as a header became the standard way of finishing off runs of Flemish bond, and was used in exactly the same way after the fashion for red dressing had passed and the whole wall was built of the same stock or marl bricks. A closer was in fact just a neat way of accommodating the brick unit to the required window spacing of the façade, while retaining a particular kind of bond. If the windows were required to be a certain distance apart, it could become impossible to use a standard-size brick and retain pure Flemish bond, so compromises had to be made. A bricklayer, required to keep the wall bonded would, for example, lay on one course between windows a header, closer, stretcher and then three headers before the next stretcher. Around window openings the closer was generally placed as Batty

Langley described, but sometimes it changed places with the header and was laid immediately next to the window void or, very rarely, laid elsewhere in the course (see plates **6, 7, 8**).

The actual jointing of the brick was also made into a fine, even art during the Georgian period. The London builder had no choice but to build with brick, unless he was working for a rich client who could afford to import stone to face his house, but bricks did not naturally lend themselves to the creation of cool, broad, classical planes on which the various architectural ornaments could be displayed to their best advantage. In the early part of the 17th century bricks were warped or uneven and had to be laid in thick layers of mortar and the resultant thick pointing and irregular bricks made it clear that the façade was made of very many small busy units which distracted the eye from appreciating the classical repose of the composition.

Wren, with his brick building, solved this problem. The most expensive solution was to build the whole façade with fine, colour-matched bricks which could all be rubbed to make their corners square and then be laid with very thin putty joints. The aim here was to reduce as much as possible the impact of the individual units and increase the impression of the façade as a smooth-planed cliff. There was a cheaper solution, however, which took the form of tuck pointing (see plate **9**) and was used throughout the Georgian period. Very simply, it was an illusion. A builder, especially if he were a speculator, could or would not afford to buy rubbing bricks and hire bricklayers just to rub them down for a façade and so instead, he built the front in ordinary stock or marls, but mixed a little brick dust with the mortar to make it match the colour of the bricks used in the façade. This mortar was used for all the joints but was used proud and then rubbed down flush with the surface of the bricks, after which operation, the actual thick joint would be disguised. The disguised joint was then scored and an imitation joint in the form of $\frac{1}{8}$ inch-deep strip of white lime putty would be stuck on. When well done this process must have been convincing, but during the early 19th century when Londone was expanding rapidly and terraces were being run up by the mile, tuck pointing became merely a device to

6 Plate from the 1748 edition of Batty Langley's *London Prices of Bricklayers' Materials and Work* showing the accurate bonding of a façade and arch: 1 is a closer, 2 a header and 3 a stretcher. Interestingly enough, the proportions of the window in *Fig. 1* is based on the Golden Section. *Fig. 2* shows how the splay of an arch could be accurately calculated

7 A built example based on the methods shown in plate **6**

8 Detail of brickwork from a house built *circa* 1730 in Neal Street, Covent Garden, London WC 2. Unusually, the closer is not placed next the edge of the windows, but set two half-bricks into the pier

9 An example of tuck pointing

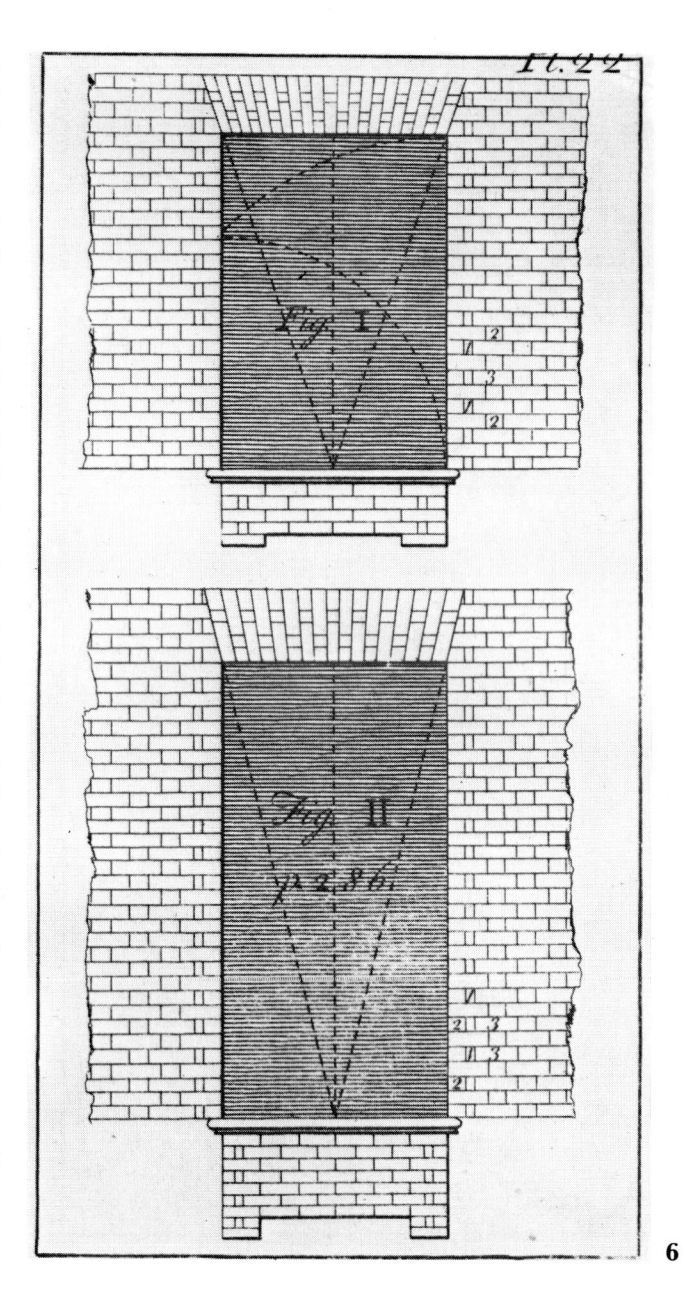

hide the excessively poor quality of the bricks being used. Nor was it only the quality of bricks that was declining in the early 19th century for, according to Peter Nicholson in 1825, so was the composition and use of mortar itself.

The essential nature of gauged brickwork then, was the adaptation by cutting or rubbing, of fine bricks to form part of a decorative design. But this technique could also be used structurally and Batty Langley in his *London Prices of Bricklayers' Materials and Work* of 1748 described, "Plain walling with rubbed and gauged red stock bricks set in putty", as a "kind of walling, when well performed . . . that was above . . . all others the most beautiful and especially when every course is laid with headers . . . To perform this kind of walling in the most substantial manner, the workmen must gauge and rub down the red stock bricks so that every five courses of them shall come level with every four courses of place bricks worked up with them within side".

This header bond described by Langley as beautiful, was of course also more expensive since more bricks and more cutting were necessary. It was used occasionally in London, NO. 13 St. James's Square being an example, and was known as bastard bond since the Bastard Brothers who rebuilt the Forum, Dorset, after the fire of the 1730s had used this header bond exclusively. If the use of header bond was exceptional, so was the use of gauged brick for *entire* façades for it was a rich device capable of producing architectural indigestion. The most effective use that could be made of fine gauged work was to decorate the plain walling that made up the majority of façades during the 18th century. It was during the days of Wren that gauged work had reached the height not only of its quality but its quantity, this popularity declining during the 18th century so that after *circa* 1730 gauged work was principally used in window arches.

Throughout the 18th century the pattern books analysed the cutting and setting up of brick arches in great detail, explaining not only the technical procedures involved, but indicating the changing fashions in window shape. Although throughout the Georgian period preferences moved from straight arches to segmental, back to straight and semi-circular, the basic techniques for cutting the bricks remained the same. The width of the window opening having been decided, the bricklayer would draw the proposed arch full size upon the floor with all the joints marked in and referring to this patterning process, Joseph Moxon suggested in 1703 that the whole piece of geometry be drawn out ". . . upon some smooth floor, or straight plastered wall, or such like. . . ." The bricks were then cut and shaped with the brick axe and rub stone to fit this pattern and when the arch was formed, as regards the shaping of its component parts, it would be fitted into a wooden template. The template containing the arch was then raised into position above the window opening for which the arch was ultimately intended, the template securing the shaped bricks until they were bonded with mortar into the façade. The arch could be executed with various types of qualities of brick and, of course, with varying degrees of skill. Isaac Ware wrote in 1756 of this variety, "The red stocks and the grey are frequently put

Bricklaying.

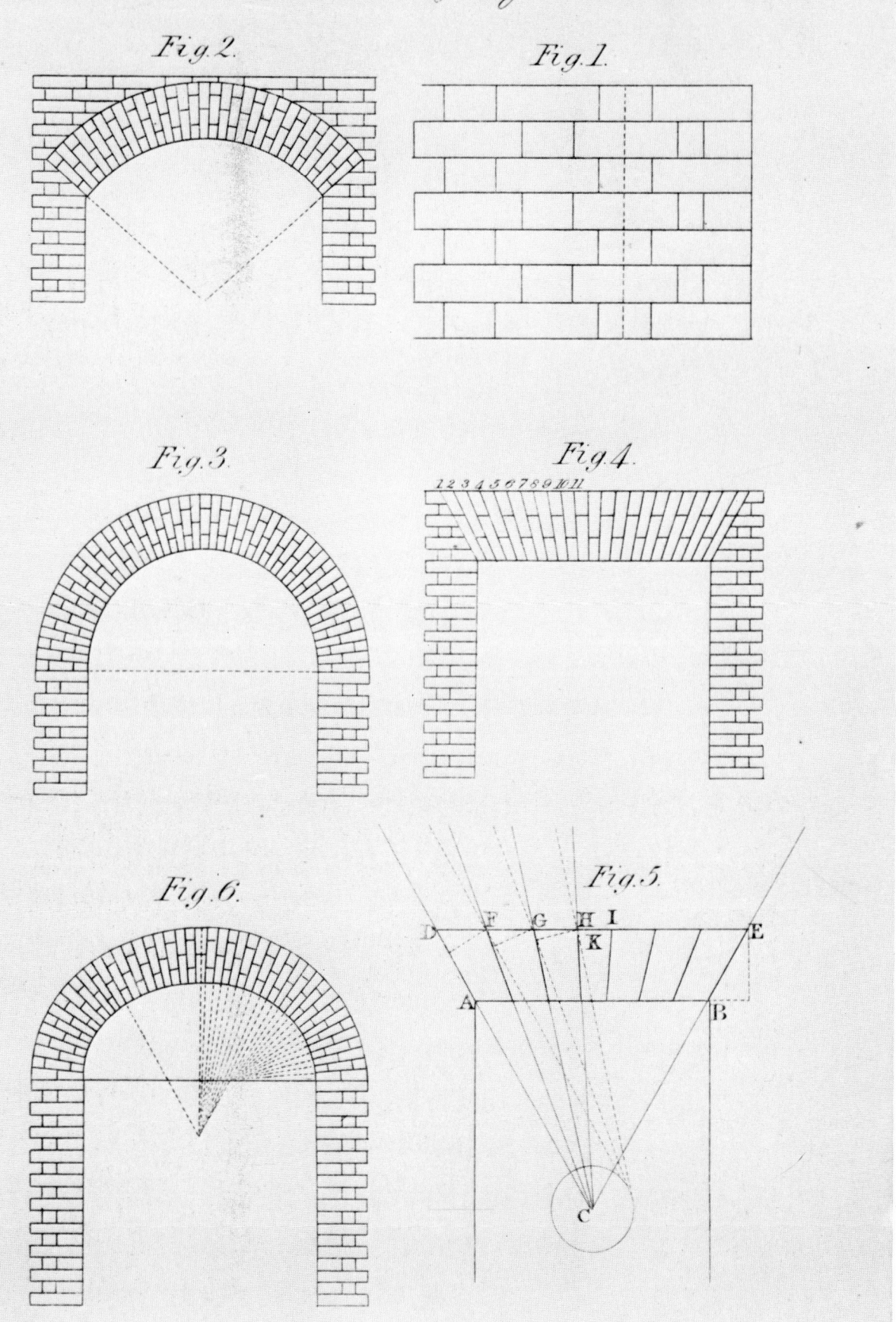

Fig. 2.   Fig. 1.

Fig. 3.   Fig. 4.

Fig. 6.   Fig. 5.

10 Plate from Peter Nicholson's *Mechanic's Companion* of 1823 showing various forms of brick arches. The figures are described as follows: "*Fig. 1* parts of the upright of a wall, at the return, laid with Flemish bond; *Fig. 2* a scheme arch, being two bricks high; *Fig. 3* a semi-circular arch two bricks high; *Fig. 4* a straight arch, which is usually the height of four courses of brickwork: the manner of describing it will be shown in the following figure; *Fig. 5* to draw the joints of a straight arch, let AB be the width of the aperture; describe an equilateral triangle ABC upon this width; describe a circle around the point C equal to the thickness of the brick. Draw DE parallel to AB at a distance equal to the height of the four courses and produce CA and CB to D and E. Lay the straight edge of a rule from C to D, and with a pair of compasses, opened to a distance equal to the thickness of a brick, cross the line DE at F, removing the rule from the points C and D. Place the straight edge against the points C and F, and with the same extent, between the points of the compass across the line DE at G: proceed in this manner until you come to the middle, and as it is usual to have a brick in the centre to key the arch in, if the last distance which we will suppose to be HI is not equally divided by the middle point K of DE the process must be repeated till it is found to be so. Though the middle brick tapers more in the same length than the extreme bricks it is convenient to draw all the bricks with the same mould, which is a great saving of time, and though this is not correctly true, the difference is so trifling as not to affect the practice. It may however be proper to observe, that the real taper of the mould is less than in the middle, but greater than either extreme distance, but even the difference between this is so small, that either may be used, or taking half their difference will come very near the truth. This difference might easily be shown by a trigonometrical calculation, the middle being an isosceles triangle, of which the base and perpendicular are given, the base being a certain part of the top line. In the triangle upon the sides you have one angle equal to 60 degrees, and the side DF is given and DC = $(DK^2 + KC^2)$ one half, can easily be found, so that in this triangle the two sides and the contained angle are given; *Fig. 6* an elliptic arch, the top is divided into equal parts, and not the underside"

11 Carved brick Ionic capital on a house in Took's Court, London EC 4

12 A rubbed red brick cornice and window arch on a house built during the 1730s in White Hart Lane, Tottenham, London N 22. The dentils in the cornice are made from specially cut and moulded bricks

Bricklaying

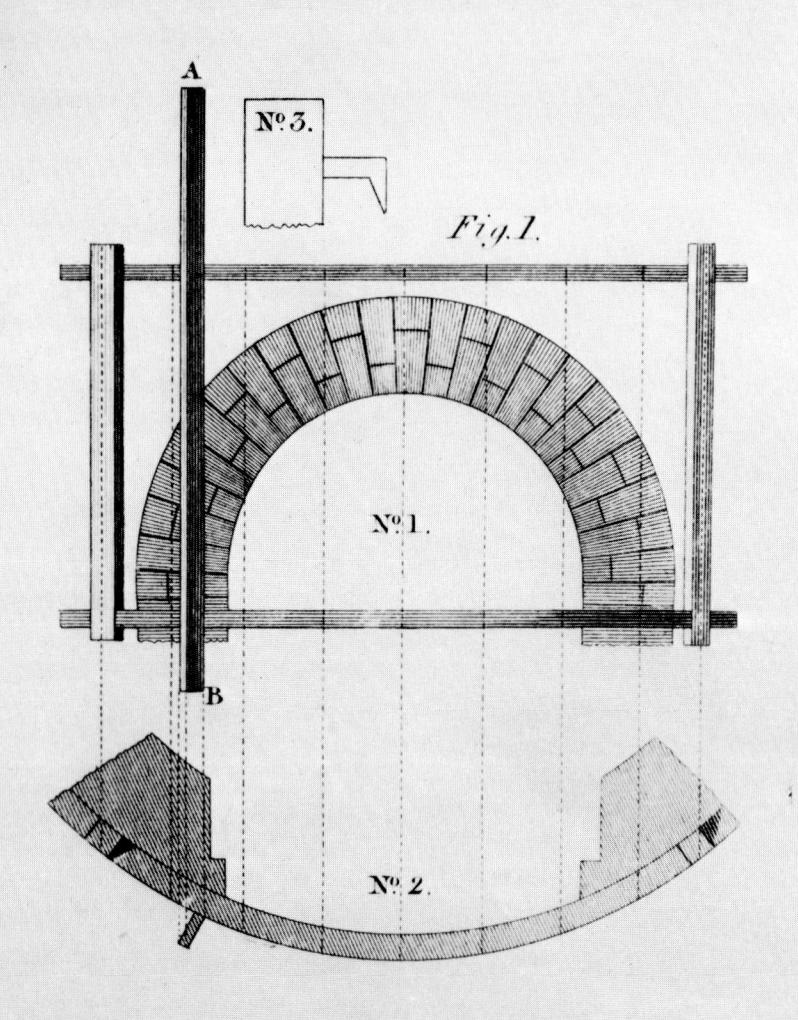

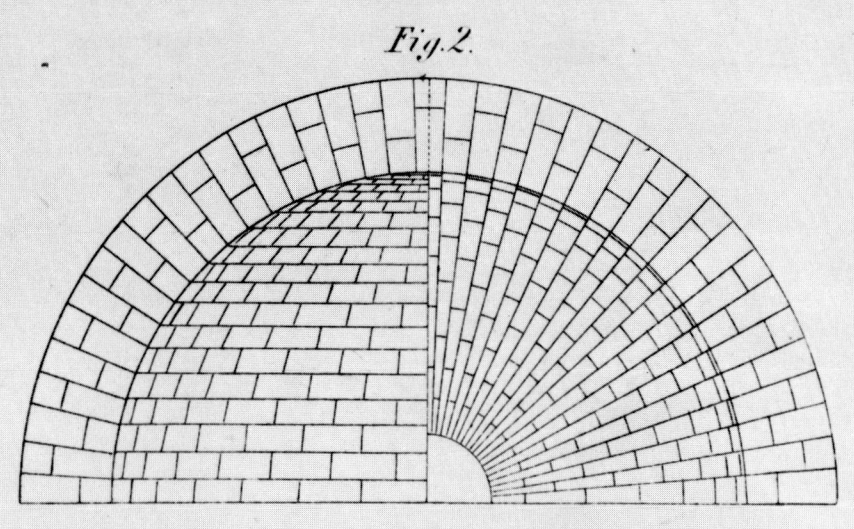

Plate 7

Fig. 1.

Nº 3.
Nº 1.
Nº 2.
A
B

Fig. 2.

in arches gauged—the one as well as the other set in putty instead of mortar... The fine red brick is used in arches rubbed and set in putty in this manner and, as it is much more beautiful, is somewhat more costly."

As to faults, Peter Nicholson presents a pessimistic view of contemporary builders in his *The New and Improved Practical Builder and Workman's Companion* of 1823. "Another great defect is frequently seen in the fronts of houses, in some of the principal ornaments of brickwork, as arches over windows etc, and which is too often by a want of experience in rubbing the bricks... the faults alluded to, are the bulging or convexity in which the faces of arches are often found, after the houses are finished, and sometimes loose in the key or centre bond. The first of these defects, which appears to be caused by too much weight, is, in reality, no more than a fault in the practice of rubbing the bricks too much off on the insides; for it should be a standing maxim: (if you expect them to appear straight under their proper weight) to make them the exact gauge on the inside; that they may bear upon the front edges, by which means their geometrical bearings are united, and all tend to one centre of gravity". Nicholson also adds, as a useful tip, that the proper skew (or angle) for all camber arches ought to be one third of their height.

Arches were, however, not the only decorative features in Georgian building that could best be executed in the finest of rubbers and the carved brick Ionic capitals from Took's Court, City of London (see plate **11**) form such an example. These capitals were made of brick lumps deeply carved like stone, but shallower carvings were simply cut into standard bricks that were built up to make a basic shape. Similarly, the niche illustrated by Peter Nicholson (see plate **13**) also could only be composed of fine rubbers, for, to achieve its effect, absolute accuracy of cutting combined with fineness of jointing was essential. The brick pilaster and columns published by William Halfpenny in his *Art of Sound Building* of 1725 are further examples of decorative features with which the virtuoso bricklayer enhanced many an ambitious façade in the early 18th century (see plate **14**). To achieve the necessary tapering of the column with neatness and to form a contrast with the rest of the façade, these elements had to be constructed of gauged bricks. Halfpenny explains how to work a diminishing pilaster in brick, "First make a diminishing rule to fit the whole side of the column, or pilaster, and if it be large so that a board will not reach the whole length, you must make it several lengths, always observing to keep the rule in its proper place, according to what part of the column it belongs, then begin to work. The example F is the first course, and the example G the second, and these continue perpendicular all of the same bigness to one third part of the height of the whole column, that is, from the base to the course AB, and from thence it diminishes something to the collar of the capital."

As to the trade of bricklaying itself, Richard Neve in his *City and Country Purchaser* of 1703, informs us how hard contemporary craftsmen could work, "A bricklayer and his labourer (having all his materials ready) will lay in a day about 1000 bricks... and some very expeditious fellows will lay 12 or 15 hundred."

And R. Campbell in his *The London Tradesman* of 1747 comments on the fact, and fact it was, that master bricklayers were designing and running up the great mass of mid 18th-century London. He wrote, "Bricklayers, carpenters, etc. all commerce architects: especially in and about London, where there go few rules to the building of a city house... A master bricklayer thinks himself capable to raise a brickhouse without the tuition of an architect: and in Town they generally know the just proportions of doors and windows, the manner of carrying up vents, and the other common articles in a city-house, where the carpenter, by the strength of wood, contributes more to the standing of the house than all the bricklayers labourers".

Bricklaying was, Campbell said, "... a very profitable business, especially if they confine themselves to work for others, and do not launch out into building projects of their own, which frequently ruin them: It is no new thing in London for these master builders to build themselves out of their own houses, and fix themselves in jail with their own materials".

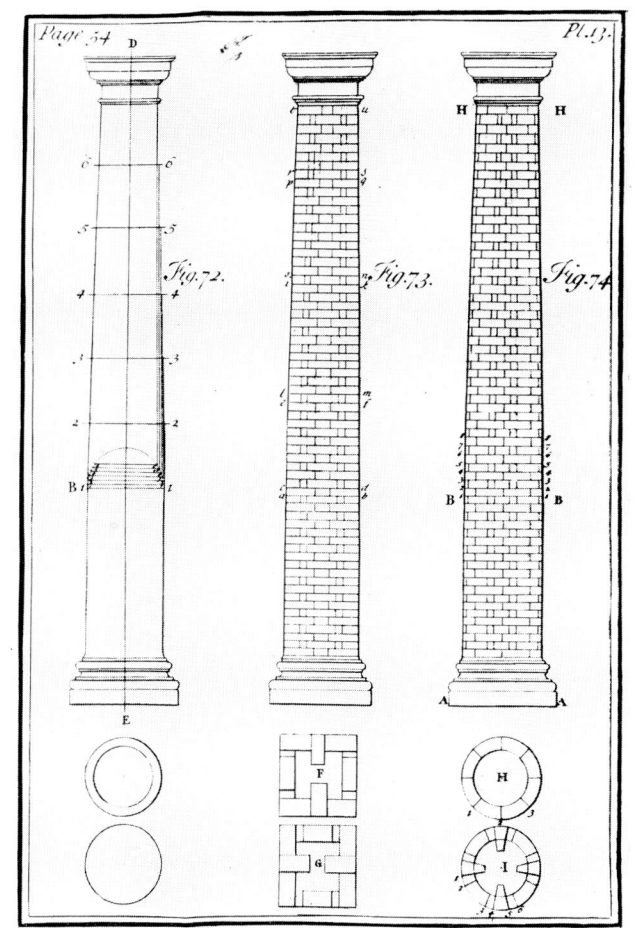

13 Plate from Peter Nicholson's *Mechanic's Companion* of 1825 showing the construction of brick niches

14 Plate from William Halfpenny's *The Art of Sound Building demonstrated in Geometrical Problems* published in 1725, showing the elevation and plan of a brick pilaster and columns. This plate also illustrates a means of calculating the entasis of a column

15 Isometric of a post-1709 Building Act gauged brick segmental arch. The segmental arch was almost universal during the 1720s, and this isometric shows how it was constructed with gauged headers, closers, and stretchers. The standard cutting brick measured a little over 8 inches long by a little over 4 inches wide and, after being rubbed, the arch would consist of units of 8 inches, 4 inches and 2 inches.

The wooden wall plate ran behind the arch, resting on the interior structural pier of place bricks (see page 181) and supporting the floor joists. The arch was merely dropped in front of the wall plate and its splay keyed it into the good facing bricks of the outside skin. Often the arch would be botched and rather than being built to one brick's depth, the headers and closers would be snapped so the arch would only be half a brick deep. A stronger, and more unusual, constructional method than that shown, was to position the wall plate above the arch and then to actually bond the facing arch into a rough brick arch of place bricks springing from the inside structural piers

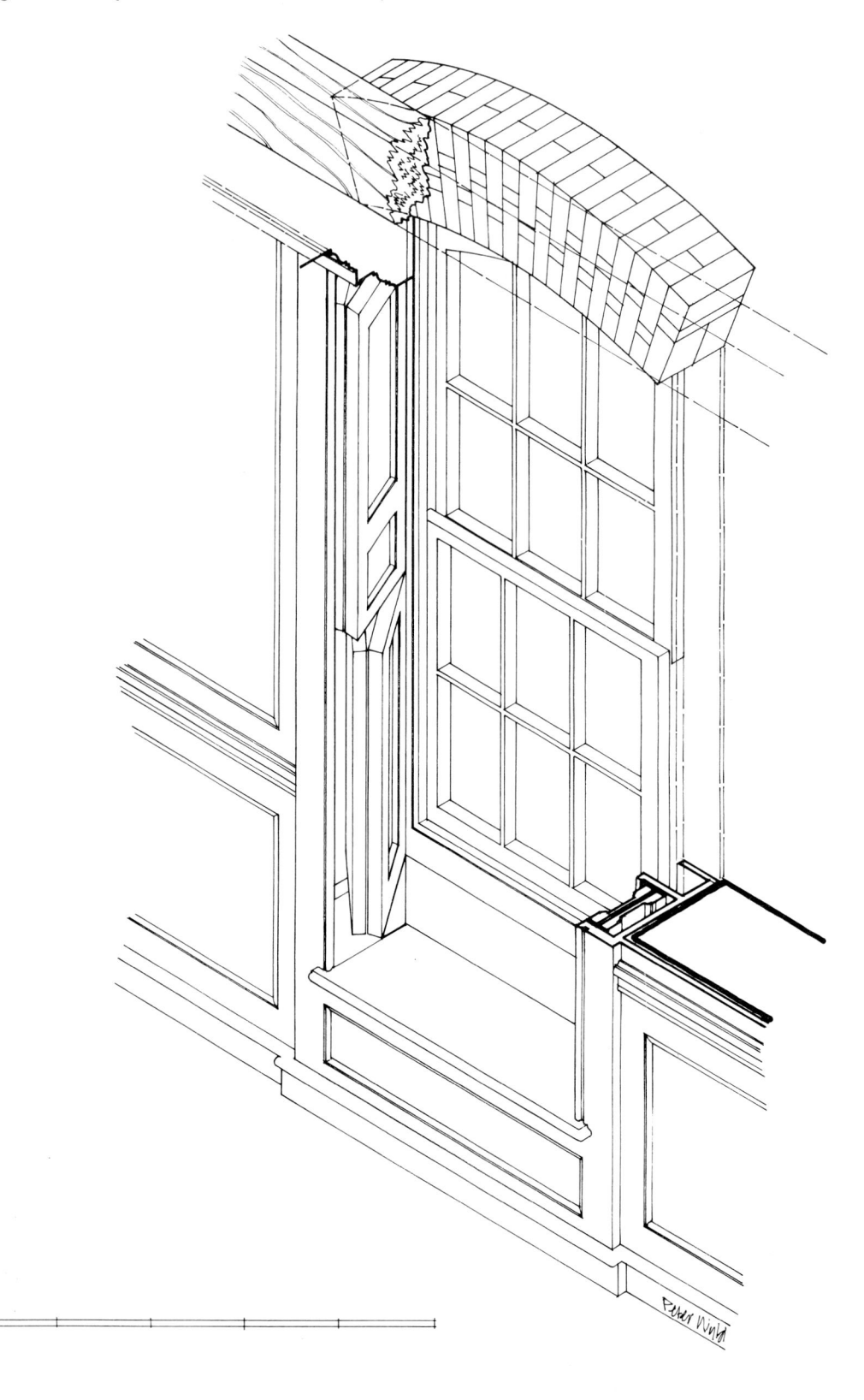

MAJOR STATUTES passed during the Georgian period to control abuses in brickmaking, to enforce the sound construction of brickwork and to provide State revenue from the brick trade
N.B. Dimensions given refer to brick sizes after firing

Date of Statute	Effect of Statute	Remarks
1725	• Place bricks to measure $9 \times 4\frac{1}{2} \times 2\frac{1}{2}$ inches • Stock bricks to measure $9 \times 4\frac{1}{2} \times 2\frac{1}{8}$ inches • Under-fired stock bricks (i.e. usually those from the perimeter of the kiln) no longer to be sold cheaply as place bricks • Brick earth no longer to be mixed with 'Spanish' (i.e. ground sea-coal ashes)	The extra depth on stocks, plus the fact that place bricks were often warped and therefore had to be laid with thick joints, exaggerated the difficulties of house construction. Since place bricks were generally used for the structural piers behind a handsome façade of stocks, the difference in size made it impossible to achieve a regular bond between two brick skins
1729	• Ban on selling under-fired stock bricks as place bricks and mixing 'Spanish' with brick earth lifted • Bricks made within 15 miles of London to measure $8\frac{3}{4} \times 4\frac{1}{8} \times 2\frac{1}{2}$ inches	
1770	• Bricks made within 15 miles of London to measure $8\frac{1}{2} \times 4 \times 2\frac{1}{2}$ inches	
1776	• Bricks throughout England to measure $8\frac{1}{2} \times 4 \times 2\frac{1}{2}$ inches	The wording of this statute gives the following reason for this nationwide control: "Inconveniences have arisen to the public by frauds committed in lessening the size of bricks under their usual proportions without diminution of price"
1784	• Imposition of the first brick tax	This tax was partly levied to offset the expense of the contemporary war with the United States and had two novel results. The tax was levied per 1000 bricks used and since it dealt with quantity rather than individual brick size, the tax was evaded by dramatically increasing brick size to approximately $10 \times 5 \times 3$ inches. The tax was also evaded by the use of Mathematical or rebate tiles, which were exempt from the tax and could be cut and hung on a façade to give the appearance of fine bonded brickwork
1803	• Bricks having a volume greater than 150 cubic inches to be double taxed at 10 shillings per 1000	This statute, which was not repealed until 1850, was intended to counter evasions of the 1784 brick tax. To avoid being double taxed, brick manufacturers started making bricks well below 150 cubic inches, the average size being $9 \times 4\frac{1}{2} \times 3$ inches (or approximately 121 cubic inches)

Stucco

"Stucco, in building, a composition of white marble pulverised and mixed with plaster of lime; and the whole being sifted and wraught with water, is to be used like common plaster." So stucco is described in the 1797 edition of the *Encyclopaedia Britannica* but after this very brief description there then follows a three-page recipe for Mr Higgin's newly patented stucco which was considered good enough for James Wyatt to use at NO. 9 Conduit Street, London W 1, one of the earliest stuccoed houses in London. The method is as follows:

"Drift sand, or quarry . . . let the sand be sifted in streaming clear water . . . Let the sand which thus subsides in the receptacle be washed in clean stream water through a finer sieve . . . Let the lime be chosen which is stone lime, which heats the most in slaking and slakes the quickest when duly watered . . . which dissolves in distilled vinegar, with the least effervescence . . . Let 56 pounds of the aforesaid chosen lime be slaked by gradually sprinkling on it, or especially in the unslaked pieces, the cementing liquor, in a close clean place . . . Let bone ash be prepared in the usual manner, by grinding the whitest burnt bones".

Stucco had a good pedigree. Vitruvius wrote of it as being made of best slaked lime, it was used by Palladio, and Inigo Jones coated several of his buildings with lime mortar, in the early 17th century: his Queen's House, Greenwich was stuccoed by the 1640s, and the building records for the Queen's Chapel, St. James refer to stucco "drawn like ashlar." In 18th- and 19th-century England stucco had two different personalities. In the first place it was simply a tidy way of surfacing a brick or rubble wall and secondly, it was used as part of a sophisticated illusion to disguise brick walls as walls of expensive and fashionable stone. It was in this latter role that stucco rose to fame in England and the supreme example of stage-scenery stucco architecture may be found in John Nash's Regent's Park terraces in which his designs combine with stucco to create the illusion of turning brick terraces into stone palaces.

An early statement on the illusionary qualities of stucco come from Richard Neve's *The City and Country Purchaser* published in 1703: "Caseing of Timber work is a plaistering of a house all over on the outside with mortar; and then striking it (by a ruler) with the corner of a trowel, or the like to make it resemble the joynts of stone". Neve then goes on to give two recipes for his mortar or cement. To make cold cement "for cementing of bricks, for some kinds of mouldings," he suggests one should, "Take half a pound of old Cheshire cheese, peel, grate very small, put into pot. Then a pint of cow's milk, let stand all night. Then get whites of 12 or 14 eggs, then $\frac{1}{2}$lb of best unslaked or quick lime, and beat to powder in a mortar, then, sift it through a fine-hair sieve into mixture, stir well, breaking knots of cheese, then add whites of egg and temper all well together. This cement will be white—add brick dust if brick colour required."
To make hot cement, Neve prescribes,
"1lb of Rozin, $\frac{1}{4}$lb of beeswax, $\frac{1}{2}$oz fine brick dust, $\frac{1}{2}$oz of chalk dust (sift both of these through a fine-hair sieve). Boil all together for about quarter of an hour. Stir and let stand for 4 or 5 minutes—then use."

Robert Campbell in his *The London Tradesman* of 1747 describes briefly the technique of decorating a stucco front: "Mouldings and other ornaments are put upon the fronts of houses, only by laying on plaister to the height of the designed figures; then running a mould of wood over them of the shape of the intended decorations. This is the method in which the Stucco fronts etc. are performed. They appear very agreeable to the eye; and if the workmen does justice in the materials, is not sparing in different thin coats, and the brick work sound upon which it is laid, it may last as long as some soft stone".

As the 18th century progressed, the illusionary character that stucco possessed, the power to turn brick to stone, was increasingly emphasised as civic improvers saw in it the saviour of London's architectural dignity. John Gwynne in his *London and Westminster Improved* wrote in 1766, " . . . no public edifice ought to be built with brick unless it is afterwards stucco'd, for a mere brick face in such buildings always makes a mean appearance . . . As the building with stone is so very expensive in this metropolis, it is to be lamented that encouragement is not given to some ingenious person to find out a stucco or composition resembling stone, and in which exterior ornaments might be easily wraught at a very easy expense." This was very much the feeling of the time, and it was not long before Gwynne's lamentations were answered. In 1763 David Work patented his form of Oil Mastic Stucco, and in 1773 Liadet patented another Stucco mixture, both of which were acquired by the Adam Brothers who renamed the mixture 'Adam's New Invented Patent Stucco'. This version became known as Adam's cement and was used by them in Hanover Square in 1776, Portland Place in the 1780s and by the Bedford Estate in Bedford Square also in the 1780s. In 1783 Nash first used stucco when converting the 17th-century houses in the corner of Bloomsbury Square and although he went bankrupt during this development and retreated to Wales, this work still stands. In 1796 'Parker's Roman Cement' was introduced and capturing the market for a while, it was used by Nash for such developments as Park Crescent in 1812, until he changed to Hamelin's and Dehl's mastic *circa* 1820. Christopher Dehl had patented his mastic in 1815. It was made of linseed oil boiled with litharge and mixed with porcelain clay finely powdered and coloured with ground brick or pottery, turpentine being used as a thinner. 'Hamelin's Cement', patented in 1817, consisted of basically similar ingredients and was used by Nash on his United Services Club, Pall Mall in 1828, and by Decimus Burton for the frieze sculpture of his Atheneum Club in 1829.

To make the illusion complete, the freshly stuccoed surface could be, and often was, frescoed in imitation of weathered stone and following Nash's example, it became the fashion to paint it as Bath Stone, although the real thing had never been a popular building material in London. Of these techniques Peter Nicholson wrote in his *Practical Builder* of 1823: "When the works are finished, they should be frescoed, or coloured, with washes, composed in proportions of five ounces of copperas (sulphate of iron) to every gallon of water . . . Where these sorts of works are executed with judgement, and finished with taste, so as to produce picturesque effects, they are drawn and jointed to imitate well-bonded masonry and the division promiscuously touched with rich tints of umber, and occasionally with vitrial, and, upon these colours mellowing, they will produce the most pleasing and harmonious effect, especially if dashed with judgement, and with the skill of a painter who has profited by watching the playful tints of nature, produced by the effects of time in the mouldering remains of our own ancient buildings."

Roman cement (which Nicholson recommended) mixed with sharp clean grit sand to form stucco plus colouring cost 4s 9d per yard superficial.

Stone

London was a city built of wood and plaster, then a city built of brick. Historically it progressed to a city *almost* built of iron and is now becoming a city built of concrete but it was never a city built of stone for unlike Bath or Edinburgh, London simply did not have any good building stone near at hand. This was a deficiency with which 18th-century London architects were never entirely able to come to terms, because on such occasions when money was available for a prestigious building, they automatically turned to stone as a facing material and the churches of Wren, Gibbs and Hawksmoor and the public buildings of Kent and Chambers are obvious examples. If they could afford it, private citizens too commissioned stone-faced houses, notable examples being 15 St. James' Square by James Stuart and Chandos House by Robert Adam. Neve, in his *City and County Purchaser* of 1703 stoutly advises builders about the general lack of stone in England, "... I would not have English men be disheartened that we do here want those firm and solid stones which nature hath furnished other nations with; but rather to exercise their ingenuity to supply ourselves by art". He then makes it clear that this lack of stone is no excuse for bad building. "T'is not the baseness of our English materials, but want of skill, and deligence in managing them, that makes our English buildings in the least measure inferior to any foreign ones."

If one looks at some of the best brickwork of the early 18th century where all the bricks are rubbed, gauged and finely pointed to make a surface almost as smooth as regular masonry, it is obvious that the workmen did "exercise their ingenuity" to supply themselves by art and when stone was used in London it was, almost without exception, Portland stone. There were attempts to introduduce Bath stone early in the 18th century (Burlington cased his Westminster school dormitory with it in 1722 and Gibbs used it for St. Bartholomew in 1730), but it never caught on and Portland remained supreme, being used for everything from facing the Horse Guards (see plate **10**, page 197) to coping stones and even fireplaces. The first recorded use of Portland stone in London on a large scale is by Inigo Jones who used it in 1615 for part of his Banqueting Hall, but it is to that other ubiquitous architectural inventor, Sir Christopher Wren, that Portland stone owes its sudden monopoly as the fashionable building stone. Not until the 1660s, with the development of the frame-saw and water power, was it possible to quarry large blocks of Portland Stone and when Wren needed large blocks of stone he used Portland Stone almost exclusively for his extensive rebuilding programme in the City of London.

Viewing the buildings of London from above in the mid 18th century one would have seen almost nothing but brick of many various colours, qualities and combinations, tiled roofs and a few of slate and, dotted here and there, white stone-faced churches, public buildings, or mansions. But if one had looked a little harder one would have seen the solid brick areas to be laced in fact with a fine mesh of Portland stone copings, string courses, cornices, quoins, doorcases, urns and keystones (see plates **1** and **2**) for although devoid of stone for structural or facing purposes, London was a city in which its purely decorative qualities were not overlooked.

The decorative use of stone in Georgian London fell into two distinct types: the work of the mason who simply cut stone for such features as coping and quoins and the work of the stone carver who would enrich houses with grotesque keystones, fancy urns, or scrolled consoles for doorcases. The rusticated façade of Kent's Horse Guards gives a good idea of the kind of work the mid 18th-century mason would hope to do (see plate **3**). Rustication, a method of laying stones so that the joints are emphasised, usually by bevelling their surface at a 45° angle, was a classical device much used by Renaissance masters and had, of course, also been used by Inigo Jones. One of the chief aesthetic functions of rustication was to make the ground floor appear to be a sturdy basement forming a visually strong support for the large and usually enriched first-floor windows which formed the *piano nobile*. The use of a rusticated ground floor readily lent itself to terrace houses with high first-floor windows but this did not become the vogue until the late 18th century when it was exclusively executed in stucco. This stucco rustication, or occasionally just plain stucco, on ground floors became a feature of early 19th-century terraces which did much to determine the proportioning of a house built according to classical canons for, by treating the ground floor as a basement, the house could be very tall, without appearing to abandon the classical ideal which based proportioning on the relationship between breadth and height. The principle for proportioning a column was that its height should be determined by the multiplication of its diameter. This principle was also applied to houses but by raising the position of the base of the supposed column up one level so that it stood on a false ground floor on top of the rusticated ground floor proper, the proportioning simply started one storey up.

The form of rustication used on the early 19th-century terrace was often very simplified and one variety, known as banded rustication, consisting only of a horizontal joint was particularly common (see plates **4** and **5**). The texturing of stone was a typically Baroque architectural technique and an example of vermiculated rustication may be seen on Kent's Horse Guards (see plate **3**). If the stone mason was underworked in London the stone carver was hardly employed in external work at all. Nearly all decorative carving was produced in wood but the series of grotesque keystones in Queen Anne's Gate, Westminster of *circa* 1700 shows the kind of work he was capable of (see plates **6–9**).

1 Brick and stone combined in an early 18th-century house in Wanstead

2 Rustic quoins on a gatehouse in Arlington Street, London SW 1

3 Detail from the Horse Guards, Whitehall, London SW 1. William Kent's last building, it was executed after his death by his friend and associate John Vardy between 1750–58

1

2

3

4

5

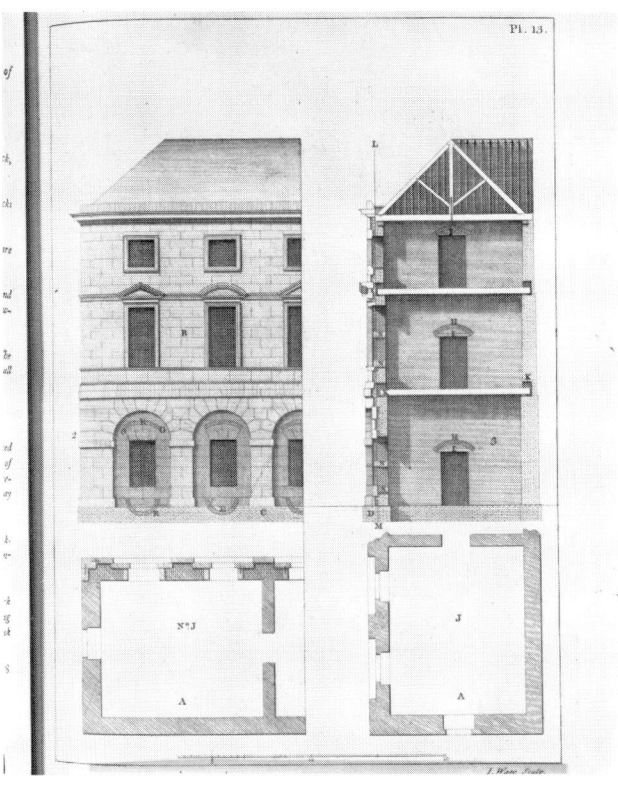

4 Early 19th-century banded rustication produced in stucco on a house in Drummond Street, Euston, London NW I

5 Very bold stuccoed rustication in a house on Commercial Road, Stepney, London E I

6, 7, 8, 9 Keystones with grotesques carved between 1700–05 in Queen Anne's Gate, Westminster, London SW I

10 Detail of the Horse Guards from Isaac Ware's *Complete Body of Architecture* published in 1756, which gives an interesting analysis of the way in which a stone-faced building was put together. The key to the plate is as follows:
"A Ground; B Elevation cased with 9 inch thick ashlar; C, D Foundations of front wall 4½ bricks thick; E Inverted arches under all apertures. Gives strength and stops cracks; F Arches turned over windows behind stone work which, springing from G bond stones, that go through walls, discharge weight from window heads, and prevent the straight stone arches from sinking; H Scheme arches over doors, pine lintels should first be laid. Arches spring from outside and so when timber decays, brick arches will keep their places; I Lintels; K Arches turned over end of all beams in walls so they have air under. Lintels pieces of oak or fir called templates; L, M Perpendicular line of wall. When diminishing, wall must be on each side still perpendicular; N Bond stones which tie the ashlar and keep the brickwork from sinking, which it otherwise would do more than the stone facing for there being so many more joints and those joints so much thicker than in stone, this must sink more, and consequently draw the front out of upright"

197

Coade stone

The history of Coade stone reflects with extraordinary accuracy the changing architectural tastes of the late 18th century as newly acquired, though not fully developed, techniques of mass-productions opened up a promising new world of decorative possibilities. The Coade Company was the first to significantly align the new techniques with the demands of architectural fashion, and the almost immediate popularity of Coade's wares shows just how acceptable the idea of mass-produced decoration was to the highly discriminating public of the late 18th century. From *circa* 1775–1810 Coade's designs were used all over London for all grades of houses and no doubt the Building Act of 1774 helped this dissemination for it put new emphasis on fire prevention and banishing even more wood from the façade, left a decorative vacuum which Coade stone readily filled. The mass-produced wares of the Coade Company were not merely seen as cheap substitutes for hand-made work, but were considered for aesthetic, intellectual, and economic reasons, to be a definite improvement on the more individualistic decorations that had been used earlier in the century. Classical architecture demanded a secure repetition of elements, and mass-production was eminently well suited to the achievement of this decorative goal. Every time the occupier of a house walked through his Coade stone decorated door he could, if inclined, ponder with satisfaction upon the technical achievements of emergent English industry, and the merits of mechanics who were able to produce such suitable, beautiful and relatively cheap decorations.

The history of artificial stone in the Georgian period began in 1722 when Richard Holt and Thomas Ripley filed a patent for the manufacture of, "... a certain compound liquid metal ... by which artificial stone and marble is made by casting or running the metal into moulds of any form or figure ... and which being petrified or vitrified and finished by strong fire became more durable and harder than stone and marble".

Later in the same year Holt took out a second patent, this time with Samuel London, for, "... a certain new composition or mixture (without any sort of clay) for making of white ware ..." and an "... earthenware of more exquisite shape than the present method of turning could ever perform."

To spread his ideas and drum up business, Holt published in 1730 *A Short Treatise on Artificial Stone* in which he commented on the natural weaknesses of real stone and claimed that the Ancients had possessed a secret formula for strong artificial stone. During the 18th century it was a usual ploy to gain respect for any new product or idea by claiming the Ancients as precursors, but Holt went so far as to claim that the pyramids and Stonehenge were really made of a marvellous artificial stone. Holt said he had re-discovered the lost formula and kept it a secret, despite the way his workmen had been questioned by, "... a pretending architect, a meddling busy man ..." who of course turned out to be Batty Langley. Langley, however, must have been merely curious rather than anxious to steal the formula because, even with Holt's claim that he could produce a stone to any strength and make it do anything that could be done with stone, lead, or cast iron, his business did not take off. Holt had not only come up with the idea before the general pattern of architectural taste was ready for it but there also appeared to have been technical problems, or at least aesthetic problems, about the finish of Holt's wares. Daniel Pincot, in his *An Essay on the Origin, Nature, Uses, and Properties of Artificial Stone, Clays, and Burnt Earth in General* published in 1770, put it simply, "Holt's work met with tolerable encouragement for some years till, the projector dying, the whole affair died also." According to Pincot, "Holt's products were durable but without taste," and were, "all covered on one side with an earthen glaze; and some of it is poorly painted with blue ornaments, baskets of flowers etc."

Pincot, after dismissing Holt, stated his own theories about artificial stone and made it clear that he did not believe in a mysterious secret formula. As far as he was concerned no natural clay alone was suitable for producing artificial stone and all varieties needed some strengthening with an artificial clay or grog. By 1767 Pincot had an artificial stone manufactory in Whitechapel, but in 1771, when he exhibited a piece of his work at the Society of Artists, he gave his address as Coade's, Lambeth and beyond this combining of addresses nothing more is known of Pincot's relationship with the Coade Company.

Coade's Lithodipyra, Terra-cotta, or Artificial Stone Manufactory, was opened at Narrow Wall, Lambeth in 1769 and the following year George Coade died. His wife, Eleanor, was then 60 and their daughter, also called Eleanor, was aged 36 and unmarried. She was a modeller in clay, and the fact that the business grew so quickly and successfully is generally attributed to her. Eleanor Coade the elder died in 1796, when her nephew, John Sealy, was taken into partnership and the firm became known as Coade and Sealy. Sealy died in 1813 and another relative, William Croggon, took his place. Eleanor Coade died in 1821, by which time William Croggon had assumed control. After that date the firm gradually became known as Croggon & Company, but many of the moulds were still stamped Coade, presumably because the name retained design *cachet* and as late as 1837 the lion cast for the Red Lion Brewery, Lambeth, still bore the name Coade scratched on his paw. The main ingredients of Coade stone were china clay mixed with finely ground grog. (Grog was prepared from broken Coade stone and was either mixed with or used alternatively with sand.) Analysis of pieces of Coade stone shows that there were other, more subtle additions, which still remain unidentified but it is now impossible to say whether there in fact was a secret ingredient or whether the Coade Company simply encouraged their competitors to think there was.

In 1824 the Coade–Croggon works were visited by a journalist from the *Somerset House Gazette* who wrote that "There was some shyness about the materials of the

1, 2, 3, 4 Keystones in Wimpole Street, London W 1, showing a range of subtly differing Coade stone sea-gods

composition of this artificial stone, but chiefly in the proportions of the ingredients". He records that the articles were first formed roughly in a mould and "... then polished by the chisel while in the soft state, which they endeavour to preserve by wrapping the blocks carefully in wet cloths. In some cases particular enrichments prepared in matrices are added; and in others the whole is nearly the work of the hand". This hand finishing, at least in part explains how the same basic motif, such as the sea-god keystones shown in plates 1–5 could have so many slight variations. Because mass-production techniques were not fully perfected and a strong tradition of individual workmanship still survived, the products of the Coade manufactory formed a transitional stage in design between hand-made one-offs and the now familiar machine-made identical products of contemporary mass-production. The visitor to the Coade manufactory also saw scagliola work in progress in which a facing of artificial marble was applied to artificial stone on a wood frame. Such an article, finished by hand, was then ready for firing but, according to the journalist, if it were large, the figure, after being "... completed in all its parts ... is cut into separate pieces, and is afterwards put together, firmly cemented, and iron rods introduced into the arms and other parts that may require to be strengthened". A description of the firing technique was given by Llewellyn Jewitt in his *The Ceramic Art of Great Britain* published in 1878. There were three sizes of kiln, the largest being 9 feet in diameter and 10 feet high. "Firing was done with Hartly coal; it continued for four days and nights, and the moment the goods were fired up he stopped all openings close without lowering the fire". Such firing was a very tricky operation for, since no thermometer was used, the success of the operation depended entirely on the skill and experience of the fireman.

The test of time has shown that Coade stone could endure weathering, but in the 1770s this was only a claim, and it was certinly not this quality that sold Coade's wares. The almost immediate success of the Coade Company lay instead in the design and versatility of its products and means of production for Coade did not merely supply the newly fashionable Neo-Classical motifs that the public demanded, but introduced motifs and made fashionable innovations. In this respect the Company was very fortunate in having from the start a technically skilled and obviously fashion-conscious sculptor, John Bacon, to produce a wide variety of models and moulds. He could produce copies of famous classical pieces, design one-off pieces in the classical style (carving the stone when soft, before firing was much easier than working in real stone), handle commissions from architects for specific motifs, or supervise the production of standard keystones, urns or imposts. John Bacon served an apprenticeship from 1754–1762 to a Lambeth potter called Crisp and when the Royal Academy was founded in 1768 Bacon entered it as a student and in the same year won a gold medal from the Society of Arts. It was almost certainly due to Bacon's skill and prestige that Coade products won their immediate acceptance by the leading architects of the day. Robert Adam used Coade at the Adelphi in the early 1770s and at Syon House. It was also used by James Wyatt for his own house, and later by John Nash.

The building boom of the late 18th century was checked by the prolonged war with France that began in 1793. With less building, obviously less Coade was used, but the fall off in the use of Coade was not in proportion to the fall off in building. The war and the consequent dissipation of wealth led to a change of fashion in decoration and Coade became something of a luxury with the job being taken over by brick, stucco, cement, or cast iron. The business carried on however, under William Croggon until 1835 when he sold it to Messrs. Routledge, Greenwood, and Keene and although no longer in fashion, the quality of Coade's artificial stone was, in the 1830s, still higher than that of its competitors.

5 Plate from Eleanor Coade's *Etchings of Coade's Artificial Stone*, a sales catalogue published in 1799, showing a selection of popular keystone motifs commonly used throughout London. The small, helmeted female head in the second row was used for example, at Kennington Common (see plate **106**, page 145) while the bearded male head in the bottom right-hand corner was used over many doorways in Bedford Square and Wimpole Street.

Such delightful ornaments as these were fairly expensive additions to a façade. The river god, measuring 2 feet 3 inches at the top and 3 feet 2 inches deep, cost £5 5s 0d, while satyrs measuring 1 foot 6 inches at the top and 1 foot 8 inches in depth cost £2 2s 0d.

Other dimensions and prices were: goat: 1 foot by 1 foot 7 inches £1 10 0d; lion: 1 foot 1¾ inches by 1 foot 5 inches 16s 0d; comic mask: 10 inches by 1 foot 2 inches 15s 0d; female head: 6¾ inches by 8 inches 6s 0d; rustic stones for an arch: 5 inches long by 1 foot 2½ inches wide at the top 5s 0d each; arch jambs 1 foot 5 inches long by 1 foot 2½ inches wide at the top 4s 0d each

Corinthian capitals: 12 inches in diameter at the neck £1 5s 0d and 8 inches in diameter at the neck 18s 0d; fluted and patera decorations 16½ inches high for a frieze 5s 0d per foot; griffen arch ornaments in very low relief 15 inches high 10s 0d per foot; projecting water-leaf mouldings for imposts 7 inches high by 19½ inches long with an 8½ inches return 12s 0d each.

These were, however, among the cheapest items in the Coade catalogue. Amongst the most expensive was a river god with urn, adapted by John Bacon from an etching by William Blake, which measured 9 feet in height and cost £105 (one of these stands in the grounds of Ham House, Richmond)

6 Coade stone decorative panels in relief on a coach house in Camberwell Road, London SE 5

7 Coade stone rustication on a modest house in Lambeth, now demolished. Note also the Coade scallop shell heading the large window

8, 9 Details of vermiculated rustication in Coade stone at Kennington Lane, London SE 11, **9** and the watch house, St. Matthews Church, Bethnal Green, London E 1, **8**

6

7

8

9

201

Wood

Until the early 1600s London had been a city both built of, and decorated with, wood. But during the 17th century, not only because of the changing architectural aesthetic, but the more mundane requirements of fire prevention together with the rapidly dwindling supply of wood, London, began to be built of brick. From 1619 onwards, this transition was enforced in London by various Building Acts to such an extent that by the beginning of the Georgian period, wood was used only for the framing of floors, stairs, and partitions within the brick shell, and for roof trusses, while outside the brick shell of a building wood survived in a limited and controlled way for decoration. Before 1707 such decoration included the carved cornice, but after that date and for the remainder of the century, wood decoration was used primarily for doorways, shop fronts and window sashes.

The different emphasis on the use of wood, depending on whether it was used inside or outside the brick shell, reflects a natural division in the craft of carpentry. Interior woodwork was in the main structural and was framed in the joiner's shop while in the early 18th century at least, that on the exterior, more the product of the artist than the technician, was from the wood carver's bench. The joiner however, was not totally excluded from the façade. He made the frame to which the carver's work was fixed and constructed the sash windows, but the exterior was, until about 1725, quite definitely the realm of the carver who would produce pieces for doorcases, cornices and anything else that was to be enriched or emphasised. During the Baroque period, when architectural taste demanded highly individualised carving, there were many details for the craftsman to enrich.

1 Console, carved in 1709, from the Drapers' Almshouses, Priscilla Road, Bow, London E 3, showing the typical Wren motif of a cherub with folded wings

2 Console with a cherubic head on a house in Richmond Green, Surrey

3 Profile of a console with cherubic head on a doorcase in Albury Street, Deptford, London SE 8. Albury Street was developed between 1709–20 and it is possible that the woodcarvers working on nearby St. Paul's, Deptford who had been trained during Wren's rebuilding programme for the City churches, were employed in this street

4 Consoles from Albury Street, Deptford, London SE 8, decorated with shell motifs

5 The cherub was a common motif in Albury Street, particularly when combined with naval or marine motifs. This console shows cherubs holding charts, sextants, calipers and set-squares

6 Detail from the cherubic naval group shown in plate 5

3

5

4

6

203

Carving
Both branches of the wood-working craft generally used the same woods and so both were influenced by the change that took place *circa* 1700 from the use of English oak, which was fast being devoured by the ship building industry, to the use of imported Baltic pine and fir. Superficially the effect was greater on the carver, for it changed the possibilities of his work and of this situation Isaac Ware wrote in 1756 in his *Complete Body of Architecture*. "Our father's worked in oak, a wood unfavourable to the tool, but which, in their masterly hands, admitted every stroke, and repayed the toil with immortality. We . . . use fir, the weakest, worst, and poorest of all woods . . . and we can give for this but two reasons equally mean . . . these are that it comes cheap, and cuts easy. It will not admit those delicate strokes which have eternalised the chisels of our fathers, nor support itself in those tender parts into which they cut their fine works".

By 1756 wood carving, at least for exterior work, was very little used—except for the occasional Ionic volute and recognising this Ware explained, "It is partly the badness of the work, and partly the destruction of it by frequent colouring, which has put carving so much as it is out of use at present".

The "frequent colouring" refers to the fact that, being a soft wood, fir, unlike oak, had to be regularly painted with white lead to stop it rotting and of course, coat after coat of this thick paint soon obscured any of the finely carved details that fir could hold. After 1700, therefore, the relationship between carved wood and paint was essential, both inside and out and although not necessary from the point of view of preservation, interior woodwork was painted because of the unpleasant anaemic colour and knotty grain of fir.

Isaac Ware saw the deteriorating quality of carving as a reflection of the age generally, which, he said, was, ". . . growing at once frugal and magnificent . . . They are great in their designs, and they content themselves with the poorest execution of them". This falling off in performance had already been marked, a few years before by Robert Campbell in his *The London Tradesman* of 1747. He recognised that, "The taste of carving has of late years prevailed much", but also notes that, "The carving now used is but the outlines of the art; It consists only in some unmeaning scroll, or a bad representation of some fruits and flowers. The Gentry, because it is the mode, will have some kind of carving; but are no judges of the execution of the work: They bargain with the masterbuilder, or architect for something of this kind; he, to make the most of it, employs such hands as can give him a slight flourish for his money; no matter how it is done . . . The taste is now for something light and easy . . . and is likely to continue so till the Gentry acquire a taste themselves".

At the time Campbell was writing, carving had, because of the swing of architectural fashion to Palladianism, ceased to be the major ornament of façades and where wood was used the joiner had taken over as the primary executor, but 25 years earlier, the results of the bargaining Campbell describes in which the builder "employs such hands as can give him a slight flourish for his money" were in fact immensely imaginative and skilled and one of the most impressive qualities of the early 18th-century carver was his ability to produce endless variations upon a theme. The cantilevered doorcase, for example, with its brackets and scrolls, was a standard design into which an enormous variety of motifs and energetic variations were fitted. Each bracket worked on the same structural principle, either cantilevered straight out of the façade or supported on pilasters, but each was a quite individual product of the carver's imagination (see pages 84–89).

7 Cantilevered doorcase with brackets and consoles built between 1725–30 at NOS. 2–4 Fournier Street, Spitalfields, London E 1

8 Detail of a cantilevered doorcase on a house in Hermitage Road, Richmond, Surrey

9 Detail of a carved bracket with lion's head on a house of 1704 in Laurence Poultney Hill, City of London EC 4

10 Detail from the back door of NOS. 2–4 Fournier Street, Spitalfields, London E 1

11 Built during the 1750s, this detail from a doorcase in Walnut Tree Walk, Kennington, London SE 11, suggests the work of a joiner rather than a carver. Its interesting Gothic details invite comparison with Batty Langley's shotgun marriage of classicism and Gothic shown in plate **14**, page 16

8

9

10

11

205

Joinery

The actual practice of joinery, like that of carving, continued in its traditional form as the Georgian period began and the effect of design innovations were relatively slight on wood carvers because all they did, at first, was to substitute classical motifs for vernacular or Gothic forms. The effect of architectural classicism on the joiner was even less for he was, in the early 18th century, still primarily concerned with the joinery of the roofs and guts of houses and only supplied a small amount of decorative joinery to supplement the work of the necessarily more fashion-conscious carver.

As regards façades therefore, the main work of the joiner in the early 18th century was concerned with the construction of window sashes, the panelled door, and the basic frame of the door case, but, despite his minor rôle in decorating the fashionable façade, it was the work of the joiner, just as much as that of the bricklayer, that kept the façade standing. Not only did he frame the joists and beams which formed the binding floors or build the trussed roof which anchored the house together, but he was also responsible for strengthening the foundations, "In works where the foundations is supposed soft, the carpenter drives piles down to support the edifice". Robert Campbell also noted that, "In brickworks he places bearers, where the chief weight of the building lies".

12 Wooden modillioned eaves cornice on a house *circa* 1710 at The Green, Richmond, Surrey

13 Plate from Peter Nicholson's *The New Practical Builder and Workman's Companion* published in 1823 showing the timber joisting of a modest terrace house. A is a girder; *a* a bridging joist; *b* a binding joist; C a wallplate; *d* a trimmer; *e* a joist on landing

NAKED FLOORING

AND LENGTHENING OF BEAMS.

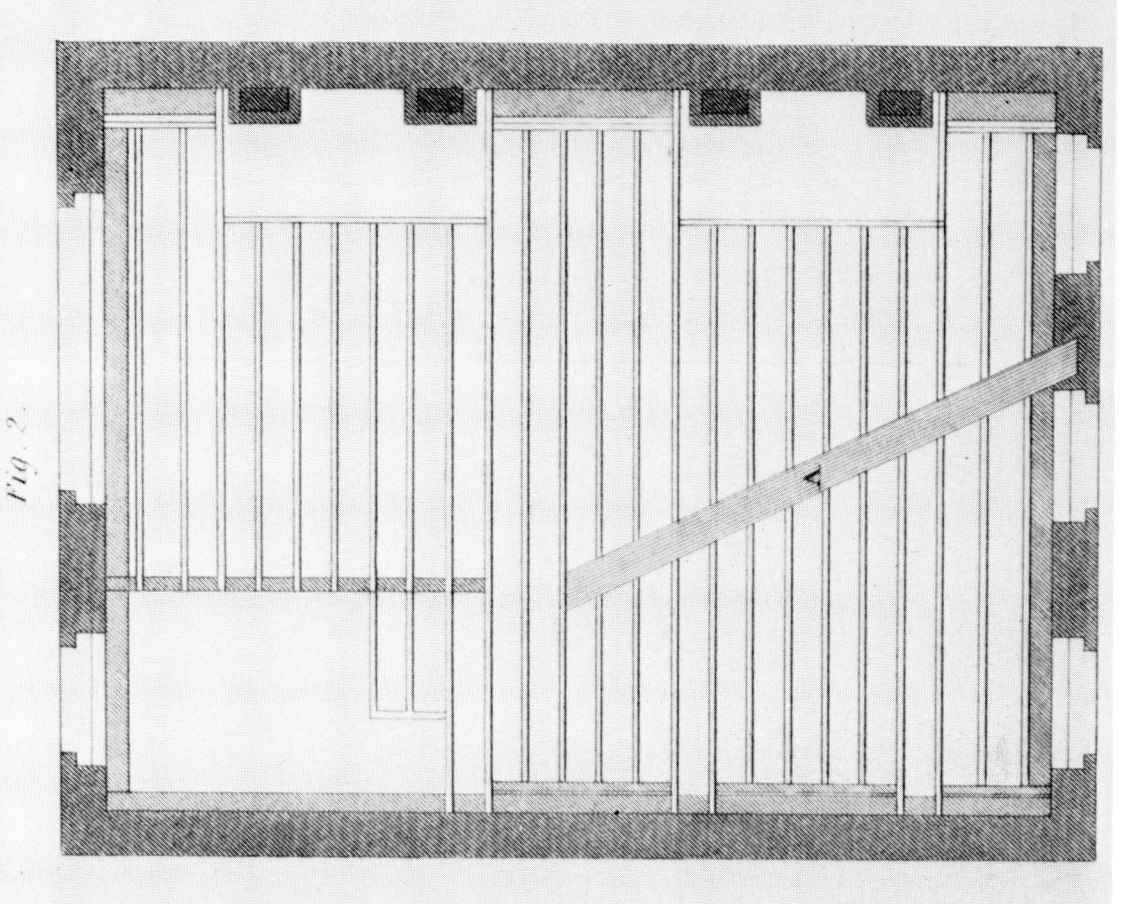

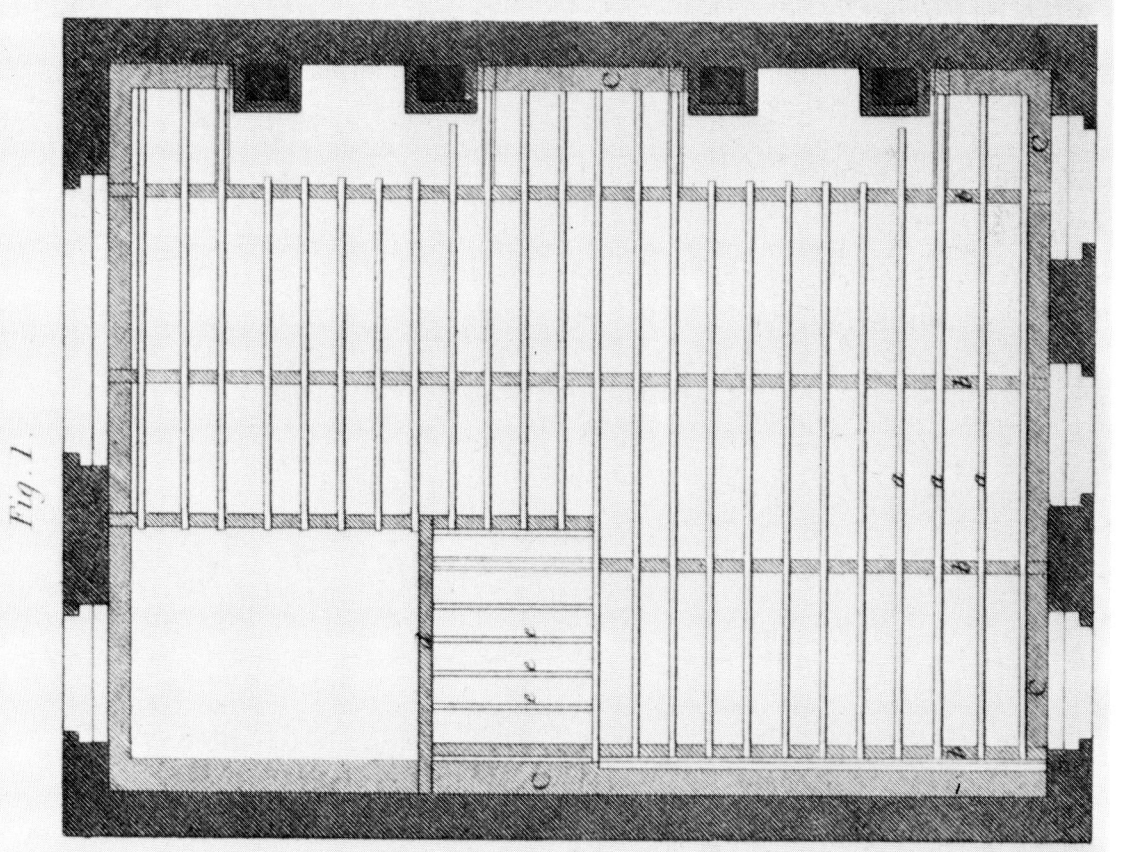

Fig. 1.

Fig. 2.

13

As the 18th century progressed, the wood carver practically became extinct whilst the joiner became increasingly responsible for decoration as well as structure to such an extent that after 1760 all the wood work in the façade came from the joiner's workshop. The most difficult of his jobs was the rendering of classical motifs by joinery, and of these the problem that produced the most ingenious solution was the production of columned doorcases. Such elements as the mouldings of the three parts of the entablature could be run off by machine, the dentils and mutules could be produced in strips and pinned or glued onto the appropriate moulding. Similarly, the pediment could be joined to the cornice and the whole thing pinned to the façade; fluted pilasters were generally made out of a pine plank chiselled with flutes and the panelled soffit around the door was a simple piece of joinery. It was only when it came to the columns with their entasis and curve that the technical repertoire of the joiner was stretched.

In 1756 Ware wrote that, "... the columns may ... be either of solid timber, or of pieces glewed together" and later this became the usual solution, with the columns being built up rather like barrels. Each plank used to form the column, was individually shaped so as to form, when glued together the tapering entasis. The curve of the column was achieved by putting the multi-facetted column into a kind of lathe and cutting the curve out of the thickness of the plank (see plate **15**).

As the century reached its end so did the decorative use of wood on façades. Although it remained supreme for internal construction and finishes, stucco and Coade stone dramatically invaded the exterior to such an extent that by the end of the Georgian period the only wood one could see from the street were the glazing bars of the sashes (and sometimes even these were of brass) and the robust panelled door.

14 The shameful demolition of these houses, built *circa* 1720, in Millman Street, Bloomsbury, London WC 1, reveals the construction of their timber flooring (see plate **13** for comparison). The main beams run from the brick piers between the windows (usually they ran from party wall to party wall) and the joists run from them into wallplates or timmers

15 Plate from Abraham Swan's *A Collection of Designs in Architecture*, published in 1757, showing how the column for a wooden doorcase should be shaped and glued together. If the column was to be fluted it had to be made up either of 8 or 12 parts to avoid flutes occurring over joints and *fig. 6* shows the jointing of an 8-piece column and *fig. 7* that of a 12-piece column.

When it had been decided whether an 8- or 12-piece column was required, each plank was shaped as if for the construction of a barrel, so that when the pieces were joined together the entasis of the column was formed. The sides of the planks were then glued together and strengthened with wedges (*fig. 3*). *Fig. 4* shows an 8-piece column glued up and this multi-planed object was then put on a kind of 'spit' (also *fig. 4*) and turned. The curve of the column was cut out of the thickness of the plank (*fig. 6*) and presumably the flutes were cut out of the column while it was on the same 'spit' by running a gauge along a parallel bar (*fig. 1*). The most difficult part of this operation was to reflect the entasis of the column in the width of the flutes, which necessarily needed to be wider in the middle of the column than at each end

14

fig. 1

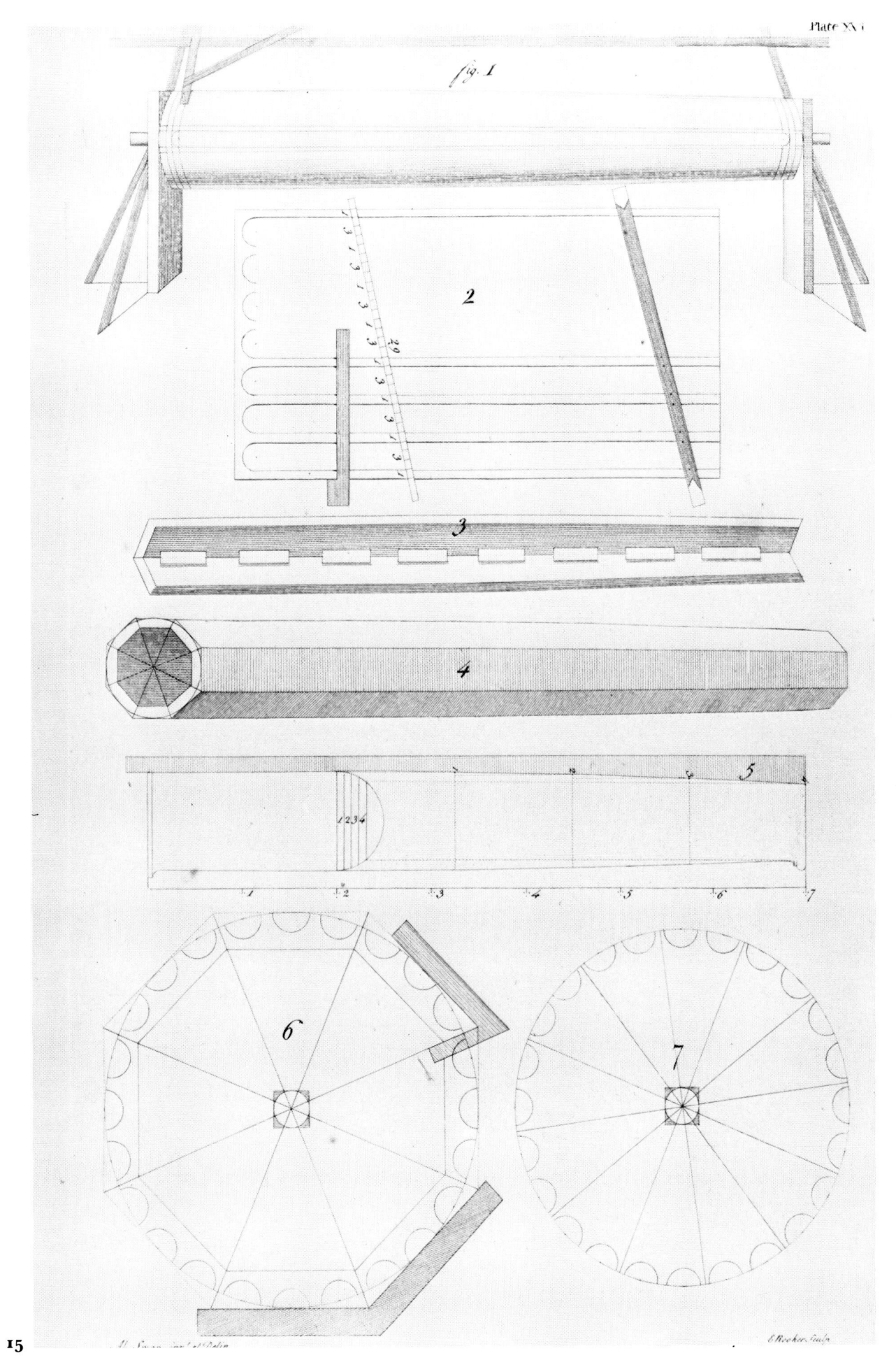

Metalwork

William and Mary were crowned in 1689 and for once in British history there was a significant relationship between the beginning of a reign and the beginning of an aesthetic trend. Although like most European monarchs William and Mary were respectable architectural patrons, they are best remembered for their patronage of metalsmiths and in particular the Huguenot Smith, Jean Tijou. Tijou, whose work included screens at Hampton Court and altar rails for St. Paul's Cathedral, had a great influence on the design of English ironwork in the first quarter of the 18th century and in 1693 as a tribute to his royal patrons he published his *A New Booke of Drawings Invented and Designed by Jean Tijou*. The frontispiece of this publication shows Queen Mary, dressed as Minerva, reclining on a cloud whilst viewing with the assistance of a hammer-clenching Vulcan, an iron panel held up for her inspection by two smiths.

As the 18th century began ironwork moved away from the functional rôle it had occupied, becoming more an element of architectural decoration and enrichment and here the influence of Tijou was great. It became the fashion to lay over the structural grid of iron great beaten and wrought lumps of iron in the form of shields, scrolls and acanthus leaves, etc., hammered into relief from the reverse side. Repoussé, as this form of metalworking was known, made the visual consideration of ironwork very two-dimensional with an interesting back and front, but little possibility of an interesting silhouette. During the first half of the 18th century there was a move away from such expensive and heavy Baroque repoussé work to a more linear type of design in which emphasis was placed on the three-dimensional possibilities of ironwork and its architectural effect in silhouette and this move towards simplicity, typical of all aspects of architecture in the mid 18th century, was instrumental in the development of cast-iron decorative details.

1 Late 18th-century fanlight in Fournier Street, Spitalfields, London E 1

2 Looped fanlight dating from the 1820s at NO. 136 Camberwell New Road, London SE 5

3 Plate from J. Crunden's *The Joiner and Cabinet Maker's Darling* of 1770 showing four designs for Gothic door tops

Cast iron
Cast iron was first used in England in the 16th century in cannon foundries and one of its earliest architectural uses occurred in 1714 when St. Paul's Cathedral was surrounded with cast-iron pallisades which were made at Lambhurst in Sussex and cost £11,000.

Similarly, in 1726 James Gibbs specified cast-iron railings for his church of St. Martin-in-the-Fields. In 1756 Isaac Ware wrote in his *Complete Body of Architecture* "... that cast iron is very serviceable to the builder and a vast expense is saved in many cases by using it; in rails and balusters it makes a rich and massy appearance when it has cost very little, and when wraught iron, much less substantial, would cost a vast sum."

The growth of the cast-iron industry and the emergence of the architectural profession drove the smith into obsolescence in the late 18th century for he was no longer his own man. Patrons were not prepared to pay for his work and architects became increasingly inclined to design or specify all the elements of their buildings. As early as 1728 James Gibbs had published in his *Book of Architecture* his own designs for ironwork details and in his *Ancient Masonry, both in the Theory and in the Practice* of 1736, Batty Langley pretended to do so, although his plates were in fact plagiarised from a German book. But it was the comprehensive approach to design as practiced by the Adam Brothers which reduced the status of the smith to that of just another instructed craftsman. In the late 18th century cast iron was not considered as a tolerable substitute for wrought iron but was genuinely liked. It was cheap and good not 'cheap and nasty' and this 'reasonable' economy was as much in keeping with the spirit of the age as the repetitive nature of cast-iron detail was in keeping with current architectural attitudes. The ability to produce simple, well-designed decorative ironwork by the yard was precisely what was needed for a rapidly growing metropolis in which speculative terraces were being run off by the mile along new radial roads. Even in rich and fashionable developments, such as Bedford Square, Bloomsbury, of 1780, the fruits of mass production were also found to be totally satisfactory. In the late 18th century the essence of classicism was seen not in the vigorous and highly individualistic work of Gibbons, Tijou or Hawksmoor, but rather in an ability to coolly and effortlessly produce perfectly proportioned houses with equally cool and perfect mass-produced details. This became so universally accepted that doubtless the common architect of the 1780s must have found the personal expression put into early 18th-century details not only academically unsound and irrelevant but rather vulgar.

Fanlights
The influence of the Adam Brothers in establishing the acceptance of cast iron and the mass production of architectural details is expressed in the development of the fan light, for originally having been made of wrought iron, lead or wood, it was an obvious subject for 'improved' methods of mass production. Some of the Adams' early fanlights were composite metal designs using cast and wrought iron, copper and brass together, but as the pace of speculative building quickened they found it necessary to mass produce and began designing fanlights in cast iron (John Adam was in fact a partner in the Carron Iron Foundry). Their designs were excellent and the Adams developed the London fanlight to its most huge and showy form. After the Adams ceased designing, the cast iron fan light went on under the impetus they had given it and by the 1820s this architectural detail had been reduced to a pretty and repetitive series of mass-produced loops and segments of loops.

Balconies
Elaborately designed iron balconies first began to appear in England in the mid 17th century and Jean Tijou is thought to have been responsible for the fashion. Certainly, if balconies were required, it was considered preferable to construct them out of iron and Le Clerc remarked in his *Treatise on Architecture* of 1732, "... balconies of iron will do as much better than those of stone, as being lighter and less subject to decay".

The Adam Brothers designed some balconies for their Adelphi development of the 1760s in wrought iron, but, as with fanlights, they very soon switched to designing them in cast iron.

The balcony was a truly characteristic feature of early 19th-century terrace houses and very accurately reflects the power of early 19th-century mass-production and sales techniques for the same designs are to be found stretching across the first floor of terraces from one end of England to the other. The plates from L. N. Cottingham's *Smith and Founder's Director* of 1824 show some of the standard designs (see plates **10, 11, 22**).

4 Heavy cast-iron balcony with anthemion motifs at NO. 7 Adam Street, Adelphi, built by Robert Adam between 1769–72

5 An example of a basic balcony at NO. 24 Queen Anne's Gate, Westminster, London SW 1. Built during the 1770s this design appears to be a combination of cast and wrought iron

6, 7 Two delicate examples of cast-iron balconies at NOS. 21 and 27 Manchester Street, London W 1. Note also the rustication technique and the Coade stone keystones and imposts

8 The anthemion leaf motif of this cast-iron balcony at NO. 23 Mornington Crescent, London NW 1, was the most commonly used pattern for early 19th-century cast-iron balconies throughout England

9 An attractive spider's web effect in an early 19th-century cast-iron balcony at NO. 35 Mornington Crescent, London NW 1

6

7

8

9

213

10, 11 A virtuoso display of patterns for cast-iron balconies from L. N. Cottingham's *The Smith and Founder's Director* published in 1824. The pattern for the anthemion leaf balcony shown in plate **8** may be seen in the bottom right-hand corner of plate **10**

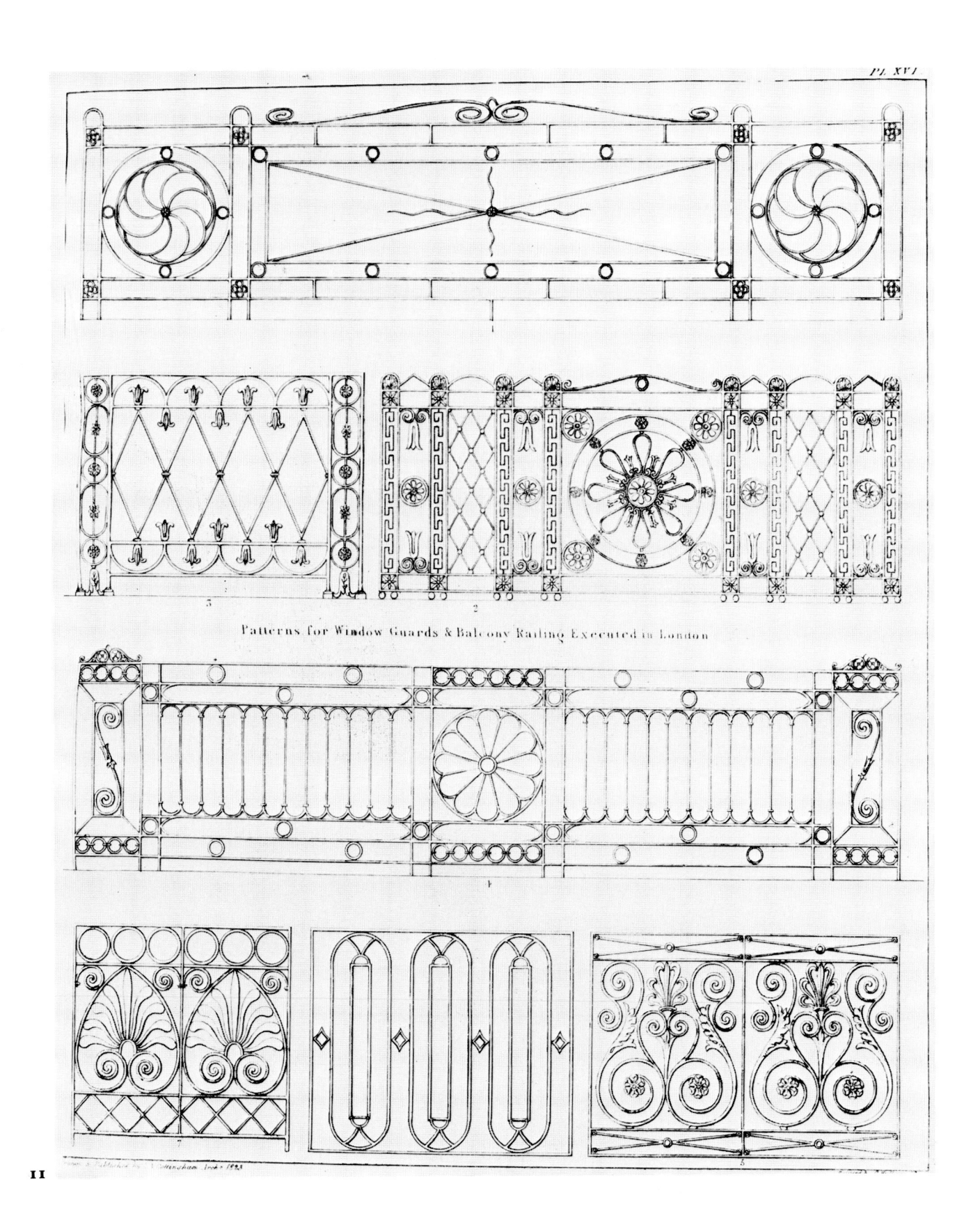

Patterns for Window Guards & Balcony Railing Executed in London

Railings
Very early in the 18th century the cast iron industry provided miles of railings and thousands of spearheads, halberds, pineapples, acorns, and urns to fence off the 'moats' in front of London terraces from the pedestrian and thief. The appearance of these pallisades was noted by Heinrich Meisler of Zurich in 1792, "The English have indeed more reasons than one for calling their houses their castles. If the areas immediately before their houses require a defence of this kind, the sight of a number of heavy black iron bars is not less offensive. During the riots occasioned by Lord George Gordon's mad flights, the mob put these bars to a very cruel use. But there is no necessity of recurring to that perilous crisis to discover that this practice of setting up iron rails have a dull, clumsy appearance; perhaps gilding might make them more lovely, or painting them of a gayer colour".

12, 13, 14 Details of finials from area ironwork showing a variety of designs from thistles to urns. The examples in plates **12** and **13** date from 1725 in Fournier Street, Spitalfields. The example in plate **14** belongs to Bedford Square, London WC 1 and dates from 1775

15, 16, 17 Details of area ironwork in Tavistock Place, London WC 1, developed by James Burton in 1810, showing the variety of motifs introduced by a builder in one terrace

18 A perfect acorn on the early 19th-century area ironwork of a house in Mecklenburgh Square, London WC 1

19 Truly Greek finials of *circa* 1830 on area ironwork in Woburn Square, London WC 1

20 An urn finial on early 19th-century area ironwork in Britton Street, Clerkenwell, London EC 1

217

21

21 A cast-iron lampholder designed by Robert Adam for Fitzroy Square, London W 1

22 Plate from L. N. Cottingham's *The Smith and Founder's Director* published in 1824, showing a series of patterns for cast-iron lampholders

23 Detail of an early 19th-century cast-iron decorated pallisade at Ham, Surrey

24 Lead rainhead from a warehouse in Wapping, London E 1, built in 1804

Glass

Many types of glass were used by glaziers during the Georgian period and Richard Neve in his *City and Country Purchaser* of 1703 names seven as commonly used: "Crown Glass, Normandy Glass, German Glass, Dutch Glass, Newcastle Glass, Staffordshire Glass and Bristol Glass". Of these crown glass was by far the most widely used and Neve subdivides it into two varieties, Ratcliff and Lambeth. "Ratcliff is the best and dearest sort of crown glass which sort was first made at the Bear Garden in the Bankside". He describes Ratcliff glass as being of a "light blue colour" and "sold at 9d per square foot in London", whilst Lambeth he describes as "inclined towards green and sold at 8d per square foot". A great deal of good-quality crown glass was also made on Tyneside, particularly at Newcastle, and Neve writes of it, "Newcastle glass is most in use here in England, but it is subject to have specks and blemishes, and streaks in it, and is very often warped crooked".

To make crown glass the glazier would blow molten glass into a bubble at the end of a long tube and he would then spin the bubble with one hand and with the other beat the bubble into a disc about 4 feet in diameter. This sheet, or table, of glass would then be cut up into panes. Tables were thicker towards the central 'bull's eye' where the tube and bubble had been joined and although considered picturesque today, in the 18th century this deformity was either thrown away or used to glaze an unimportant attic or workshop. The varying thickness of the glass, plus the concentric circles formed by the spinning, gave crown glass its characteristic reflective quality and sparkle and since it came into contact with no other material during manufacture, it retained its fine finished lustre.

William Salmon in his *Palladio Londinensis: or, The London Art of Building* of 1734 gives some prices for crown glazing, "Sashes glazed with Crown glass, puttied on both sides, and brads included, from 12d to 14d per foot; Ditto., with Newcastle glass at 7d or 8d per foot. Ditto. with waned or jealous glass at 2s 6d per foot". Salmon then quotes an advertisement from the *London Evening Post* of June 27th, 1732, "Thomas Lovett, glazier, at the Green Lamp in Red-Lion Street, Holborn, sells the best Crown Glass for forty shillings the half case, likewise the same proportions by the single table, and those that have a mind to have it cut to any dimensions for 7d per foot; and for the second sort of Crown Glass for 6d per foot; also wainscat sashes 1 inch and a half thick, ready glazed, for 1s per foot, to any dimensions".

Jealous glass was described by Neve as, "... a sort of wrinkled glass of such a quality, that one cannot distinctly see what is done in the other side of it ... This sort of glass is commonly used, in and about London, to put into the lower lights of sash windows etc. where the windows are low against the street, to prevent people seeing what is done in the rooms as they pass by."

There was however an earlier form of manufactured glass than crown known as cylinder glass. In this process, as the name implies, a cylinder, or muff of glass was blown and then split lengthwise and as the glass cooled, it was unrolled to form a flat plate. This glass was cheaper than crown but, due to its inferiority, its manufacture practically ceased by the mid 18th century. Towards the end of the 18th century a third type of glass appeared. A French invention, it was the thing of the future—plate glass—and was first made in England at Ravenford, St. Helens, Lancashire, in 1773. This type of glass could be made as a cylinder or as a casting but its importance lay in its thickness which meant that the plates could be ground and polished to remove all flaws. Early plate glass remained too expensive for too long for it to play a significant part in window design during the Georgian period and it was not until 1838 that a thinner and cheaper form of plate glass, called sheet glass, was introduced. Peter Nicholson, in his *Practical Builder* of 1823 confirms that the "... glazier now uses chiefly what is called Crown Glass" but also admits that plate glass "... is the most beautiful glass made ... being nearly colourless, and sufficiently thick to admit being polished in the highest degree".

To turn from glass to the glazier himself, it must be said that unlike the other building trades, the glazier was very much a middleman. He simply bought sheets of glass from a manufacturer or wholesaler, cut them and puttied them into the glazing bars which had been run off by the joiner. Consequently, he could neither command high wages nor much respect. In his *The London Tradesman, being a compendious view of all the trades, professions, arts, both liberal and mechanic, now practised in the cities of London and Westminster* of 1747, R. Campbell wrote of glaziers, "He buys the glass from the glass house in chests and his profits arise from the difference between the buying and selling price. This brand of Mechanics requires neither great strength, nor much ingenuity, and it is, in fact, but a poor business."

Glass was taxed in 1740 and the Act was not repealed until 1845. There was no reaction comparable to the blocking up of windows when the window tax was introduced in 1696: glass was essential and payment of the tax was unavoidable.

Paint

"Painting, if not the chief, is as necessary a Part of Building as any other whatever, both for Use and Ornament, the doing of which well and often being the surest way of preserving all the rest, instances of which may be seen in several Buildings, about London, where the Misfortunes of the Builders have prevented them from finishing their Works, it may be observed that the Sash-Frames, Sashes, Window-Shutters, Doors, and Door-Cases, for want of Painting, in a very few Years, are so much decayed, that were those Buildings to be made tenantable most of the outside Timber-Work must be renewed; Iron-Work, tho' of a much stronger nature than timber, if not well secured by Painting, is likewise subject to the same misfortune". Thus wrote William Salmon in his *Palladio Londinensis* of 1734 and in doing so he points out the two functions of external paintwork during the Georgian period: those of decoration and preservation.

From the beginning of the 18th century traditional oak was replaced, in both structural and decorative work, by the cheaper softwoods then being imported from Scandinavia of which pine and fir, both known as deal, were the most common types. The introduction of this foreign wood brought about a revolution in domestic wood decoration. Being softer than oak, deal was easier to carve, but it was also less able to hold deep carving without splitting and these properties coupled with its vulnerability to the weather led to a form of simpler and painted external wood decoration. Deep wood carving could be, and was, attempted with softwood, but it had to be so heavily and regularly painted that the quality of the carving was soon lost under inches of lead paint. However, even if these newly introduced softwoods had not possessed this tendency to decay quickly, 18th-century taste would still not have allowed softwoods to remain naked for their knotty and anaemic surface was not at all in keeping with the robust dignity then required of English classical architecture. Only oak, because of its traditional prestige and the fact that exposed oak hardens with weathering, was sometimes suffered to remain in its natural state.

The major ingredient of all protective paint during the Georgian period was white lead and in the plain white paint which was the most commonly used colour for external woodwork throughout the 18th century white lead, according to Peter Nicholson, was used neat. He also explained that white lead was "used in all stone colours", and that, "... all fancy colours have a portion of white lead in their compositions; but chocolate, black, brown ... have no portion whatever." Presumably, therefore, one of the major reasons for white being the most common colour for external woodwork was that it contained most white lead and therefore gave the maximum protection. Nicholson also explains how white lead was obtained. Sheets of lead were rolled into coils with ½ inch gaps and placed vertically in earthen pots with vinegar and the pots were then moderately heated so that the vapour of the vinegar corroded the lead. When the coils of lead were taken out of the pots they were beaten and the flakes of lead which fell off were then bleached, ground, and saturated with linseed oil to form white lead paint. This mixture had to mature for two or three years before use.

The method of applying lead-based paints to timber is also explained by Nicholson. It was recommended that the primer should be made of a little red lead mixed with linseed oil while the second coat was a mixture of white lead, a small portion of red, linseed oil and a little spirit of turpentine. This coat was left for some days before being rubbed down with fine sandpaper by which time cracks were filled with old putty if necessary and knots disguised with silver leaf and japan gold size. Problem knots were 'killed' by the use of lime, turpentine, and a scraper. The third coat consisted of white lead mixed with linseed and turpentine in equal parts, while the fourth coat was of old white lead thinned with bleached linseed and turpentine in proportions of 1:2. This procedure varied slightly for the treatment of stucco. Here the fourth coat consisted of half white lead and half turpentine and linseed and in the treatment of stucco a fifth coat consisting of turpentine and flatting was also thought to be necessary.

PART IV AXONOMETRIC SUMMARY

So far *London: the Art of Georgian Building* has examined the 18th-century house as a series of isolated elements. This axonometric of a pair of houses in Rugby Street, London WC 1, built during the 1720s, brings together all the elements mentioned earlier and shows how they related and determined each other's form and design.

Door. The doors are built to a typical early 18th-century pattern (see plate **7**, page 88) and are made of painted pine with carved decorations

Window. Although constructed during the 1720s the windows in these two houses are still of the pattern made illegal by the 1709 Building Act (see page 162). The boxes are exposed and are set flush with the façade

Roof. The roof is of a constructional type common throughout the Georgian period (see page 168). It is of a low double pitch to prevent it from being seen from ground-level and disturbing the symmetry of the façade. A king post links the tie beam to the ridge pole and to a collar beam. A gutter, taking water from the parapet gutter, through the valley gutter and then down a pipe on the rear elevation runs through the roof. The drawing shows the roof clad in slate although originally it would have been tiled

Brick. The façade is constructed to the wall-thickness and building-height regulations laid down in the 1667 Building Act (see page 22). It is constructed in two skins with a facing skin of good bricks randomly bonded into a load-bearing skin of cheaper place bricks. The wall thickens out below the water table and its foundations are merely corbelled-out 'feet'.

Decoratively, the façade is typical of the 1720s. The stock bricks are purplish-brown with red brick dressings around the windows and forming the quoins. The window arches are constructed of finely cut and rubbed red bricks. Although the near house has straight arches, the segmental arches displayed by the other were more common during the 1720s

Stone. In London little stone was used in speculative domestic building during the Georgian period. In these houses the only visible stone is that forming the coping of the parapet, the window cills and the blocks into which the area railings are set

Stucco. This material was not used generally before the late 18th-century (see page 192). However, the basement walls are rendered

Coade. Coade stone does not appear on this pair of houses.

It was not manufactured until the late 18th century (see page 198) and none of the earlier artificial stones were in use before that period

Wood. Apart from the front, rear and party walls, a typical house of the 1720s was entirely constructed of wood (even the walls contain a good deal of wood in the form of wall-plates and bonding-timbers).

Here we see the main beam running from party wall to party wall, (with the framing for the partitions between the front and back rooms standing on it.) Running from this main beam to the wall-plates in the façades, are the joists and over these are laid the floor boards. In the hall is a run of panelling with a good box cornice

Metal. Until the late 18th century, when balconies and verandas became the fashion, the only large use of metal in buildings was for the creation of area railings, and fanlights. Railings were made of cast iron (see page 211) while fanlights were either cast or consisted of a co-ordination of cast and wrought iron. Faltering façades were generally tied together with metal rods and, of course, external pipes, gutters, and rain-water heads were made of lead

Glass. When originally built, these houses would have been glazed with crown glass (see page 220)

Paint. In the early 18th century oak was becoming very expensive and soft woods, which were imported from Scandinavia, were becoming cheaper. Consequently, for both decorative and structural uses, soft wood was taking over (see page 221). Soft wood, unlike oak, needs protection when exposed to the elements and all external wood-work was covered with lead-based paint. Internal decorative soft wood was also painted, for its grained, knotty, and anaemic surface was unsightly to the 18th-century eye.

The door cases and sashes in these houses were very likely painted with white paint which contained the highest proportion of lead

223

Map to show the extent of London at the end of the Georgian period

Regents Canal
HAGGERSTONE
Bishop Bonners Hall
Charter House
S.Pauls
CHEAPSIDE
CORNHILL
LEADENHALL STREET
WHITECHAPEL ROAD
COMMERCIAL ROAD
LONDON DOCK
New Dock
Grand Surrey Inner Dock
BOROUGH ROAD
KENT ROAD
Bermondsey Spa
Seven Islands
Claremont Pl.
Seven Houses
Manor Row
Scale of One Mile
0 1 2 3 4 5 6 7 8
Boun.y of the City of London
Bou.y of the City of Westminster
d.o d.o Boro' of Southwark
Boundary of the New Boro's

BIBLIOGRAPHY

For convenience of reference this bibliography is divided into the following categories:
1 Architectural pattern books, treatises and records of Grand Tours pertaining to speculative building in Georgian London
2 History and topography of London
3 General

1 *Architectural pattern books, treatises and records of Grand Tours pertaining to speculative building in Georgian London*

Adam, Robert *Ruins of the Palace of the Emperor Diocletian, at Spalatro, in Dalmatia* The Author: London 1764

Adam, Robert and James *The Works in Architecture of Robert and James Adam*, 3 vols. J. Tiranti & Co.: London 1931

Alberti, Leon Battista *L'Architettura . . . Tradotta in lingua Fiorentina da Cosimo Bartoli . . . Con la aggiunta de disegni at alti diversi trattati del medesimo auttore*, (*La Pittura tradotta per M. Lodovico Domenichi*). L. Torrentino: Monte Regale 1565
Ten Books on Architecture by Leone Battista Translated into Italian by Cosimo Bartoli, and into English by James Leoni . . . Edited by Joseph Rykovert. A reprint of The Ten Books of Architecture from the 1755 edition, with the addition of the Life from the 1739 edition. Alec Tiranti: London 1955

Barozzi, Giacomo, called Il Vignola *Regola delli cinque ordini d'architettura* G. Porro: Venetia 1596 further editions, 1607, 1617, 1620, 1635, 1795, 1805, 1806, 1811 etc.

Campbell, Colin *Vitruvius Britannicus, or the British Architect, containing the plans, elevations, and sections of the regular buildings, both publik and private, in Great Britain, with variety of new designs, in . . . . . large folio plates (with explanations)*. The Author: London 1717–25

Campbell, R. Esq. of London *The London Tradesman, being a compendious view of all the trades, professions, arts, both liberal and mechanic, now practiced in the cities of London and Westminster.* J. Gardner: London 1747

Chambers, Sir William *A Treatise on the Decorative Part of Civil Architecture (in which the principles of that art are laid down). Illustrated by fifty original, and three additional plates, engraved by old Rooker, old Foudninier (sic) Charles Grignion and other eminent hands . . . The third edition, considerably augmented.* Joseph Smeeton: London 1791
Designs of Chinese Buildings, Furniture, Dresses, Machines and Utensils, Engraved by the best hands, from the originals drawn in China . . . To which is annexed a description of their temples, houses, gardens, etc. Published for the Author: London 1757

Coade, Eleanor *A Descriptive Catalogue of Coade's Artificial Stone Manufactory . . . With prices affixed* London 1848 (*Etchings of Coades's Artificial Stone Manufacture, Narrow Wall, Lambeth, published for private circulation under the superintendence of John Bacon?*) (London 1777–79) The title is from a MS note in the British Museum

Cottingham, Lewis Nockalls *The Smith and Founders' Director. Containing a series of Designs and Patterns for Ornamental Iron and Brass Works.* L. N. Cottingham: London 1824

Crunden, John *Convenient and Ornamental Architecture, consisting of Original Designs . . . The whole . . . engraved on seventy copper-plates, by Isaac Taylor.* Printed for the Author: London 1770.
The Joyner and Cabinet-maker's Darling, or Pocket Director. Containing sixty Different designs, entirely new and useful . . . the whole designed and engraved by J. Crunden. A. Webley: London 1770

Elsam, Richard *The Practical Builder's Perpetual Price-book* London 1825

Entick, John *A New and Accurate History and Survey of London, Westminster, Southwark and Places adjacent, etc.* 4 vols., London 1766

Gibbs, James *A Book of Architecture, containing Designs of Buildings and Ornaments.* London 1728

Gwynne, John *London and Westminster Improved, illustrated by Plans, to which is prefixed a Discourse on Public Magnificence, with Observations on the state of Arts and Artists in this Kingdom* (With a dedication by Samuel Johnson). London 1766

Halfpenny, William *The Art of Sound Building demonstrated in Geometrical Problems shewing Geometrical Lines for all kinds of arches, niches, groins and twisted rails . . . with several . . . draughts of buildings and staircases.* London 1725
Useful Architecture, in Twenty-One New Designs for erecting Parsonage-houses, Farm-houses, and Inns etc. Robert Sayer: London 1752

Halfpenny, William and John *The Modern Builder's Assistant; or, a concise epitome of the whole system of architecture . . . Engraved on eighty-five folio copper plates, from the designs of William and John Halfpenny . . . Robert Morris . . . and T. Lightoler.* James Rivington and J. Fletcher and Robert Sayer: London 1757

Hoppus, Edward *The Gentleman's and Builder's Repository: or, Architecture Display'd. Containing the most useful and requisite problems in Geometry. The designs drawn by E. Hoppus.* London 1738

Langley, Batty *Ancient Masonry, both in the Theory and in the Practice . . . Illustrated by . . . examples engraved on . . . copper plates* 2 vols, Printed for the Author: London 1734–35, 1736
The Builder's Chest-Book; or, a Compleat Key to the Five Orders of Columns in Architecture J. Wilcox: London 1727
The Builder's Director, or Bench-Mate: being a Pocket-Treasury of the Grecian, Roman, and Gothic orders of Architecture . . . Engraved on 184 copper plates, etc. H. Piers: London 1746, 1751, 1767

The City and Country Builder's and Workman's Treasury of Designs: or, the Art of Drawing and Working the Ornamental Parts of Architecture London 1740, 1741, 1750, 1756. Also available as a facsimile reprint published by Gregg International Publishers Ltd.: Farnborough, Hampshire 1969

The London Prices of Bricklayer's Materials and Works ... justly ascertained. London 1747, 1748, 1749, 1750, 1818

Langley, Batty and Thomas *The Builder's Jewel: or, the Youth's Instructor, and Workman's Remembrancer. Explaining short and easy rules ... for drawing and working, etc.* R. Ware: London 1746, 1754, 1768, 1787, 1808

Gothic Architecture Restored and Improved, by Rules and Proportions. In many Grand Designs of Columns, Doors, Windows. London 1741

Le Clerc, Sebastien *Traite d'Architecture avec des remarques et des observations, etc.* Paris 1714, London 1732. Translated by Mr Chambers

Leoni, Giacomo *The Architecture of A. Palladio ... Revis'd, Design'd, and published by Giacomo Leoni, a Venetian: Architect to his most Serene Highness, the Elector Palatine.* London 1715, 1721

Morgan, Morris Hickey *Vitruvius: the Books on Architecture. Translated by Morris Hickey Morgan ... With illustrations and original Designs prepared under the Direction of Herbert Langford Warren.* Harvard University Press: Cambridge, Mass. 1914

Morris, Robert *The Architectural Remembrancer: being a collection of New and Useful Designs of Ornamental Buildings and Decorations to which are added, a variety of chimney-pieces ... the whole ... engraved on fifty copper plates.* London 1751

An Essay in Defence of Ancient Architecture; or, a Parallel of the Ancient Buildings with the Modern; Shewing the Beauty and Harmony of the Former, and the Irregularity of the Latter, to which is annexed an Inspectional Table, universally useful. London 1728

An Essay upon Harmony, as it relates chiefly to Situation and Building. London 1739

Lectures on Architecture, Consisting of Rules founded upon Harmonick and Arithmetical Proportions in Building. London 1734-6, 1759

Moxon, Joseph *Mechanick Exercises, or, the Doctrine of Handy-works, etc.* 2 vols. London 1683

Vignola: or, the Compleat Architect. Shewing in a Plain and Easie way the Rules of the Five Orders of Architecture ... Translated into English by J. M. London 1655

(translator) *The Theory and Practice of Architecture: or Vitruvius and Vignola abridg'd. The first by ... Mr Perrault ... and carefully done into English. And the other by J. Moxon; and now accurately publish'd the fifth time.* London 1703

Neve, Richard *The City and Country Purchaser, and Builder's Dictionary; or the Compleat Builder's Guide.* Philomath (i.e. R. Neve): London 1703

Nicholson, Peter *An Architectural Dictionary, containing a Correct Nomenclature and Derivations of the Terms employed by Architects, Builders and Workmen ... and the Lives of the Principal Architects, etc.* 2 vols. London 1819

The Builder and Workman's New Dictionary London 1824

The Carpenter's and Joiner's Assistant London 1792

The Carpenter's New Guide London 1792

The New and Improved Practical Builder and Workman's Companion London 1823

Treatise on the Construction of Staircases and Handrails London 1820

Pain, William *The Practical Builder, or Workman's General Assistant: shewing ... Methods for Drawing and Working the Whole or Separate Part of any Building.* London 1774

Pain, William and James Pain *British Palladio; or, The Builder's General Assistant. Demonstrating, in the most easy and practical method, all the principal rules of Architecture ... Engraved ... from the original designs of W. and J. Pain.* London 1786

Palladio, Andrea *I quattro Libri dell' Architettura* Venetia 1570. See also: Leoni, Giacomo

Price, Francis *The British Carpenter: or, a Treatise on Carpentry.* C. Achers: London 1733. Second edition enlarged with the addition of sixteen copper plates 1735

Rawlins, Thomas *Familiar Architecture; consisting of original Designs of Houses for Gentlemen and Tradesmen; Parsonages; Summer Retreats; Banqueting Rooms; and Churches To which is added the masonry of the semicircular and elliptical arches, etc.* London 1768

Richardson, George *A Treatise on the Five Orders of Architecture ... With Observations ... on several of the Antiquities of Rome, and various parts of Italy, at Pola in Istria, and the Southern Provinces of France, made in the years 1760–63.* London 1787

Salmon, William *Palladio Londinensis: or, The London Art of Building* London 1734. Also available as a facsimile reprint published by Gregg International Publishers Ltd., Farnborough, Hampshire 1969

Scamozzi, Vincenzo *The Mirror of Architecture: or the Ground-rules of the Art of Building ... Reviewed and inlarged ... by J. Schuym ... Translated out of the Dutch by W. F. Hercunto to which is added the description and use of an ordinary Joynt-Rule ... by John Browne.* W. Fisher: London 1669

Serlio, Sebastiano *Tutte l'Opere d'Architettura di S. Serlio ... dore ... hora di nuovo aggiunto (oltre il libro delle porte) gran numero di case private ... el un indice ... raccolto per via consideratione da ... G. D. Scamozzi.* Venetia 1584

Shute, John *The First and Chief Groundes of Architecture ... first printed in 1563. A facsimile of the first edition with an introduction by Lawrence Weaver.* Country Life: London 1912

Stuart, James and Revett, Nicholas *The Antiquities of Athens measured and delineated by James Stuart, F.R.S. and F.S.A., and Nicholas Revett, Painters and Architects* (vol. 2 edited by W. Newton; vol. 3 by W. Reveley and vol. 4 by J. Woods). London 1762–1816

Swan, Abraham *A Collection of Designs in Architecture: to which are added ... Designs of Stone and Timber Bridges.* 2 vols. London 1757

Interior Decoration of the Eighteenth Century from the Designs of Abraham Swan, selected by Arthur Stratton. Alec Tiranti: London 1923

Tijou, Jean *A New Booke of Drawings ... Reproduced with the Addition of a Brief Account of the Author and His Works, and Description of the Plates, by J. S. Gardner.* B. T. Batsford: London 1896

Vitruvius Pollio, Marcus *The Architecture of M. Vitruvius Pollio: Translated from the Original Latin by W. Newton.* 2 vols. James Newton: London 1791

Ware, Isaac *A Complete Body of Architecture adorned with plans and elevations from original designs . . . in which are interspersed some designs of Inigo Jones, never before published.* T. Osborne and J. Shipton: London First edition n.d., 1735, 1756, 1760

Designs of Inigo Jones and others published by I.W. London. First edition n.d., 1735, 1743, 1756

(translator) *The Four Books of A. Palladio's Architecture.* London 1738

Wilkins, William *The Civil Architecture of Vitruvius; comprising those Books which relate to the public and private Edifices of the Ancients, translated by W. Wilkins . . . with an Introduction, containing an Historical View of the Rise and Progress of Architecture among the Greeks.* London 1812, 1817

Wood, John *A Dissertation Upon the Orders of Columns and their Appendages.* London 1750

The Origins of Building, or the Plagiarisms of the Heathens Detected. London 1741

Wood, Robert *The Ruins of Balbec, otherwise Neliopolis, in Coelosyria.* London 1757

Wotton, Sir Henry *The Grounde-rules of Architecture collected from the Best Authors and Examples.* London 1686

2 History and topography of London

Allen, Thomas *The History and Antiquities of London, Westminster, Southwark and parts Adjacent. With engravings* 5 vols. (Vols. 1-4 by T. Allen; vol. 5 by T. Wright) G. Virtue: London 1827-37

Allgood, Henry G. C. *Stray Leaves from the Past of our Village. A history of Bethnal Green, from the earliest times to 1680. To which is added an account of the Poor's Land Charity.* Reprint of a series of articles which appeared in the *North Eastern Leader.* J. S. Forsaith: London 1894

Annual Record, The see: London Topographical Society

Archenholz, Johann Wilhelm von *A Picture of England: containing a description of the laws, customs, and manners of England . . . Translated from the original German.* For the Booksellers: London 1797

Bell, Walter George *The Great Fire of London in 1666 . . . with forty-one illustrations including plans, etc.* John Lane: London, New York 1920

Besant, Sir Walter *East London . . . With illustrations by Phil May, Joseph Pennell and L. Rowen-Hill.* Chatto & Windus: London 1901

Birch, John Godfrey *Limehouse through Five Centuries.* Sheldon Press: London 1930

Braun, Hugh Stanley *Old London Buildings.* Convoy Publications: London 1949

Chancellor, Edwin Beresford *The History of the Squares of London, Topographical and Historical . . . with thirty-six illustrations.* Kegan Paul & Co.: London 1907

Clunn, Harold Philip *The Face of London. The Record of a Century's Changes and Development* Simpkin Marshall: London 1932

Cunningham, Peter *A Handbook for London, Past and Present* 2 vols. John Murray: London 1849

Dodsley, R. and Dodsley, J. *London and its Environs described; Containing an Account of Whatever is most Remarkable in the City and in the Country Twenty Miles around it, etc.* R. & J. Dodsley: London 1761

Dupin, Francois Pierre Charles Baron *The Commercial Power of Great Britain; exhibiting a compleat View of the Public Works of this Country, under the several heads of Streets, Roads, Canals, Aqueducts, Bridges, Coasts and Maritime Ports.* 2 vols., translated from the French. London 1825

Ellis, Sir Henry *The History and Antiquities of the Parish of Saint Leonard Shoreditch and Liberty of Norton Folgate.* London 1798

Feltham, John *The Picture of London for 1802; being a Correct Guide to all the Curiosities, Amusements, Exhibitions . . . in and near London, with a Collection of Appropriate Tables, etc.* London 1802

Gavin, Hector *Sanitary Ramblings; being Sketches and Illustrations of Bethnal Green. A Type of the Condition of the Metropolis and Other Large Towns.* London 1848

George, Mary Dorothy *London Life in the XVIIIth Century.* Kegan Paul & Co.: London; A. A. Knopf: New York 1925

Godfrey, Walter Hindes *A History of Architecture in London. Arranged to illustrate the course of architecture in England until 1800, with a sketch of the preceding European styles . . . With a preface by Philip Norman . . . With 250 illustrations, 7 maps and Descriptive Guide to the Buildings.* B. T. Batsford: London 1911

Greater London Council, The *Survey of London* vols. 1-37. Athlone Press: London

Harrison, Walter *A New and Universal History, Description and Survey of the Cities of London and Westminster, the Borough of Southwark and their adjacent parts, including not only the Parishes within the Bills of Mortality, but the Towns . . . Villages, Seats and Country, to the extent of twenty miles round, etc.* London 1775

Hatton, Edward Gent. *A New View of London (by E. Hatton) etc.*, 2 vols. London 1708

Heal, Sir Ambrose *The Sign Boards of Old London Shops. A Review of the Shop Signs employed by the London Tradesmen during the XVLLth and XVIIIth Centuries. Compiled from the Author's Collection of Contemporary Trade-cards and Billheads . . . Illustrated, etc.* B. T. Batsford: London 1947

Hobhouse, Hermione *Lost London.* Macmillan: London 1971

Kent, William Richard Gladstone *An Encyclopaedia of London.* J. M. Dent & Sons: London 1937

Knowles, C. C. and Pitt, P. H. *The History of Building Regulation in London 1189-1972 with an account of the District Surveyors' Association.* The Architectural Press: London 1972

Lambert, B. *The History and Survey of London, and its Environs; from the Earliest Period of the Present-Time,* 4 vols. London 1806

Lewis, Wilmarth Sheldon *Three Tours Through London in the years 1748, 1776, 1797.* Yale University Press: New Haven 1941

Lillywhite, Bryant *London Coffee Houses. A Reference Book of Coffee Houses of the Seventeenth and Nineteenth Centuries.*

George Allen & Unwin: London 1963

London Topographical Society, *Annual Record... including the reprints of the... annual meetings, etc.* London 1901–

Lysons, Daniel *The Environs of London, being an Historical Account of the Town, Villages and Hamlets, within twelve miles of that Capital... with Biographical Anecdotes*, 4 vols. London 1792–96

Maitland, William *The History of London from its Foundation by the Romans to the present time... With the Several Accounts of Westminster, Southwark, and other parts within the Bill of Mortality.* London 1739

Malcolm, James Peller *Anecdotes of the Manners and Customs of London, during the Eighteenth Century... with a Review of the State of Society in 1807. To which is added a Sketch of the Domestic and Ecclesiastical Architecture, and of the various Improvements in the Metropolis. Illustrated by fifty engravings.* London 1808

Londinium Redivivium; or, an Ancient History and Modern Description of London, etc. 4 vols. London 1802–7

Malton, Thomas the Younger *A Picturesque Tour through the Cities of London and Westminster, illustrated with the Most Interesting Views executed in aquatinta*, 2 vols. London 1792

Meister, Jacques Henri *Letters written During a Residence in England. Translated from the French of H. Meister ("Souvenirs de mes Voyages en Angleterre"). Together with a letter from the Margrave of Ansbach to the Author.* J. N. Longman: London 1799

Mills, Peter *The Survey of Building Sites in the City of London after the Great Fire of 1666... With an introduction by W. H. Godfrey.* London 1946

Morris, Corbyn *Observations on the Past Growth and Present State of the City of London. To which are annexed a Complete Table of the Christenings and Burials within this City from 1601 to 1750... together with a Table of the Numbers which have Annually Died of each disease from 1675 to the present time, etc.* London 1751

Noorthouck, John *A New History of London, including Westminster and Southwark. To which is added, a General Survey of the Whole, describing the Public Buildings, late improvements... With copper-plates.* London 1773

Page, William *London: its Origins and Early Development.* Constable & Co.: London 1923

Pevsner, Nikolaus *London Volume I: The Cities of Westminster and London.* Buildings of England Series, Penguin Books Ltd.: Harmondsworth 1973

London Volume II: Except the Cities of London and Westminster. The Buildings of England Series, Penguin Books Ltd.: Harmondsworth 1969

Phillips, Hugh *Mid-Georgian London. A Topographical and Social Survey of Central and Western London about 1750.* Collins: London 1964

Powell, Rosamund B. *Eighteenth-Century London Life.* John Murray: London 1937

Readaway, Thomas Fiddian *The Rebuilding of London after the Great Fire.* Jonathan Cape: London 1940; republished by Edward Arnold & Co.: London 1951

Richardson, Sir Albert G. and Gill, Charles Lovett *London Houses from 1660–1820. A Consideration of their Architectural Detail... Illustrated by Drawings and photographs specially taken.* B. T. Batsford: London 1911

Salvin, Arthur Knowles *The Silk Weavers of Spitalfields and Bethnal Green. With a catalogue and illustrations of Spitalfields silks.* Victoria and Albert Museum: London 1931

Seymour, Robert *A Survey of the Cities of London and Westminster... the whole being an Improvement of Mr Stow's and other surveys, etc.*, 2 vols. London 1734, 35

Sinclair, Robert George, *East London. The East and North. East Boroughs of London and Greater London.* Robert Hale: London 1950

Small, Tunstall and Woodbridge, Christopher *Houses of the Wren and Early Georgian Periods.* The Architectural Press: London 1928

Smith, Sir Hubert Llewellyn *The History of East London from the Earliest Times to the End of the Eighteenth Century.* Macmillan & Co.: London 1939

Strype, John *A Survey of the Cities of London and Westminster... brought down from the year 1633... to the Present Time by J. Strype. To which is Prefixed the Life of the Author by the Editor, etc.*, 2 vols. London 1720

Summerson, John *Georgian London.* Pleiades Books 1945; Penguin Books Ltd.: Harmondsworth 1962

Totton, Stevens *The Humble Representation of S. Totton to the... Lord Mayor... Aldermen and... Common Council of... London June 1795 (relative to a plan for constructiong sewers in the City of London).* London 1795

Vale, George Frederick *Old Bethnal Green.* Blythenhale Press: London 1934

Vale, George Frederick and Smith, Stanley *Bygone Bethnal Green. Handbook to an Exhibition held at Bethnal Green Central Library, May 29th to June 12th 1948*

Wheatley, Henry B. *London Past and Present... Based upon the Handbook of London by the late P. Cunningham.* London 1891

3 *General*

Braun, Hugh Stanley *The Restoration of Old Houses.* Faber & Faber: London 1954

Briggs, Martin Shaw *Goths and Vandals. A Study of the Neglect and Preservation of Historical Buildings in England.* Constable: London 1952

Clifton-Taylor, Alec *The Pattern of English Building*, new edition, Faber & Faber Ltd.: London 1972

Crossley, Frederick Herbert *Timber Building in England, from Early Times to the End of the Seventeenth Century.* B. T. Batsford: London 1951

Davey, Norman *A History of Building Materials.* Phoenix House: London 1961

Gardner, John Starkie *English Ironwork of the XVIIth and XVIIIth Centuries: an Historical and Analytical Account of the Development of Exterior Smithcraft... With 88 collotype plates from photographs chiefly by Horace Dan... and upwards of 150 other illustrations.* B. T. Batsford: London 1911

Gloag, John Edwards *Georgian Grace. A Social History of Design from 1660–1830.* Adam & Charles Black: London 1956

Gloag, John Edwards and Bridgewater, Derek Powley *A History of Cast Iron in Architecture.* George Allen & Unwin: London 1948

Godfrey, Walter Hindes *Our Building Inheritance. Are we to lose it?* Faber & Faber: London 1944

Innocent, Charles Frederick *The Development of English Building Construction* The Cambridge Technical Series, General editor: P. Abbott. University Press: Cambridge 1913–40.

Lindsay, John Seymour *Iron and Brass Implements of the English House* Alec Tiranti: London 1964

Lloyd, Nathaniel *A History of English Brickwork* H. G. Montgomery: London; William Helburn: New York 1925

A History of the English House from Primitive Times to the Victorian period. The Architectural Press: London; William Helburn: New York 1931

MacGrath, Raymond and Frost, Albert Childerstone *Glass in Architecture and Decoration . . . With a Section on the Nature and Properties of Glass* by H. E. Beckett. The Architectural Press: London 1937

Powys, Albert Reginald *Repair of Ancient Buildings.* J. M. Dent & Sons: London and Toronto 1929

Summerson, John *Architecture in Britain, 1530 to 1830.* Penguin Books: London 1953

(ed.) *The Microcosm of London (with coloured plates by A. W. N. Pugin and Thomas Rowlandson) of 1808).* Penguin Books: London, New York 1943

Walpole, Horace, Earl of Oxford *Anecdotes of Painting in England, with some account of the Principal Artists; . . . collected by . . . G. Vertue and now digested and published from his original MSS by . . . H. Walpole. (To which is added, the History of the Modern Taste in Gardening (by the latter)) 4 vols.* Strawberry Hill: 1762–71

Warnes, Arthur Robert *Building Stones: their Properties, Decay and Preservation.* Ernest Benn: London 1926

STREET INDEX

Figures in italics refer to pages in which illustrations occur

Adam Street, Adelphi, WC2 *65*, 65, 132, *132*, 212, *212*
Albert Embankment, SE11 *66*, 66, 151, *151*
Albury Street, Deptford, SE8 *43*, 47, 82, 95, *95*, 102, 202, *203*, 204
Alie Street, Whitechapel, E1 157, *157*
Arlington Street, St James's, SW1 58, *59*, 194, *195*
Ashfield Street, Whitechapel, E1 142, *142*

Batty Street, Stepney, E1 *138*, 139
Bedford Square, Bloomsbury, WC1 138, *138*, 139, 192, 211, *216*, 217
Bedford Way, Bloomsbury, WC1 *146*, 147
Berkeley Square, W1 2
Bloomsbury Square, WC1 2, 192
Bloomsbury Way, WC1 60, *60*
Brabant Court, City of London, EC1 127, *127*
Brick Lane, Spitalfields, E1 157, *157*
Britton Street, Clerkenwell, EC1 38, *38*, 217, *217*
Broadway, Hammersmith, W6 125, *125*

Camberwell New Road, SE5 2, 74, 75, 78, 80, *81*, 147, *147*, 152, *152*, 166, *166*, 168, 210, *210*
Camberwell Road, SE5 200, *201*
Cannon Street Road, Stepney, E1 89, *89*, 103
Caxton Street, SW1 180, *180*
Charles Square, Hoxton, N1 *53*, 53
Church Row, Hampstead, NW3 82
City Road, Islington, EC1 70, 72
Clapham Old Town, SW4 40, *41*, *126*, 127
Commercial Road, Stepney, E1 2, *196*, 197
Coram Street, Bloomsbury, WC1 *69*, 69
Covent Garden Piazza, WC2 2, 21
Croom's Hill, Greenwich, SE10 119, *119*
Cross Street, Islington, N1 115, *115*, 133, *133*

Dean Street, Soho, W1 58
Denmark Street, WC2 40, *40*
Devonshire Square, EC2 114, *114*
Dock Street, Stepney, E1 104, *104*
Dombey Street, Bloomsbury, WC1 62, 102, *102*
Dover Street, W1 83
Drummond Street, Euston, NW1 85, *85*, *196*, 197

Eastern Avenue, E11 *44*, 47
Elder Street, Spitalfields, E1 112–13, *113*, 123, *123*, 128, *128*, 181, *181*
Elliot Road, Camberwell, SW9 77, 78

Fitzroy Square, W1 *218*, 219
Forest Road, Walthamstow, E17 150, *150*
Fournier Street, Spitalfields, E1 55, 82, 86, *87*, 89, *89*, 99, 102, 112, *112*, 129, *129*, 136, *146*, 147, 176, *176*, 204, *204*, *205*, 210, *210*, 216, 217
Foxley Road, Camberwell, SW9 71, 72

Grafton Street, W1 140, *141*, *146*, 147

Grafton Way, W1 *68*, 69
Great James Street, WC1 82, 111, *111*
Great Ormond Street, Bloomsbury, WC1 82, 111, *111*, 114, *114*, 168, *169*
Greatorex Street, Whitechapel, E1 102, *103*
Greek Street, Soho, W1 99, *99*, 102
The Green, Richmond 82, 202, *202*, 206, *206*
Grove Terrace, Hampstead, NW5 123, *123*
Guilford Street, Bloomsbury, WC1 *68*, 69

Hackney Road, E2 152, *153*
Hanover Square, W1 47, *47*, 134, *164*, 165, 192
Harpur Street, WC1 62, *62–3*, 121, *121*
Helmet Row, Finsbury, EC1 130, *130*
Hermitage Road, Richmond 204, *205*
High Street, Deptford, SE8 152, *152*
High Street, Islington, N1 102, *102*
Huntley Street, Holborn, WC1 140, *140*

Kennington Common, SE11 145, *145*, 200
Kennington Lane, SE11 100, *101*, 140, *141*, 159, *159*, 200, *201*
Kennington Road, SE11 66, *67*, 123, *123*
King's Bench Walk, Temple, EC4 106, *107*

Lambeth Road, SE1 132, *132*
Laurence Pountney Hill, City of London, EC4 86, *87*, 204, *205*
Leman Street, Aldgate, E1 113, *113*
Lincoln's Inn Fields, Holborn, WC2 114, *114*
Long Lane, Bermondsey, SE1 124, *124*, 129, *129*, 130

Manchester Street, W1 212, *213*
Mansfield Street, W1 *64*, 65, *144*, 145
Maple Street, W1 145, *145*
Mare Street, Hackney, E8 *45*, 47, *122*, 123, 148, *148*
Meard Street, Soho, W1 36, *37*, 55, *56–57*, 58, 82, 96, *97*, 102
Mecklenburgh Square, WC1 217, *217*
Millman Place, Bloomsbury, WC1 17
Millman Street, Bloomsbury, WC1 96, *96*, 133, *133*, 208, *208*
Monmouth Street, Covent Garden, WC2 176, *177*
Montague Street, Bloomsbury, WC1 70, 72
Montpelier Road, Twickenham 86, *87*, 106, *106*
Mornington Crescent, NW1 212, *213*
Mount Pleasant, WC1 168, *168*

Narrow Wall, Lambeth, SE1 198
Neal Street, Covent Garden, WC2 184, *185*
New Road, Whitechapel, E1 139, *139*
Northdown Street, King's Cross, N1 148, *148*

Old Kent Road, SE15 80, *80*
Ormond Road, Richmond 82, 136

The Paragon, Hackney, E9 78, *79*, 142, *143*
Parkshot, Richmond 136, *136*
Parliament Street, Westminster, SW1 60, *61*, 120, *120*
Percy Street, W1 150, *150*
Portland Place, W1 192

Princelet Street, Spitalfields, E1 55
Priscilla Road, Bow, E3 202, *202*

Queen Anne's Gate, Westminster, SW1 194, *197*, 212, *212*
Queen Anne Street, Marylebone, W1 150–51, *150*
Queen's Square, Bloomsbury, WC1 69

Redman's Row, Stepney, E1 84–5, *85*
Rotherhithe Street, Bermondsey, SE16 116, *117*, *158*, 159
Rugby Street, Bloomsbury, WC1 48, *49*, 82, *88*, 89, 222, *223*
Russell Square, Bloomsbury WC1 *146*, 147
Russell Street, Covent Garden, WC2 163, *163*

St George Street, W1 134, *134*
St James's Square, SW1 2, *58*, 58, 194
Sekforde Street, Clerkenwell, EC1 76, 78
Silver Street, Edmonton, N18 115, *115*
Southampton Place, WC1 2, 172, *172*
Stepney Green, E1 95, *95*, 131, *131*
Stepney Way, Whitechapel, E1 140, *141*
Stoke Newington Church Street, N16 *98*, 99
Stoke Newington High Street, N16 *46*, 47
Strand, WC2 9

Suffolk Street, Strand, WC2 116, *117*
Surrey Street, Strand, WC2 103, *103*
Syon Road, Twickenham 136, *136*

Tavistock Place, WC1 *216*, 217
Took's Court, Chancery Lane, EC4 50, *51*, 187, *187*, 189
Tottenham High Road, N17 48, *48*
Tottenham High Street, N17 *86*, 86, 113, *113*, 116, *117*, 124, *124*

Vassall Road, Camberwell, SW9 72, *72*

Walnut Tree Walk, Kennington, SE11 *100*, 100, 102, 204, *205*
Wandsworth Place, SW18 130, *130*
Wardour Street, Soho, W1 58
Whitechapel Road, E1 135, *135*
Whitehall, SW1 194, *195*
White Hart Lane, Tottenham, N17 116, *117*
White's Row, Spitalfields, E1 *52*, 53, *92–3*, 93
Wilke's Street, Spitalfields, E1 50, *50*, *54*, 55, 82, 103, *103*
Wimpole Street, W1 199, *199*
Woburn Square, Bloomsbury, WC1 148, *149*, 217, *217*
Wyndham Place, Marylebone, W1 72, *73*